The Journey
THROUGH
FOUR SEASONS
OF LIFE

SIN MONG WONG

The Journey Through Four Seasons of Life

Copyright © 2021 by Sin Mong Wong.

Paperback ISBN: 978-1-63812-101-5
Ebook ISBN: 978-1-63812-102-2

All rights reserved. No part in this book may be produced and transmitted in any form or by any means, electronic, or mechanical, including photocopying, recording, or by any information storage and retrieval system, without permission in writing from the copyright owner.

The views expressed in this work are solely those of the author and do not necessarily reflect the views of the publisher hereby disclaims any responsibility for them.

Published by Pen Culture Solutions   08/19/2021

Pen Culture Solutions
1-888-727-7204 (USA)
1-800-950-458 (Australia)
support@penculturesolutions.com

Contents

Acknowledgements and Preface xi

Chapter 1 Introduction 1
Simple Philosophy of Life 3
Some Secrets of Life 8
Overcoming Obstacles in Early Stages of Life 12
The Power of Saying No and the Benefits of Saying Yes 12
Meditation and Visualisation 13
Humanising the Teaching of Mathematics 16
Living a Healthy and Happy Life 17
An Interesting Story 19
Self-Awareness Strategy 21
Affluent Attitude and Poverty Consciousness 24
Some Secrets to Happiness 26
Simple Approaches to Do Things Better 29
The Three Stages of My Life 35
The Wonders of the Four Seasons of My Life 36
A Simple View of a Successful Life 41
The Wonder of Infinity and the Infinite
Power of the Mind 42
A Simple Purpose of Life 45
Assertiveness as an Important Social Skill in My Life 47
Relationship and Happiness 49
The Key to Normal Growth Is Love 50
Family Life 54
Retirement Life 56
Family Achievements 58
How I Manage My Time 63

Chapter 2 Introduction to Financial Security 65
How I Create Lifelong Streams of Income 70
Providing Mathematics Tuition and
Lecturing Part-Time as a Source of Linear Income 72
Writing Mathematics Textbooks as a Source
of Residual Income 74
Investing in Properties as a Stream of Residual Income ... 79
Dividends of Stocks as another Stream of
Residual Income and Growth 80
Joint Venture as another Source of Residual Income 83
Advantages of Residual Income over Linear Income 88
Investment Life during Retirement 91
Position Sizing and Risk Management 102
A Big Secret in Investing 105
Technology Stocks for the Future 107
Trading and Investing Golden Rules 109
    Rule One 110
    Rule Two 111
    Rule Three 112
    Rule Four 114
    Rule Five 115
    Rule Six 115
Knowledge and Information Key to Investment 117
Strategies to Find Best Growing Stocks 121
The Demon Fear and Greed in Trading and
Investments 123
Four Common Mistaken Beliefs Traders and
Investors Make 126
A Good Strategy to Make Big Money in Stock 128
Guillotine and Sandpaper Phases 130
Three Possible Factors Affecting Investors
Making Bad Decisions 131
    Availability Bias 131
    Loss Aversion 132
    Probability Neglect 133
Life Expectancy of a Bull Market 133

	Time for Holidays from Stocks 135
	Four Dumb Mistakes Most Investors Make 137
	Properties as Alternative Investment.............................. 140
	Some Characteristics of Rich People 143
Chapter 3	Healthy Lifestyle... 145
	Heart Disease and Cancer.. 150
	Misconception of Heart Disease and Cholesterol 151
	Cancer as a Killer.. 152
	A Simple Peanut Butter Odour Test for Alzheimer's Disease.. 153
	Simple Steps to Improve Your Digestive System and Boost Your Metabolism and Energy Levels..... 154
	Steps Taken to Prevent Diabetes 156
	Preventive Medical Services 158
	Recognising Symptoms of Stroke 158
	Medical Screening.. 158
	Alzheimer's Disease.. 159
	Nature's Brain-Protecting Miracle - Curcumin 163
	Danger of Turmeric Consumption during Pregnancy ... 164
	Natural Treatment for Memory Loss, Dementia, and Alzheimer's Disease................................... 165
	Health Benefits of Omega-3 Fatty Acids from Fish Oil.. 165
	Super Antioxidant from Brown Seaweed 166
	Form the Habit of Eating One or Two Apples a Day..... 168
	Weight Control Using Insulin Sensitivity and Carbohydrate Tolerance 169
	Strategy for a Slim Body and Flat Belly.......................... 170
	Natural Cure for Many Types of Cancer........................ 170
	Other Alternative Cures for Cancer 171
	Iodine: the Anticancer Agent 172
	Key to Living Longer and Healthier Life....................... 172
	Include Walking into the Good Life Style for Older People 176
	Knee Joint Pain and Osteoarthritis 177
	The Length of Telomeres and Overall Health 178
	Never too Old to Learn New Things 179

	The Values of Meditation and Mental Training	182
Chapter 4	The Wonders of the Four Seasons of My Life	189
	Early Childhood as the Economic Winter Season	189
	Primary Education	193
	The Wonders of the Spring Season of My Life	195
	Playing Basketball during Secondary School Days	197
	Secondary Schooling in Penang	200
	Teacher Training at the Technical Teachers Training College	210
	Developing Ways to Increase My Will Power	213
	Two Years of Teaching Industrial Arts after College	215
	University Education	217
	Playing Basketball at the University	218
	Meeting My Soulmate at the University	220
Chapter 5	The Wonders of the Summer Season of My Life	222
	Two Years of Teaching at Kuantan, Pahang	222
	Teaching Life in Petaling Jaya, Selangor	228
	Investment Life during Working	232
	A Successful Career as a Teacher	233
	Office Politics Affecting Your Career	239
	What Predict Success in a Career?	242
	Student Exchange Programme with Junshing College, Japan	244
Chapter 6	The Autumn Season of My Life	246
	Retirement Life	246
	A Born-Again Christian	248
	A Memorable Trip to Watch Tiger Woods at the Master Golf Tournament at Augustus, USA	250
	A Few Memorable Visits to the United States	252
	Touring Europe for Seven Weeks	254
	Simple Steps to Influence People to Like You	255
	The Award of Ph.D.	258
Chapter 7	Enjoying the Fruits of Life and Keep Learning	260
	Searching for Fulfilment in Life through Quantum Jumping	264
	Quantum Jumping for Healing	264

My First Successful Quantum Jumping to
Heal My Headache 266
Quantum Jumping to Learn a Figure of Speech............ 267
Quantum Jumping to Overcome Illogical Fear 268
Quantum Jumping to Enhance Happy Marriage 270
Quantum Jumping to Enhance Abundance 271
Quantum Jumping to Enhance Spirituality 273
  Everyday Enlightenment, which states the following: ... 275
Quantum Jumping to Experience Flow.......................... 275
Quantum Jumping to Overcome Negativities
or Difficult Situations 277
Quantum Jumping to Search for Happiness.................. 279
First Lesson to Learn the Skill of Happiness.................. 280
Second Lesson to Learn the Skill of Happiness 283
Third Lesson to Learn the Skill of Happiness 286
Quantum Jumping to Overcome
Unhappiness over Issues of the Past............................... 288
Quantum Jumping to Reinvent Yourself 289
Quantum Jumping to Find Ways to become a
Better Leader 292
Quantum Jumping to Attract Wealth 294
Quantum Jumping into Absolution 295
Quantum Jumping into a Long and Happy Life 297
Quantum Jumping to Imitate the Habits of
Happy People... 298
Quantum Jumping to Be a Successful Investor 300
Quantum Jumping to eliminate Emotion
from the Investment Decisions' Equation..................... 304
Quantum Jumping to Help My
Doppelganger How to Use Creative
Visualisation to Realise His Dreams 306
Quantum Jumping to Seek Joy in Life 310
Quantum Jumping to Help a Beginner to
Start Meditation 310

Conclusion..313
Summary 315

Acknowledgements and Preface

Most importantly, I acknowledge my wife, for her home management and other supports to enable time to write this motivation book related to my journey through four seasons of my life. I acknowledge her complaints regarding her private life, which was initially included in my draft. Subsequently, I have removed some of them for the sake of meeting her wish halfway. I learn that cooperation and gratitude are necessary keys to a happy life. I have learnt from her that gratitude inclination will pave the way for a more joyful life. I love her for who she is. I am thankful for her contribution to my success and happiness. I may have made some mistakes, I say sorry.

First and foremost, I would like to thank Professor Ann for reading the manuscript and her verbal comments. I greatly appreciate the contribution of my daughter and son for providing their working credentials to be included as the family achievements. I also thank them for reading through the manuscript. My career as a humble teacher was satisfying and rewarding. Part of the intention of this book is to change the concept of the image of a poor teacher and encourage talented people to take up teaching as a career. Singapore is doing the right thing. The country is encouraging the best 30 per cent of its students to take up teaching as a career. Teachers are well rewarded in Singapore. Malaysia is following suit. But too much damage has been done as many of its teachers are from the lower 50 per cent of its students. The practice of pay peanuts and get monkeys to be teachers are over. Teachers should be well rewarded if we want our society to advance.

The purpose of this book is not only to provide the journey of the three stages of my life but also to encourage the next generation to live a healthy, happy, financially independent, and fulfilled life by early planning followed by actions. Choose your career carefully, and love what you do.

Happiness at work increases productivity and eventually produces success in your life. What constitute a successful life? This book will shed some light regarding the notion of a successful life. Financial independent is one of the three metrics for a successful life. While you are working, try to create as many streams of income both linear and residual as possible to enable you to invest for retirement. Always live beneath your means so that you will not be in debt. Live well by being aware of the foods you eat. Learn meditation to increase your spirituality and concentration in your life. A new concept of meditation known as Quantum Jumping will help to expand your visualisation and imagination. In our universe, Google provides a level playing field for us to assess information. In a parallel universe, the imaginary quantum library will provide an infinite knowledge to help you in living a life of abundance. Your responsibility is to download the necessary information into your subconscious mind and begin to practice such strategies to help you living a life of success. Try to exercise regularly to complement your good health. Preferably take up a sport to ensure regular exercise and add excitement to your life. In addition, exercise your idea muscles regularly. This will ensure that your brain always function the way you wish. Finally, try to add funs, excitements, and purpose to all stages of your life. Encourage healthy relationship to achieve not only happiness but also a long and healthy life. Do not allow age to be an obstacle to your learning. Learning is a lifelong process. Take up anything you like. The simple philosophy is that if you like it, enjoy it. If you do not like it, avoid it. What happen if you do not like it and you cannot avoid it, then change your attitude to like it. By doing this simple feat, you will be properly laying the foundation of your happiness and eventually your success in life.

Chapter One

INTRODUCTION

My name is Dr Sin Mong Wong. Before I tell you my life story, I must admit that I am just an ordinary person who chooses every day to make extraordinary decisions and take actions. I know taking actions may not be enough. I have to get the feedback constantly to assess my progress. Actions that produce results are maintained. Those actions which are not productive are avoided. I have to do something productive every day that moves me towards my goals and dreams. In both academic and sports, I just be in action. I am aware of forming good habits and avoid bad ones that will not help to enrich my life. This awareness that if I were caught and taught bad habits, then my mind would be programmed to continue to follow these bad habits throughout my life. And when I realised this, I made some profound changes in my life. It all started when I began my secondary school in Penang. I begin to believe in myself. I am aware that if I believe that I am unsuccessful and unimaginative, then that is exactly the type of person I am going to be. I am lucky that I believe and behave as if everything I venture into is possible, all opportunities in my game and study seem to appear at my doorsteps. To help me succeed in life, I must focus on what I love. I enjoy playing basketball, and I also enjoy learning. I finally found success as a basketball player and became an outstanding state player. I also found success in academic. I had found a model for success in both sport and academic. I knew sport will not last long, but the skill set for learning has no limit. So my dream of becoming a teacher began to take shape. So the research began, and it all started with awareness. The pursuit of knowledge is fundamental to my success as an educator. Knowledge or information is power, but without implementation, it falls short. I am determined to use any knowledge available.

I must admit that I am not afraid of making mistakes. Yes, I made many mistakes in my life. I am still making mistakes. But I usually learn from each mistake and try not to repeat it. Each mistake becomes a lesson for me to do better when I face the same situation. I like to ask for help, and my wife now tells me that I am too dependent. For things that I know, I am always ready to help others. In short, I render help before I seek help. One thing I discover is that most people are keen to help me. I will continue to ask for help when I am unable to understand or do a certain thing. I learn from others, and I never tell myself that I can't do it! Once I learn a thing, I am not shy to put myself on stage or in the game. My positive attitude enables me to avoid living a life in dress rehearsal. I am ambitious because I am blessed with drive and the right attitude. I do not just hope but act instead. I also aspire to be physically, emotionally, and spiritually healthy. Every day I try to do a little bit better.

Another thing I learn is that whenever I undertake a project, I never give up. I will do it consistently, persistently, playfully, and disciplinarily. Until now I can't recollect any instant that I abandon a planned project. I always remember what my mother told me when I was a young boy. She inspired me to try to be the best I could at whatever I do. Her words encourage me to pursue everything that interests me with true passion. All these help me to live an exceptional life and become more than an ordinary person. In my life, both game and work, I always think that I can win. I went into tough challenges planning to come out victories. To me thinking like that often seems to turn into a self-fulfilling prophecy. If you care to follow some of my footsteps, you can also live an exceptional life in whatever job you do. By sharing the journey of my life, I hope my experiences can provide some directions for you in integrating various areas of life to live a productive, healthy, and happy life.

Simple Philosophy of Life

I always follow a simple philosophy of life. First, I do what I love and love what I do. If I love what I do, I'll do more of it, and I'll gather more confidence and more energy and get better at it. I enjoy teaching, writing, and investing. I have started my career as a tuition teacher when I was a student in secondary school. I love helping other students learn. I love to exercise my idea muscles every day. I have the habit of writing down ideas every day: some good and some bad. This love builds more confidence, and I love it more. And I grow in my capability and skills. Ultimately, I am able to choose what I want to do in my life. When I was a secondary school student, I enjoyed teaching my neighbours' kids and a couple of my classmates. Naturally, I chose to be a teacher. I became a sixth-form mathematics teacher for twenty-three years. I loved the job, seeing my students achieving their dreams. Eventually, I became the school principal, and I liked the job, helping others to become better teachers. I also love to write and choose to be a good mathematics writer. Since I enjoy writing, now I choose to become a motivation writer. Hopefully, I will be able to influence others to live a healthy, meaningful, productive, and fulfilled life. My experiences tell me that success alone does not bring happiness but happiness increases productivity and will eventually bring success in whatever I do. Happiness and sadness, just like success and failure, coexist in our life. Usually, a sudden success will bring temporary happiness for a while. Soon you will strive for a bigger one and another one. Failure will soon show its ugly face, and your happiness will evaporate. And you will start again to look for another success. My life experiences tell me that we should instead do the things we love and success will follow. I will put my hand up and be bold and courageous. I am always prepared to back myself and be prepared to have a go. I will not allow the feeling that I am not good enough, not adequate, and not going to do well in my job as a writer and a teacher to control me. I do not worry about failure! I will take courage in my own hands by telling myself that I will back myself and others out there will support me and want to see me win the race. It is about bringing my true self to the forefront and banishing the insecurity, fear, and indecision that will hold me back. I do not have to pretend to be someone I am not. I will not just hope but bring action into what I dream off. I believe in a fair go. Most people are under achievers because of their own decisions. They think that the universe is unfair to them. But it is you who makes the choice how to deal with it. If you choose to stay where you are, play a victim and believe that is not what you deserve or stand up, brush off, and take action. Remember that there is no one else who creates the reality you're under achieving.

I would like to share some of my simple tips helping me to be a happier, more productive, and more successful person. Other than doing the things I love, I usually try to list the things that I am grateful for and the things that interest me. I use to give support to others, and I always gain more support in whatever I do. Some of these experiences are valuable, and they help me grow. I learn to meditate to enhance spirituality and creative visualisation. What is creative visualisation? To me creative visualisation is simply using my imagination to create what I want in life. I use it to experience what I

want in life including my spiritual growth. Do not confuse spirituality with religion! Stories and beliefs in any religion are relative truths. Not all people believe them. There is another truth known as absolute truth which everyone shares the view. Personal realisation is enhanced by indulging in meditation, yoga, prayer, and other forms of spirituality. People who involve in such practices experience invisible sensation like feeling peaceful and empowered. Through meditation, I become a witness, as if another person watching the traffic of my mind, seeing the thoughts, memories, concerns, and dreams. By just observing these thoughts, my self judgement departs and my life moves towards peace, calm, and acceptance. I become an observer of my own life and all life around me. Here spirituality and creative visualisation becomes part of my life. It does not necessarily belong to people believing in relative truths, though it can be part of religious practice involving prayer. I use creative visualisation to attract the abundance, the health, and the relationship I want during meditation. By visualising during meditation, I begin to invite new experiences into my life. In a way, my visualisation practice enhances my intuition. During visualisation, I am seeing the outcome in my mind's eye before things actually happen. This practice provides the fun translating into a state of expanded energy in my real life. This state ushers my intuitive guidance to function smoothly. When I visualise writing a new book, I actually experience a lot of intuitive responses because my intuitive mind looks for patterns and presentations that aligned with my creative visualisation experiences. I do not stop there but take action to fulfil my dreams. Perhaps the reverse is also valid! If I am more in tune with my intuition, I will see better results from my creative visualisation. All of us are born with the gifts of intuition. But sadly, a very few actually take advantage of it and use it to live life fully. I hope I have triggered your awareness to use the gift. I will not allow obstacles to prevent me from benefiting fully. For example, intuition can come in a subtle feeling about whether or not you can trust someone. Other times, it can be a 'knowing' of someone who is in deep pain. Intuition sometimes can be a voice that protects us from imminent danger. In investment, it can be an early alert system for spotting industry trends, business opportunities, and lucrative niches. This is what Sir Richard Branson said,

> 'I rely far more on gut instinct than researching huge amount of statistics. We all have intuitive sense of what is best and follow it.'

People who meditate may agree with me that this strange phenomenon that a certain clarity of mind regarding plaguing problems seem to simply feel clear. And we have sudden burst of amazing insights. It may be a subtle form of intuition which meditators experience at one or more pivoted points in their life. In the words of Edison, the American inventor,

> 'Ideas come from space. It's hard to believe but it's true.'

> The late Apple founder Steve Jobs challenged us to 'have the courage to follow your heart and intuition, because everything else is secondary'.

I do not neglect my well-being as I build my abundance. I play my game basketball or tennis to enjoy it, and I do regular exercise to ensure fitness. Now in my retirement, I still do what I love. I still play my game tennis to keep fit and enjoy the game. I still love reading, writing, and investing. I always remember people who help me, and I am still very grateful to them. So it is important that when you choose your career, pay particular attention to what you love to do. Any job you love is more important than the glamour of the job. I love to move my body by playing the games I enjoy. I played basketball from the first day I entered primary school, throughout secondary school, college, and university. I played basketball in the veteran international games until I was well over fifties. I took up tennis and golf later on. I still play tennis in my seventies. I walk almost every day. All these activities keep me fit in my entire life. If you want to live a healthy life, start playing a game seriously or take up any movement activity which will always keep you fit.

I always stay connected with people with common interest. Lasting friendship is important. I have a few good friends since university days. After more than forty years, we are still good friends and enjoy deep heartfelt relationships with them. I still make good friends with those who play tennis with me now. Hanging out with friends adds values to your life just like meditation and prayer. If you want to resist stress, increase productivity, or get a promotion, don't just seek social support but provide it to others. Be aware that your attitude has a huge effect on your success. Here attitude refers to our action, thinking, and feeling. Our words and body language reveal most of them. The influence of significant persons like parents, teachers, and peers plays an important part in our attitude. So be aware that developing a positive attitude will be more important than all our qualifications and knowledge. So worry less about your academic grades, but increase your optimism that is the belief that our behaviour and attitude matter in the midst of challenge. Start building social connection with focus on depth and breadth related to attitude and the way you perceive stress. I used to dance with my fear, and now I try to read more books to enlighten me. I choose to have positive attitude and embrace the grace of gratitude.

I believe I am what I eat! I live on a good diet and eat moderately. That's what I do to keep me healthy. I am empowered and clear rather than overwhelmed by the food that passes my lips. I want to live a healthy life, and I follow good eating habits. Detailed discussion regarding nutrition and healthy lifestyle is discussed in Chapter Three.

I have a rewarding family life. I have two children. But during my working life, I had provided financial and moral support to my brothers, sisters, and relatives to fulfil their educational goals. A happy family is an important ingredient in any one's life. In my family life, we disagree on many things, we argue on many issues, but we thrive together. We learn to live with our differences. If you want a fulfilled life, have a rewarding family life, no matter how dysfunctional it may be.

I keep learning throughout my whole life. I was a late starter in life. I never regret that I spent too many years in my learning stage. I believe I was well prepared. Slow and steady wins the race. I manage to sharpen my brain to keep me on my game for my entire life. Learning has become a lifelong process for me. I read and read about everything that interests me. I write and write about anything that I know best. I play and enjoy every game that I happen to encounter. So if you intend to keep your brain sharp, my life experiences may be valuable. I consistently stick to the basics such as quality sleep, regular exercise, good nutrition, and freeing my mind from unnecessary distractions. These habits provide the building blocks for my optimum brain function and give me a strong physical disposition.

The economic well-being of my family is my top priority when I started working. I worked hard, but I enjoyed the process. I looked back with great satisfaction because I had created economic independence to support my extended family, my dreams, and the world around me. I wanted financial security for my family, so I had to do something extraordinary while I was working. First, I did not get into debt by spending what I haven't earned. I used to put aside any surplus by creating parallel careers to generate extra income for investment. I did all these when I was young and working. My grandmother told me this. Time and tide waits for no man. One inch of time is more valuable than one inch of gold because one inch of gold cannot buy one inch of time. I did all these extra activities willingly and consistently to help me succeed in my life and gain financial independent.

Now in my retirement, I begin to appreciate the magnificence in everything. I had taken an extra step to map out my exceptional life to a higher level. I am still trying to make the rest of my life the best. I continue to do things that I love. I do research, write, invest, and still enjoy playing tennis and golf. I would like to encourage you to do the same things while you are working. Try to integrate every areas of your life carefully. Try to give a balance to your career, family, nutrition, social life, and financial security, and exercise to keep fit and healthy. I urge you to push the button of your soul and join me in this wonderful ride to financial independence and live a fulfilled life without regret. So do not miss the opportunity while you are working.

I try to get rid of outdated beliefs which no longer serve my purpose. At the same time, I try to build new beliefs that help to transform my life. I also try to get rid of old habits which hinder my progress. This consciousness helps me to cultivate new habits which help to achieve my dreams. By repeating intentionally, these new habits soon become my ways of life. I share this consciousness strategy hoping that you will not miss the opportunity while you are working.

Some Secrets of Life

I am one of those lucky people who discover some secrets of life, which help me to become successful financially, mentally, and physically. I become aware of the infinite power of my mind through meditation. The more I meditate, the more my true self or capability is revealed. My 'self' is not what I have but who I am. This awareness and watchfulness helps me to ask questions, analyse the situation, and discover the answer. Going beyond my mind through meditation is where I find the emergence of my true self. There is harmony for my body, mind, and soul when I meditate. I can meditate while sitting down, standing up or walking, and laughing. There is no perfect way for me to meditate. I discover my own perfect way of meditation and follow it daily before I start studying. After many practices I discover far reaching benefits when I reach an alpha state of mind. Later, I learn that if my brain generates fewer beta brainwaves and far more alpha brainwaves, I start to perform better in almost every area of my study. I experience more well-being and peace. My creativity explodes. My stress dissolves. I am able to learn many times faster than normal. I place myself in peak performance after each meditation. Many discoveries are made. I am always in a flow state after each meditation where everything seems to magically manifest the result I want. I do not have to struggle or seemingly try to succeed. I follow a self-study strategy with ease, and it helps me achieving my educational goal. Almost every morning, I meditate first immediately after I get up. I then follow a consistent and persistent practice drill strategy to master the basic skills for my game, basketball, and it helps me to excel in the game. The combination of meditation, awareness, watchfulness, and witnessing seem to help my body, my mind, and my soul to function in harmony both in academic and in sport. Understanding this concept through meditation helps my body to accomplish certain goals in the game I play and compete. I am able to handle the ball deceptively and shoot exceptionally well. My body is able to perform these tasks even without my mind giving it step-by-step direction. All these practices and advantages have greatly enhanced my consistency and performance. The performance results in both game and study are attributed to my disciplined involvement in all these activities including meditation.

I learn very early the concept of assertiveness and use it to develop my character and confidence in social interaction. I was involved in meditation very early in my life. Meditations provide me with clarity in decision making and help me in creative visualisation. I become more aware of others and my surroundings. I also become more creative in whatever I do. When I started teaching, I discovered a teaching strategy which helps to humanise the teaching of mathematics concepts. I also happened to stumble upon a self-awareness strategy that helps me rewiring my subconscious beliefs. All the discoveries help to enhance my writing techniques by providing the human touch and mould my style of presentation. Detailed discussion of all these discoveries including the humanising strategy will be dealt with in Chapter Five.

I learn very early the strategy of using properties, value stocks, and joint venture as long-term investment. Their compounding returns in terms of rentals, dividends, and growth help to build my financial security. The secret isn't hard to grasp. It involves a little bit of mathematics. So it can take some time and patience to understand the secret of compounding. Respected physicist Albert Bartlett once claimed,

> 'The greatest shortcoming of the human race is our inability to understand the exponential function.'

This function is a mathematical way of explaining compounding. In simple term, compounding my capital is simply a way of saying that growth of my money happens over and over again at regular intervals.

To get the idea of simple compounding, I will use an example easy to understand. If I agree to give you $100 a year on a thousand dollars saving, at the end of the year you would have $1,100, a 10 per cent return. How much will you have at the end of the second year? Right, you would have $1,210 at the end of the second year. Now you are getting the idea of compounding! What would you have at the end of the fifth year? You would have $1,608 at the end of the fifth year. How many years does it take to double your money? About seven years. That's right. This is because the money we have in each time period is added to the money we started with. And then the next time, period's earned interest includes the extra money you made in the preceding period, along with the initial $1,000. We end up with more and more because we're making more and more on each little bit extra earned. We are using time as our advantage, the critical ingredient in compounding. So the more years we give it, the more our money mushrooms. Do not wait! Start immediately. A dollar invested today is more valuable than one invested tomorrow. And it's a lot more valuable than one invested next year!

I am lucky to realise that I could change my environment and destiny by involving in creative visualisation. Many thanks to my early discovery that I could use my imagination to create what I want in life. It takes a great genius like Albert Einstein to realise that everything is in a form of energy. Matter is energy ($E = mc$ square). Everything is made up of energy, and its vibrations determine its state. Human beings are no exception. How we feel and react to our environment depends on our energy level. For example, when the frequency of vibration is low, water becomes ice. Increasing the frequency of vibration, ice melts to become water. Increasing the frequency of vibration further, water becomes steam. Similarly, our life depends on our energy levels determine by the frequency of vibration. Basically, 60 per cent to 70 per cent of our body is made up of water. When the frequency of vibration is low, our energy level is also low, and so we experience sadness and other negative feelings. When our energy source improves, the frequency of vibration increases, so we feel good and inspired. We are more likely to experience acceptance, reason, love, joy, peace, and other positive feelings. I am about to share with you the experiences, discoveries, and insights of my life journey. In this book you will find valuable lessons using self-study strategy to enhance learning, using consistent and persistent drill technique to master game skills, and learning assertiveness to win friends. I learn to use the mechanism called meditation to reprogramme my subconscious mind through visualisation to experience happiness and success in life. I use the self-awareness strategy to enrich my belief systems.

    I had a big dream to become a successful teacher, writer, and investor so that I could attain financial security for my family. That is something that I had thought of for a long time. Something I wanted for a long time. I finally decided that I had to do it. Yes, I can do it. And I put all my energy to plan, to focus, to attract, to manifest, and to take action for my dream to come reality. My dream becomes my goal. It's a simple objective I try to accomplish. It gives me direction, and it gives me purpose. It points me in a certain direction, and it gives me something to strive for. Without the goal, I will more likely just drift around. This has been my long-term goal. Perhaps a long-term goal is less motivating because my current actions may have little influence. So I needed short-term goal to induce me to take actions when I was in secondary school. My short-term goal was to qualify myself to become a trained teacher and in game to become a state basketball player. This short-term goal was enough to motivate me into action, and my long-term goal gives me wiggle room to fall along the way. I would like to encourage you to start conceiving your short-term goal and your long-term goal as soon as possible. If you are keen to learn sound investment strategies to help you securing financial security, read Chapter Two of this book carefully. These experiences provide various perspectives to help you achieve this dream. See how I use a good diet and a balance active lifestyle to ensure a spectacular health. Chapter Three of this book can offer plenty of information for you to live a healthy life. I also like to encourage you to learn using the infinite power of the subconscious mind to enhance spiritual growth and creative visualisation. I learn early that life is a choice. So I choose the spirit of happiness to live a healthy, fulfilled, rich, and satisfying life. Within two decades of hardworking life, I have turned my life around to attain happiness and success. I hope the story of my life will inspire you to do the same.

Overcoming Obstacles in Early Stages of Life

In the early stage of my life, after six years of formal primary Chinese education, I was left out from the main stream of government secondary education. I was thrown into the workforce tried to earn a living by labouring as a rubber tapper. I was in that situation, tapping rubber in the morning and attending school in the afternoon, for almost three years. When opportunity for secondary education was offered to me by my eldest sister, who married a businessman in Penang, I took it with full commitment. I was way behind in my command of English, and I had a long way to catch up. It took me months of hard work, and I soon discovered my own self-study strategy, which helps me all the way in my learning process. In the field of sports, especially basketball, I stumbled upon a simple strategy involving persistent, consistent, and disciplined practices in skills which helped me excel in the game. I became a very skilful player especially in the skills of handling the ball by dribbling and accurate shooting from every corner. With consistent and persistent practice in shooting, I became well known as a sharp shooter in most tournaments I played. I represented my school, combined schools for Penang State, my country Malaya, the University of Malaya, the Penang State, and Kedah State. I was outstanding in dribbling, passing, and shooting, and these skills are essential to secure victory in any competitive game.

The Power of Saying No and the Benefits of Saying Yes

I also stumbled upon the power of saying 'no' to things that were unhealthy to me. First, I learnt to say 'no' to smoking because it was detrimental to my health. Most rubber tappers smoke because of the sheer number of mosquitoes. I also learnt to say 'no' when I was not respected and underestimated. 'No' is sometimes the hardest word to say when it involves your emotion. In relationship, I remembered, when I graduated from teachers training college, I was interested in a girl, going out with her for a period of time. I remembered the moment she told me about her new boyfriend doing a university course overseas. I knew immediately she was hinting that I was not good enough to be her special. That was the last straw. I decided to end my relationship with her. I needed to change; otherwise, I couldn't grow. I also had a choice. I did not want to be humiliated further. This well-placed 'no' had saved not only my valuable time but emotional trouble. I realised that I have the right to say 'no' to anything that is hurting me and any standard that no longer serving me. I am not going to entertain people who drain my creativity and expression. I need to be assertive and be true to my real self. I know that I have the power to create new, positive beliefs about myself.

I am grateful to my habitual practice in meditation. This experience teaches me an important lesson to follow my intuition. I am not confused regarding 'yes' or 'no'. When come to life, I always say 'yes'. I learn that in life, 'no' is a word that closes doors and may keep me away from life's greatest experiences. I am aware that in life 'yes' opens doors to many things. As I practise saying 'yes' to life, good things happen. My experiences reveal to me that opportunities I have shut out before come back to me. Even people I have kept at arm's length show up to assist me. My relationship with others improves when I adopt an aura of acceptance. Unconsciously by saying 'yes' to life, I open a space for universal good to fill. So when it comes to gaining new experiences, I prefer to leave 'no' out of my vocabulary for the day. I follow my intuition energy, and I find my advice from my inner guru, my inner master. Now I know that once my intuition starts to function, I do not need to ask advice from anybody. Intuition is in tune with oneself, totally in tune with oneself. Out of the tuning, I will find my answer. I believe that is a good solution helping me to become who I am now.

Meditation and Visualisation

I disciplined myself to pursue my goals both short term and long term for my game basketball and education. My early meditation or controlled daydreaming helped me to reprogramme my subconscious 'blueprint' through visualisation and imagination. I know very early in my life that everyone is creative. I must allow my creativity to spring forth. I focused on the power of creativity on both my game and my education. I dreamt of studying at the University of Malaya and hoped to meet my soulmate there. In sport, my dream was to be a state basketball player, and in education I wanted to be a teacher and a writer. I began to visualise that I became rich and started to invest into equities, properties, and businesses. I dreamt of becoming an entrepreneur and a businessman in my later life. So I practise meditation and visualisation daily. According to Osho,

> 'Creativity is the highest flowering of meditation and as a quality and an attitude it is first and foremost an inner expression. With this understanding we open the possibilities for a thousand and one things. Love what you do. Be meditative while you are doing it - irrelevant of the fact of what it is. A creative act enhances the beauty of the world. It gives something to the world. It never takes anything from it.'

I dare to dream big through meditation. I realise that meditation is just an open, relaxed way to assess availability and all that are going to happen to me in the future. I need to be connected with things around me, and I will deepen my connection to life. I realise that if I use my will to make something happen, it can be exhausting. Sometimes, when I face a mathematics problem, I try very hard to think of a solution. I try and try but the solution has avoided me. What I usually do is to take my attention of the solution off my mind. This does not make the problem disappear from my mind. In a relax moment, when I almost forget about the problem while I am walking or meditating, suddenly the answer pops up. What is the difference? I think the difference lies between willing something to happen and letting it to happen. The creative visualisation helps me in reconditioning and reprogramming my subconscious mind to help me grow happier, more confident, more productive, and eventually more successful. I realise that I am a designer of my own destiny. I was determined to follow my dream and began to take action by implementing the steps of my visualisations into realities. In my early life, these habits helped me to achieve my goals in both sport and education. During my early childhood, I dreamt of representing my hometown in basketball. I practised hard and achieved my goal when I was in standard six. When I started secondary school in Penang, I dreamt of representing the state in the game I loved. I took action. Every morning before my breakfast, I practised dribbling and shooting for almost an hour each day. This repeated practice became my routine each morning. Soon I was drafted into the state combined schools team and eventually the state team. I represented Penang state and Kedah state in basketball for almost four years while I was a student. I also dreamt of becoming an outstanding educationist and a writer. I did everything that was necessary to prepare myself. Every morning before I revised my lessons, my imagination and visualisation went into full steam. I practised creative visualisation almost every day. To me, at that point of time was simply using my imagination to create what I wanted in life. I imagined playing basketball in front of a crowd of many thousand spectators cheering me to shoot more. I also imagined standing in front of students and teachers trying to inspire them to strive for a better life. I enjoyed dreaming. I took actions, and after many years of struggle, I managed to become a teacher and a writer. I had written many books related to my subject of specialisation. All these imaginations eventually produce rather fantastic results in my life.

Just like everybody else, I suffered from my past conditionings from my brothers, sisters, parents, society, and teachers. They cannot tolerate my individuality because individuality will not follow like a sheep. My new environment while boarding in my eldest sister's house and my habit of morning meditation helped me to eliminate many of these past conditionings, and I became aware of my wings. And those wings helped to take me to a new reality. I started to live a life of truth, authenticity, and my original self. All types of troubles and doubts began to disappear because my inner conflicts dropped and I was no longer divided. I found my inner peace and acquired a voice of unity in all my undertaking. I let my emotion guide me as I made the transformation. If I found myself feeling grateful, self-affirming, contented, and inspired, I knew I was doing right. On the other hand, if I found myself feeling lousy in any way, I knew I was doing something wrong. So I would try to identify the thought that was creating the feeling. That thought I felt scare to entertain holds the treasure I seek. Being aware of that, I was able to concentrate in forming new habits, creating new thoughts, improving my self-study strategy, and intensifying my practice drills in my basketball game.

I enjoyed playing basketball and played well. I was a well-respected basketball player in school, in college, in the university, and for the states I represented. I enjoyed playing the game and benefited with plenty of exciting experiences in my playing days. I was fully committed to do well in secondary school. My self-study strategy involving preparing lessons before attending classes helped me in understanding most lessons well. When in secondary school, my academic achievement spoke louder than my words. I was a well-respected student in my class. Two of my classmates had faith in me. They took tuition from me. I started spreading my self-study strategy to them and assumed leadership role when I helped them to learn effectively. I became assertive and won many friendships. My friends found that I was dependable and I was trusted as their leader. I trust my emotional intelligence which will always let me know if I encountered a lie, no matter how it is disguised. The feeling of lousiness gives me the critical signal. I concentrated on learning new skills and habits, forming my character, and growing spiritually as I experience life.

Humanising the Teaching of Mathematics

When I started teaching as a form-six mathematics teacher, I stumbled upon a very important strategy, humanising the teaching of applied mathematics concepts. Hope smiled at the threshold of my teaching career whispering to me that I was on the right track. I caught the bull by its horns. Applied mathematics is a subject which most students drag. I explored practical daily experiences to explain applied mathematics concepts and principles. This approach helps students to appreciate and feel the connections between mathematics and real-life situations. A few detailed exploring examples of the humanising process will be dealt with in Chapter Five.

I also advocated that the teacher should be the curriculum maker when I lectured at the Curriculum Development Centre in Kuala Lumpur. Here a curriculum maker means an initiator and an integrator of every aspect of the curriculum. The teacher is the most important connection between the curriculum and the students. To make all these connections effective and lasting, I started to become a curriculum developer involving both textbooks and guidebooks to help connecting mathematical concepts and practical experiences. My intention was to make learning simple, interesting, and relevant. I was rewarded plentifully when my books became popular and used widely. With all these extra revenues, I started investing in properties and stocks. I was lucky that I stumbled into an algorithm of investing in value stocks that prepared well for my retirement.

Living a Healthy and Happy Life

Another discovery I made early was critical to my well-being and happiness. All the visions and achievements will be useless if I do not have good health. I need to develop a balance in all aspects of my life. I embark on a journey educating myself regarding factors affecting my health as well as my financial security. I strongly believe that if there is will, there is a way. You need to focus on what you have instead of what you do not have. My wife was a nurse, and this helped in our nutrition planning. We have a medical person at home. If you are keen to cultivate the habit of resourcefulness in order to find good health and abundance, this book has plenty to offer. You see, abundance is everywhere, but most people just don't see it. They seem to see negative aspects of the economy and society instead of seeing a world filled of new opportunities.

Abundance also includes happiness. To create this aspect of abundance, I start to form happiness ritual. I used to figure out the activities, people, places, or objects that activate my happiness, and I used to write them down. I enjoy playing games, spending time with nature, and helping others. I try to include these activities as part of my routine. These have created more stability and excitement in my life. I used to look forward to doing these activities each day. I also focus on creating a new habit each day instead of trying to achieve all my goals. While setting goals and resolutions is great, but trying to juggle them at the same time can be overwhelming when we have little time. It would be better if we focus our energy and attention into developing one positive habit at a time. By repeating it, we will soon see it becoming automatic. I practise letting go what no longer serving me. I used to make a list of people and activities that I have to let go because they represent my past and not with integrity with where I want to be in life. I learn to let go anything holding me back. I use creative visualisation as an exercise helping me feeling more connected with my goals and try to be happier about. I do not wait for things to change to be happier. I make the choice to be motivated, inspired, and fully engaged in my life. My decision is to be happy right now. I take action by focusing on my personal growth and try to develop a deeper connection with what really matters to me. It takes an experience such as good fall to really know where I stand.

These discoveries have completely changed who I am. I was rewarded because I dared to dream big. I had faced failure in my first courtship, but I accepted it well. I also had failures in other aspects of my life like investments and business ventures with friends. My first business venture with friends ended in a failure. In fact, my second business involving publication was also a failure. We did not put in enough planning and we were lacking in capital investment. Many lessons were learnt from the failures. When we shifted into our first home, we were cheated by the contractor's supervisor promising to get us plan to close the air well. He collected payment for the renovation from many of the neighbouring houses there. Being the developer's supervisor, we trusted him for the renovation with a few thousand dollars. After months of waiting, he never surfaced. He disappeared with all the money. Now I learn to look well into the matter before I invest or make payment. I soon realise that there is no sin in failure, but it will be a sin if I do not try. I also enjoyed many successes as mentioned earlier. They had brought me everything I could have asked for in life-success, talent, wealth, well-being, happiness - you name it.

I was lucky to stumble upon a critical social skill which helps me to become who I am and not what I do. I learnt the critical behaviour of being assertive very early during my secondary school days. I was drawn into leadership role among my peers helping them to succeed in their educational pursuit. Instinct and circumstance became my great teacher. I was able to differentiate between these two social behaviours: assertiveness and aggressiveness very early in my secondary school days. A detailed discussion of these two social behaviours will be dealt with later. This social skill continued to develop in my working life. This book shows the way how to be assertive and how to live the life of your dreams.

An Interesting Story

Many thanks to a wonderful story I heard from my elders when I was a small boy. This story was again told by Burt Goldman, my mentor who taught me the art of meditation called Quantum Jumping. I will share my practice of Quantum Jumping in Chapter Seven. The story I heard when I was a small boy had a very deep impression in my life. I would like to tell the story in a very simple way so that it will stay in your mind as long as you live.

There was a king in the Middle East who had many advisers to help him in administration and governing his kingdom. One day, he summoned some of his wise and learned people. He wanted to be a wiser and better king. He wanted them to include all the wisdoms of the world into a book. After much effort, they managed to come up with a big volume containing all the wisdoms the king required. The king was old then, and he looked at the book. This was too much for him to digest and understand. So he summoned them again asking them to summarise the book into a chapter. Again these wise men worked hard and came out with the required chapter. The king was getting older, and the chapter appeared to be too much for him to comprehend. He wanted them to reduce the chapter into a sentence. Being obedient they obliged and reduced the chapter into a mere sentence containing all the wisdoms of the world. Suddenly, the king died, and the sentence was forgotten. The son became a king. When he got older, he suddenly remembered the project of his father. Many of the wise men had passed away and a few were still alive. He too summoned the remaining wise men and also included some new ones. He wanted to see the sentence which contained all the wisdoms of the world. He read the sentence. It was too complicated for him to grasp. So to make things simple, he ordered them to summarise the sentence into just one *word* so that he would understand. Suddenly, war broke and everything was forgotten including the *word*. Many years had passed, and the word was discovered. Now we know that the *word* is *attitude*. All the descriptions contained in all the wisdoms of the world rotate on the attitude of a person. The king had wealth and power as his two metrics for success in his life. But he was sitting on a two-legged stool and it was not stable. He needed a third metric. According Ariana Buffington, the third metric has four pillars.

The first is focused on well-being. His well-being and that of his people are important. Is the king happy and healthy? Are his people well taken care off? Is the king happy and enjoying his life? Are his people enjoying life? So his attitude towards his people and his own family is important. A positive attitude for the king is essential to achieve well-being for his people and his kingdom. The second pillar rotates around wonders. We live in a world full of wonders and mystics. Is the king appreciating all the wonders and mysterious things of the world, many of them he never understood? Do we understand all the wonders we see every day? Appreciating these wonders and being grateful for being part of the universe will make us more human and willing to contribute without reservations. The moon is always viewed with romance and mystery. We all know that it takes twenty-eight days to orbit around the earth and the change from waxing to waning takes about fourteen days. The period before full moon is known as waxing, and the period after full moon is known waning. About three days before new moon or full moon, the pull of the moon is greatest as seen by the tide of the sea. The wonders of the effect of the moon on human behaviours are too many to mention. By experience, farmers will sow their seed during waxing period to produce maximum cropping. It is believed that meditation during the three days before new moon or full moon time can bring maximum effect. To give the benefit of the doubt, I used to mediate for abundance, good health, and good relationship during the ending of the waxing period. New moon happens when the moon, the earth, and the sun are in alignment, with the moon between the sun and the earth, and full moon is when the earth is between the sun and the moon. We only see the full moon especially during the night because the sun shines on the moon. New moon is not seen clearly but can be calculated. My new-moon programming is all about leveraging on the altered gravitational pull of the new moon. I used it to amplify my manifestation so that everything I dream of in life comes to me much easier. This lunar leveraging seems to work for me most of the time when I meditate during the particular period. I share this wonder or experience hoping that you too may also use it to optimise the effect of your meditation.

The third pillar is wisdom, which the king was seeking. Knowledge is not wisdom. The ability to use knowledge for the well-being of others and guiding others to become better human beings are essential for wisdom to grow. It is not necessary that wisdom follows our age. Most of us need guidance to allow wisdom to take root. Always put other's interest before self. The Bible has a good guild line. Do unto others what you want others to do unto you.

The last of the pillar is giving. Giving can manifest in many forms. Give a smile to cheer others up. Giving your time to help others and giving a person in need are part of our contribution to mankind. If you want support from others, then provide support first. While we benefit from others, do not forget to give back. Fulfilling all the three metrics are perhaps the prerequisite for a successful life. All these four pillars in the third metric are deep-rooted in our attitude towards life.

Self-Awareness Strategy

I wanted to be a successful and healthy person even when I was a small boy. I started my daydreaming when I was in primary school. Soon, I was able to control these daydreams now through meditations, which are helping me in visualisations. I stumbled upon the three essential elements which I thought would make me a successful person in life. First, I needed money so my visualisation was focused on creating wealth so that I would have financial security. In order to create wealth, I realised that I needed a good career which would enable me to save some money so that I could start investing for my future family. These controlled daydreams manifested into creative visualisations when I started my secondary education in Penang. Every morning after my breakfast, I began to prepare my lessons getting ready for the day's work in school in the afternoon. I closed my eyes in meditation and started visualising my journey of life through the three phases: learning stage, working stage, and retiring stage. I have a big dream. It is not negotiable. It is my birthright. Meditation is not a 'spare wheel' that I pull out when in trouble, but it is a 'steering wheel' that directs the right path throughout my life journey. I could see myself sailing through my secondary school with ease because I was fully committed to do well in my school career. Every day before I went to bed, I started to review the things I did in each day that I should have done differently to have better results. This self-awareness strategy became my daily routine not only in education but also in the game, basketball, I played. I excelled in both when I was a student. My subconscious mind was put in motion searching for a career that suited me. My interest in teaching was ignited, and I focused on the influence of my teachers on my learning. Everywhere I went I seemed to notice the role played by teachers on students' life. The subconscious mind appeared more powerful than my conscious mind in processing the data necessary for my future career. I began to visualise the important role a teacher could play besides teaching. A teacher could easily be a curriculum maker in terms of teaching strategy innovation, producer of curriculum materials, teaching aids, critical skill development, and agent of change for society. My visualisation led me to the conclusion that I needed information and knowledge. The only way to see my dreams come true is a long process of education especially higher education.

I also used the self-awareness strategy during my working life and found the strategy very effective in enhancing my career as a teacher. My creative visualisation exercises brought me to the awareness of another element in life besides wealth and position. This element has many components which in each small way will contribute to a more fulfilling life. My well-being such as been healthy and able to enjoy life is important. This encouraged me to be active in my chosen sports: basketball and tennis. I like my games, and I enjoy them. I played basketball until the age of fifty plus representing Malaysia in many veteran international games for people over forty-five. I picked up tennis and golf during my working days and played both reasonably well. In my seventies, I still play very good tennis and enjoy the game.

I made my fortune from the society I am in, and I felt the need to give back to society part of what I have gained. I started many charity projects when I was the principal of my school. I made my contributions both physically and financially secretly. Only my ex-principal, Reverence Brother Felix, could bear testimony to it. Wisdom and wonders are the components I am lacking. I am still working towards achieving them. I have another big dream in terms of contribution. I am still educating myself with all the necessary knowledge to help others by penning down the essential elements to help them live a fulfilling and enjoyable life. As usual, I had my mean goal as dictated by society. I needed a job. I chose to be a teacher. This was my starting point in my experience in life. I worked hard to earn extra money because many people depended on me. Once I achieved this small bit of financial security, I started thinking of my intellectual growth. After a few years of teaching and slotting to earn some extra money by giving tuition and part-time lecturing, I enrolled at the University of Malaya for an external master's degree in education. I had to attend lectures during the weekend on research methodologies and things related to mathematics education. I realised that I had an end goal for my life. Deep down in my heart and soul, I needed experiences, spiritual, and intellectual growth. I wanted new experiences and growth so that I could make my contribution in the field I was in. It took me two full years to accomplish my work in writing my master's dissertation related to mathematics curriculum innovation. This started my journey of growth as a curriculum maker and innovator. I am thankful that I realise that in life, I either grow or decay. If I did not make an effort to grow, I would be in decay. I am thankful that I made growth intentionally instead of waiting for it to happen.

My writing journey was given a push, and within two years, I wrote my first mathematics textbook. Subsequently, I had made more contribution by producing more than two dozens of textbooks and guidebooks related to mathematics learning. The burning desire for further growth prompted me to take my optional retirement at the age of fifty-one to pursue my doctoral study in Australia. I have a strong desire to gain more experience and growth and always try to make more contributions to society in many forms. This end goal will bring satisfaction, fulfilment, well-being, and happiness to my life. I hope by sharing my experiences will encourage you to do the same. All things in life including experiences are temporary. You need to create new experiences, and if they are going well, enjoy them because they will not last forever. If they go wrong, do not worry because they cannot last long either. This awareness serves as the driving force to me to keep experiencing new things even in my retirement.

Affluent Attitude and Poverty Consciousness

When I was working as a teacher, I stumbled upon a secret strategy to create affluent consciousness or affluent attitude in my life. I used this self awareness strategy in helping me to achieve my dream of abundance.

I do not associate abundance limiting to money alone. To me abundance includes things like useful experiences I want in life, having loving relationship, sharing positive contributions with society, financial security, and many others affecting my life. Before I went to bed, I listed down the things I had done and singled out things that I was not happy with. I used to imagine that if I had another chance, I would do them differently. As I practised this approach almost every day, these unhappy events became less and less. I was lucky to realise that these unhappy things were the main cause of my self-limitations in the subconscious mind. These limitations may be in relation to my friendship, relationship, mental growth, and others. So if this type of situation is allowed to accumulate every day, we will find that we are magnifying our limitations in many aspects of life. If things have been done wrongly, we feel guilty. This guilt is usually submerged in our subconscious mind. We begin to feel inadequate and unworthy, and it limits our motivation. Then a strong feeling soon emerges telling us that we do not deserve much in relationship, well-being, wealth, and others aspects. Soon, we would have developed a poverty consciousness or poverty attitude because of our past memories of mistakes and failures accumulated. We will begin to see things in a negative way. But if we adopt this self-awareness strategy, we will begin to take notes of our mistakes and poor decisions each day. After practising this strategy each day, soon we will discover that the things we want to do differently each day will start to decline. A stage is reached where our sense of self awareness is enhanced. Our confidence in our daily life becomes a routine. Other limitations including our abundance blocks because of conditioning and our childhood subconscious limiting beliefs, in every aspect of life, will be overcome. Soon our poverty attitude will make way for a more affluent attitude because of this awareness and we see things differently. Our creative visualisation for better things will follow, and we will experience the feeling that we have been liberated from these mental blocks. We will develop a rhythm of positive energy that will help us in getting whatever things we want. We will find that we have become a magnetic force not only attracting friendship but also attracting others aspect of life including wealth. If we give this strategy a try, we will soon embrace a positive rhythm moving towards a more positive energy to accomplish the dreams we deserve. Take note of this available strategy and do not allow fear, anger, and sadness keeping us stuck. Let this awareness empower us to embrace our true nature and free ourselves of pain, suffering, and self limiting beliefs.

It is told that if you give a person with poverty consciousness a million dollars, he will soon waste it within a few years because his rhythm is of very low energy. He feels that he does deserve it, and therefore, he cannot make it grow but eventually waste it. On the other hand, if you take away a million dollars from an affluent consciousness person, he will soon gain that million and have a few millions added to his account. He has the affluent attitude and his rhythm is positive and he is like a magnet attracting money.

I am lucky to learn about this affluent attitude early in my working life. I put the strategy to work for me and lived beneath my means. As I worked and saved, each day, I had less and less things I wanted to change in my lifestyle giving me confidence to plan for the future. I worked hard in my teaching both at school and in my tuition centre during the weekends. I started writing seriously, and my rhythm for affluence began to pick up. I started investing in properties and equities, and my confidence grew. As my energy level improves, the frequency of vibrations keeps increasing, and positive elements like acceptance, joy, peace, and enlightenment start to take root. I ventured into investments such as properties, stocks, and business. These gave me a better rhythm for affluence as time passed. I added more of my saving into these investments which take care of my retirement until today. All these happenings indicate that happiness is the prerequisite for financial success.

Some Secrets to Happiness

I am also lucky that I learn very early some secrets to happiness. We are indulged in many things in our life. I always adopt the attitude that if a thing I like, I am going to enjoy it. I picked up the game basketball during my primary school years. I played the game well, and I really enjoyed it. I started using my self-study strategy during my secondary school years. I liked it because it produced results and I enjoyed it. Similarly, I like my self-awareness strategy, and I enjoy using it all the time in my life. Being assertive in my daily life paves the way for my self-confidence and defines who I am. I realise that enjoying the things you do produce an atmosphere of happiness. If something you do and you do not like it, then avoid it. I did not like a few things in my younger days so I tried my best to avoid them. There are things that you do not like but you cannot avoid them. I was given the assignment of cleaning the toilets every week and my brother was given the task of cleaning the whole house. I changed the responsibility with my brother. He did not mind the job because it involved less time. So if a thing you can't avoid, try to change it. What happen if you can't avoid and can't change it, then you better change your attitude and develop a rhythm so that you can grow to like it. Otherwise, you will have planted the seed of unhappiness. Besides this simple philosophy, there are a few other things you need to let go for you to find lasting happiness. Be aware that happiness will not only bring financial success but a more healthy way of life. Have you ever wondered why a car's windshield is large and its rear view mirror is small? May be it has something to do with our life telling us that our past is not as important as our future.

I have friends who are at the pinnacle of their career, and they appear to be successful, but they are immensely and deeply unhappy. They have position and wealth, but they have lost along the way. They lack the third metric consisting of well-being, wisdom, wonders, and giving. They have relationship problem; they are not connected with their children. They have health problems, and they have no true friends. They lack the spirit of generosity. They do not believe in practising this spirit, and they show no respect to others' individuality. They neither support nor help others to flourish in their jobs. Perhaps they are selfish, intolerant, and always quick to pass judgements. They want to take credit of others' work. To be happy once you have climbed the ladder of your profession, do invest in your well-being and build wonders and wisdom as part of your development. Give generously by practising generosity of spirit.

When I was young I used to believe that if I could gather more stuff, happiness would follow. I wanted to impress people with what I had and what I could do. In most encountered with people, I usually wanted to be right most of the time. I also tried to speak bad about others and tried to gossip about them in order to exalt myself. I was also badly influenced by my poor childhood days with so many brothers and sisters struggling to attract attention. My self-esteem was low, and I lacked confidence even asking for directions and getting help when I was young. I was lucky when I started my secondary school in Penang. I was staying with my eldest sister far away from my family. Many thanks to the extraordinary discoveries: self-study strategy and my consistent practice in my game skills which gave me success as a student and self-esteem as a state basketballer. I became well known in both academic and sport. Soon, the secret of happiness became clear to me. I need to let go all these unnecessary negative aspects of my life for me to become a peaceful person and I will be happier.

First, I try to let go the need to impress others. Being a social creature, I do care about what people think of me. But I do not need to spend time and energy trying to impress people and get their approval. I only need to be true to myself. What I have and had are already fabulous. My achievements should be able to speak for themselves both in academic and in sports. I realise that I only need to be my real self and people will appreciate who I am.

Second, I need to let go the need to be 'right'. Many a time, I was misunderstood and mistreated. I got caught up wanting others to admit that they had wronged or misunderstood me. I normally demanded an apology or at least acknowledged that I was right and they were wrong. Now I realise that not all human beings see things from the same perspective. In my world I am right, but in their world they are also right. So it is not necessary to allow negativity to take root inside me and start spilling into other areas of my life. So I need to re-examine the question whether I need to be right! It's more important that I want to be happy. I am determined not to allow my ego that keeps me holding to past resentments and upsets. Instead I need to consider the desire to be right. With this decision, I instantly am able to restore happiness and contentment in my life. So it appears that happiness has its source from contentment and the latter also flows from the stream of gratitude or attitude. I think you can make the same decision for your happiness sake.

Third, I need to let go the desire to gossip. Thanks to my discovery that gossip is just a cheap way to make myself feel good. But the influence is so strong. People around me are doing it, and I can easily slip into the habit. The secret of the quality of my life depends on the quality of my conversation with others. I am lucky this secret was discovered by me early in life. I am convinced that we are judged not by our jobs or look but by the quality of our words. Our voice is powerful, and what we say makes a difference. By committed to having more positive conversations about things, not people, that matter will quickly brighten our outlook in life. So there is no place for gossiping when we are indulged in conversation. Friendship is like a book. It takes years to write, but it takes a few minutes to burn. Be aware of what you say.

Finally, I need to let go the past. Initially, it was difficult to let go the past when the future is so uncertain. I usually feel safe when I look at the past good or bad because I know what have happened. But I do not have the chance to change what had happened. Luckily, I realise that the past has served its purpose and it had brought me to the place I am today. The past had made the person I am now. I am now absolutely perfect. I am grateful for the experiences and know that now is all I have. I am going to do my best to enjoy each moment. This is the gift of being present! If we allow this simple philosophy to get better as part of our life, we will never miss an everlasting happiness. It's never too late to set another goal for happiness and another dream to a more healthy and happy life.

Another important factor contributing to my happiness has to do with my attitude for being grateful to others who helped me and my environments. Gratitude seems to impact my life in a very powerful ways especially my mental well-being. I have more energy, more forgiving attitude, less anxiousness, no depression, more feelings of being socially connected, better sleep, and no headache. I believe gratitude also increases my spiritualism and my self-esteem.

Simple Approaches to Do Things Better

Before I discuss the approaches to do better, I need to get to know myself first. What I am really capable of and what are my strengths? I know I have average intelligence. I am athletics, strong, and well-built. I have good discipline to become a good sportsman. I can sit down for hours to concentrate on my study. This exceptional quality will help me to do well in academics and in writing. I am also very dependable, and people can usually trust me. I have my weaknesses too. When I started my education in Penang, I was lacking in self-confidence. I was shy to ask questions and asked for help. I got the inferiority complex because of my background. I used to say things that were not exact, and sometimes, I used to make up stories. I am not proud of it. It took me years of struggle to overcome these weaknesses. Many thanks of my regular practice in meditation and my awareness strategy. I was able to review things I had done wrongly or words uttered carelessly each day. Although, the process is slow, but these consistent practices have changed my life. When I did well in my study and when I was selected to play basketball for the state, my confidence and self esteem began to take root. I became aware of my weaknesses and recognised them. I started working on these unhealthy behaviours, and soon they empowered me to explore better choices in life. My daily meditation helps to get rid of most of these weaknesses, and now I can celebrate and embrace them. Ultimately, I discover ways to become confident and assertive to help me to become a better version of myself. I realise that my strength grows out of my weaknesses.

I am lucky to learn some of the effective approaches to get better at anything I want to do. I had practised them when I was a secondary school student. I had used these simple approaches successfully in my working life, and I am still using them in my retiring life. My motivation and inspiration for success in everything I do are built on a strong foundation. I want to experience a happy and healthy life. I want to grow to my full potential whatever talents God has given. And I wanted to be able to contribute and give back to society whatever things I have benefited. I always remember that when God solves my problems, I have faith in his abilities. I also remember that when God does not solve my problems, he has faith in my abilities. I also remember the answer St. Anthony gave to a blind man who asked that whether there is anything worse than losing your sight. He said, 'Yes, losing your vision!'

I dreamt of becoming a good basketball player representing my state, and I also dreamt of becoming a successful writer and a good investor. So each step taken is fine-tuned to help me fulfil my dreams. The following are the essential steps I have taken to help me achieve my dreams. I believe that it's never too old to set another goal and dream another dream.

First, I used to love what I do especially teaching others. Of course, I should love what I do. It is not easy initially. I have to develop a positive attitude first. I always reward myself with this simple phrase. If I like it, enjoy it. If I do not like it, I will avoid it. Sometimes, it is difficult to love something when you are losing respect and people hating you for it. You may be losing friends and you may feel like a failure. The best I can do is to avoid this type of situation and find something else that I can love and enjoy. I learn to say 'no' to situations detrimental to me, and I will find the true power of 'yes' in doing things I like and enjoy. Doing things I enjoy brings happiness, and happiness increases productivity and eventually provides the foundation for a successful life.

Second, I used to connect with people who love the same thing I do. In sports, I enjoy the same interest and have plenty of common things to talk about. In writing, I love to hear their ideas. I enjoy learning different ways of doing something so that I can learn. More importantly, they are my friends and comrades with common interest. Together, we will conquer, succeed, keep healthy, and most importantly enjoy life together. I have a weak point. I feel for the weak and the poor. I am always ready to help the weak and the wounded and protect the unprotected! I had met many great friends through this process. I will continue to do so.

Third, I learn to listen to the people who love what I do. Especially in sports, teaching, and writing, I always seek the advice of others. In investment I love to listen to what others have in mind regarding the economic situations and their choice of stocks. I like people who are experts in their field giving comments regarding my game, teaching, writing, and investment. I am very thankful to them who encourage and give constructive comments. All these have helped me to succeed. I have also encountered people who offered destructive criticism. The power of 'no' helps me to ignore and dissociate with them. I do not need this category of people who look good on paper but are useless to me and my improvement. I choose to listen to people who share common interest, and I learn their self-improvement approaches with humility, the prerequisite to knowledge. I enjoy their wisdom and their role models. I always open my heart to their advice.

Fourth, I appreciate the history of what I do. I look back with pride the game, basketball, I had played, the students I had taught, the books I had written, and the investments I had made. In the game basketball, I represented my school, college, university, states, and the country. I was a teacher, vice principal, and principal of my school. I had a collection of more than twenty mathematics textbooks and guidebooks to my credit. I had written two theses: one for my master and one for my Ph.D. I have started on another book, and the quest goes on. I enjoy seeing and receiving my residual income through royalties, rentals, and dividends. Now I am looking for something unique, something old people have forgotten and look for new twists of various combinations that nobody ever thought of. I begin to read motivation books, investment books, and health conscious guides to help me live a more fulfilled and healthy life. I start to write motivation book for I want to help people live a healthy and successful life. But what constitute success in life! I have plenty to explore and more efforts to acquire new wisdom.

Fifth, I learn to be kind to people who love what I do. I started with the wrong assumption that people wanted to meet me because they thought I could do something for them especially when I was principal of my school. I have changed my attitude. If I meet someone now, I think of what I can do for him or her. I have abandoned my old selfish motive. I believe now that the more I deliver to others I will get many times in return. My own experiences are good examples. My eldest sister provided me accommodation when I was studying in Penang. My second brother-in-law provided me financial support when my saving ran out while I was in the university. My third brother-in-law helped me with the initial payment for my second investment property. I am always grateful to them. They are like charming gardeners who make my soul blossom. I feel the urge to provide help to those who need my help. When I was teaching, I helped my brothers and sisters including my wife's brothers and sisters. Many of them are very successful now. One of them is a billionaire now. Not all of them forget about our help. We are getting gifts and appreciations from them. On the other hand, I am now giving help to people who have failed and are not so lucky. I know their feelings. I have met failures before. They make me sad, and they are no fun but stink. I now realise that being kind to people who have failed and are depressed is often the best way to deliver that value that is needed most.

Sixth, I always practise what I love. It doesn't matter what you do. Do it as often as you can. Doing things we had done many times helps us to operate with confidence. For example, I loved playing basketball during my school days, and I practised most of the skills every day to excel in the game. I used my self-study strategy almost every day to prepare lessons before I attended class. All these repetitive habits are the key to my success in study and game. I love writing. I started as a mathematics textbooks writer when I was a teacher. Now I am trying to become a motivational book writer. I read and read to improve my knowledge in every aspect of life: motivation, well-being, wonders, wisdom, and others including how to create abundance. I believe in myself, and I think by reading and practicing I will be able to make my dreams come true. I also need to be aware that there is also a detrimental side to habits. They may prevent me from adapting to change. This awareness comes with my mathematical thinking that change is only constant in my life. I learn to move with necessary changes in my life. My three stages of life reflect this awareness. Even in investment, I need to adapt to change in business environment. Competition is the force that drives business to perpetually innovate. Companies that do not move with time soon become absolute. Only companies that adapt well will thrive by offering better products and services at cheaper prices. Many camera manufacturing companies had gone broke with the invention of digital phone like iPhone and the galaxy. Very soon many companies producing softwares for computers are going to be absolute when 'cloud computing' centres become popular. Every software and computing system can be obtained from the cloud computing centres. As an investor, these information and knowledge are essential in picking stocks for long-term investments.

Seventh, I practise outsource the things I don't love. Each day there are only twenty-four hours. Working hours usually range from eight to ten hours. It's hard to have time to do everything in the field you love with this time frame. I used to look into what I did when I was working. I loved to play games, I loved teaching, and I loved writing. When I was the principal of secondary schools, I had many things to do. I relied on outsource by listing things I did not have the time to do. I assigned running errands and other less important projects to my assistants. Outsourcing helped to ease my job to only critical parts of my responsibilities. This distribution of tasks helped to streamline the machinery of my administration. Even in home management, we need to distribute responsibilities to each and every member of the family.

Eighth, I used to analyse my own mistakes and failures. Even in tennis, I missed certain strokes and lost the game. I tried to figure out what was wrong with certain strokes and tried to play better with extra practice. Even now I have a sparring partner in tennis to help me rectifying my weakness in certain strokes. He is Tom Pearson, an eighty-five-year-old player who was a former corporate director. We play together very often, and we are great friends. In basketball game, when my team lost a game, I used to tell my teammates that failure is an opportunity to expand our creativity. It applies to our life too. There is a solution to any problem. We will not see it unless we look at the challenge from a different angle. In my writing now, with the computer age, I used to reread what I have written long ago and see what I can do differently. Sometimes, I have to rewrite them. In my earlier experiences as a mathematics textbooks writer, I really felt the pain when I spotted my own mistakes. I was upset many times and even had nightmares. I could not even look at my own mistakes for months afterwards. Now I realise that I get better at analysing my mistakes. I get better at doing what I love, writing and investing. Creativity is the method of problem-solving that expands your perspective and turns your imagination into reality. Even in my daily life, before the end of each day, I used to look back things I had done. I used to analyse things that I am not happy with. I used to tell myself to avoid doing such things. I think of alternative ways of doing them. I realise that my life needs constant improvement.

Another motivating trait I consistently use is to give myself the push. In my game, basketball or tennis, after every match, I always think of what else I can do to make my game better. In my teaching, I used to think of more effective ways to make learning simpler. In writing, I used to think of what else I can do with the work I am most proud of. Every day there is always a push within me to do better in helping others to learn through teaching or writing. Even in investment, there is always a push to pick the right stocks to make money. I always believe that I am the type of person who can use my skills to help, teach, and provide values in many ways I have not thought about yet. So when the push works, an entire new world will open up: new people and new experiences. Finally, it feeds right back into the very basics of doing what I love. It also adds value right back to the source.

Others like failure should be viewed as an opportunity to learn. I consider the season of failure as the time for me to sow the seeds of success. It may hurt a little bit, and just stop over thinking over it. When people succeed, they bask in glory. When they fail, they mope in defeat. But both success and failure are temporary waves in an ever-changing ocean of life. They are neither permanent nor final. Winston Churchill said,

> 'Success is stumbling from failure to failure with no loss of enthusiasm.'

I realise that I will never find someone more worthy of love than myself. So I try to practise to love myself. With the process and seeds, everything will respond to me. I try to surround myself with people with positive energy so more energy will be created and that bring me to a higher level. I will go out to meet people who inspire me.

Getting enough rest is critical for me. I learn not to do one thing all day, all week, all months, for the rest of my life. I mix them up: games, teaching, writing, and investing. I learn to read new books, meet people, and spend time with family and friends. I try to gain new experiences all the time. Not just so that I can rest. The mind is such a wonderful machine that is capable of combining ideas without us thinking about it. After enough rest if I get back to doing what I love to do, I usually do it better.

Finally, I learn not hold grudges. I stumble on the idea that not everyone is going to help me out or like me today. I had an experience where a form six mathematics teacher made a nasty comment about my first additional mathematics textbook. After using my sixth-form textbooks, she wrote back to express her appreciation on my method of humanising the teaching of applied mathematics. I am glad I did not argue with her when she made her first comments. I followed the principle of ignoring people who made destructive comments about me. I had another experience with the boss of my publication company. He threatened to sue me because my editor left the company to joint venture with me in a new project. I ignored him. He later worked with me in many other textbooks with different editors. We later became close friends. So you see, grudges and lashing back will only hurt your long-term chances of success. Success is hard enough without you cutting yourself off all your escape exits. Next time if anyone hurt you, do not turn a small burning candle into a raging fire!

Last but not least, if you believe you can do it, you probably can. If you believe you can't, you probably can't. All our possibilities and limitations are self-created. Both fear and confidence are narrative we tell ourselves. So if you want to change and improve our life, shift our thoughts and beliefs to the story we prefer and stick with it. Everything we experience is essential to our growth. All of us are looking for life experience, growth, and contribution. Living in the present moment is the foundation of all success and happiness. When I work, I work fully. When I relax, I relax fully. When I enjoy, I enjoy fully. Only a centred mind is capable of creative thinking. Whatever moment brings, embrace it and cultivate peace of mind. Followed what Lao Tzu said, 'If you are depressed, you are living in the past. If you are anxious, you are living in the future. If you are at peace, you are living in the present.'

> Living the present well is most important. How to be at peace now? I try my best to make peace with the present moment! The present moment is the ground in which the game of my life happens. By living well today, I will make every yesterday a memorable day.

The Three Stages of My Life

My life journey is exciting. Life can generally be classified into three general categories: the learning stage, the working stage, and finally the retiring or yearning stage. I spent almost twenty-nine years in the learning stage before I formally entered into my professionally working life where I spent another twenty-three years, working mainly as a sixth-form mathematics teacher, and in my free time worked as a writer, personal mathematics tutor, part-time lecturer, business initiator, and investor. When I took my optional retirement at the age of fifty-one, I unintentionally joined the retiring group to start my yearning stage of life. Many consider this age to be too young for retirement. I have been in my yearning stage for almost twenty-three years now, and I believe I will remain in this stage for many more years to come. I am still healthy and enjoying my life doing the things I enjoy. I play tennis seriously three times per week. I walk up the hill in front of my home in Brisbane almost every day. It takes about half an hour to go up and another half an hour to come down. I still maintain my garden and enjoy my daily routine. I enjoy reading, learning, doing research, writing, and investing. I believe that when a concept can be visualised in the mind, it exists. I still explore, dream, and try discoveries. All these routines plus eating moderately keep me in shape, mentally alert, and contribute to my healthy life.

I went into my yearning stage to begin another phase of life without having to clock in every day. Each of these three stages of life brings its own excitements, wonders, and challenges. I am now seventy-five and looking forward to many more exciting years to add to my enjoyable and healthy journey in life. I have just signed up to do a course in meditation involving creative visualisation and a personal development programme under the great Burt Goldman. My intention to complete my motivational book and my own autobiography on the journey of my life has motivated me to explore all possible means. I had been a curriculum developer, writing mainly mathematics textbooks for secondary schools. I was also involved in revision books and guidebooks to help students master secondary school mathematics. Now I am experimenting with motivational books.

The Wonders of the Four Seasons of My Life

The three stages of my life can be divided into four seasons. From the time I was born until I left for my secondary school in Penang, the period when I stayed with my parents for almost fifteen years, I was living in the economic winter season of my life. Life was tough and cold. With so many brothers and sisters, I had to struggle for survival. I had to work every day after school. We had to fight for food every day. Imagine you live in a family with seven brothers and five sisters. How much food and clothing your parents have to prepare for all of you? There was no time for thinking and enjoying. After primary school, I had to tap rubber in the morning and attend school in the afternoon. I attended Methodist Afternoon School in Parit Buntar, a town about fifteen kilometres from my hometown, Serdang in the state Kedah. Everything was in a rush. Every day I had to catch a bus to school. The journey took almost half an hour to forty-five minutes from Serdang to Bandar Bahru. I had to take a small boat to cross the river from Bandar Bahru into Parit Buntar and walk three kilometres to school. I did this routine five times a week for three long years. It was a missionary school helping averaged students to learn some English and other subjects. Not much learning took place because the schooling hours were short, the weather was hot, and the teachers were underqualified. Anyhow I was grateful for picking up some words helping me improving my command of English and learn other subjects in English. A full description of this stage of my life is found in Chapter Four.

The period I spent in Penang Secondary School, in teacher training college, and in university was the spring season of my life. Much has been written about the blooming of flowers during the spring season. Trees that have shed their leaves during winter season will begin to put on new leaves. This was the period when my game, basketball, was at its best. I represented my school, the combined schools, and the national combined schools teams. I played in the Penang Senior Basketball League for the champion team in Penang. Every competitive game I played, I was rewarded with small sum of pocket money. I was not a professional player. I also played for my hometown team in Kedah State Basketball League. I represented both Kedah State and Penang State in the game. All my food and travel expenses were taken care off because I was one of the key players. I travelled frequently from Penang to Kedah when the basketball seasons were in full swing. I was rewarded for all the efforts. Being a student, the money came in very handy.

In academic life, some discoveries were made. I learnt creative visualisation through meditation. I discovered an effective self-study strategy that helped me excel in my study. I became a top student in my class. I was assertive, and I got along well with most people and was very dependable. I learnt to become a leader by helping others to learn effectively. I started to become financially independent during my secondary school days by giving tuition to neighbouring boys and two of my classmates. I did not have to depend on my father for pocket money during my secondary school days.

I enjoyed two years of teacher training at the technical teachers training college (TTTC). Although I was not very interested in industrial arts education, I had enriched my life by the exposure. I only served about two years as an industrial arts teacher before I left for University of Malaya for my science degree, majoring in mathematical physics. Three and half years of university life had actually transformed my thinking and my beliefs. This is the climax of my learning stage. I do not stop learning. I am in fact more interested to help revolutionise the teaching and learning process in mathematics. I went on to get my master's degree and Ph.D. later on.

When I started working as a graduate teacher, I was working too hard and everything was hot. I began my economic summer season of my life. I had a job as a mathematics teacher. After a few years of teaching, I fell in love with my job. I began to reflect seriously to make teaching my career. It was an exploration that led me to ponder such a thing entitled calling because I wanted to make difference in teaching and learning. And does such a thing actually exist? Academic research seems to provide such evidence statistically. People's desire to pursue their true calling has tripled in the past five years. I think it represents an urgent demand among employees to work for more than just money. I believe in it by putting extra number of hours in dedication to the job to have some sort of impact on the learning stage. I wanted to make a difference, and at the same time, I wanted to leave some marks, no matter how small in the grand scheme of teaching and learning. At the same time, I am aware of the emotional consequences that arise from the desperate pursuit of a calling. To some people, such pursuit can be satisfying and life changing. It is also possible that such pursuit can lead to frustration and misery. If such a calling is near impossible to identify and attain, it may lead to feeling of personal failure. Luckily, I love what I do in my career, and I have the talent or potential competencies to follow my calling. I was also aware that such calling does not pay much. I should not be disappointed for the lack of compensation for such a calling. I am aware that I could extend my calling by using my spare time to create my financial security. I knew very early that my calling will not provide financial security. My calling is perhaps nothing more than an inspired and hopeful idea in my mind. I did not set any unrealistic expectation from the pursuit of my calling. I did not have to chase after any quixotic dream from the calling. To avoid disappointment, I began to use my spare time wisely in pursuit of knowledge, wisdom, and encouragement. I extended my calling into curriculum innovations, providing tuition for the needs of some students and textbooks production. My calling together with the sidekicks lasted for twenty-three years. It's like 'calling sidekicks' helping the fire burning in my career. Finally, I realise that chasing my calling leads to happiness and joy contrary to many people's experience of regret and disillusionment. Looking back, I can confidently say that all my efforts are worthwhile.

I was a teacher, tutor, writer, an investor, and entrepreneur. I took charge of my finance and created streams of linear (active) income and residual (passive) income. I lived a healthy life, saved any surplus, and started to invest for my future. I want to share with you the experiences I went through before I became a wealthy man. I noticed something interesting. Every single time I experienced success, I froze. I always confront a belief that held me back from achieving more. I came across people who were brilliant, talented, and passionate, but their subconscious belief system around money, their financial mindset, and their limiting beliefs caused them from achieving their dreams. Initially, I was suffering from the same limiting beliefs. I was aware why some of my father's friends were rich. They were mostly self-employed. They worked for their own profits instead for somebody else. They took charge of their own destiny and built their own confidence, knowing that confidence could boost their income. They did not necessarily choose businesses that they were passionate about or really understand. They looked for areas that were in great demand and small supply. This appears natural, but most people do not follow. They were not brilliant, but they knew how to choose wisely. They knew how to get along with people. They had strong work ethic, leadership, and very dependable. I think their self-discipline has greater advantage over their IQ. They are rich because they are thrifty and not materialistic. They usually think long term and are always money conscious. This awareness gives me an advantage when I have started to create my own areas of finding extra income. I wanted to be financially independent too and be rich. Luckily, I realised that unless I could reach a breakthrough in my own life, I wouldn't be fully able to help others. I decided to take massive action. I started to activate my brain to become money conscious. My family started to operate on an annual budget. We knew how much we spent on foods, clothing, shelter, and transport. We started to plan our monthly, annually, and life goal. A lot of time was spent in planning our financial future. I did not have much time to spend in my working life because I started very late. I started to train my brain muscles the way I trained the skills for my game. I needed a couch to assist my consistent practice in skills, strength, and conditioning. Similarly, in wealth creation, I needed role models and examples. I read widely about successful investors and writers. I learnt their rhythm and their style of investing and writing. Forming good habits and developing good strategies of writing and investing were my immediate concern. These helped me to breakthrough all limits and created a life of non-stop success. The economic summer season of my life ended when I took my optional retirement.

The economic autumn season of my life started when I took my optional retirement at the age of fifty-one. Everything cooled down. I left Malaysia for Australia. During autumn many leaves turn yellow. This period is most attractive and beautiful. I sensed and enjoyed this new beauty immediately. I was back at the University of Queensland to pursue my doctoral study. It took me almost three and half years to complete my thesis. I went back to teaching for a short period, and then I became self-employed. I started writing and investing again as my new phase of life. As I had mentioned before, I had created a few streams residual income which kept flowing. I am still doing the same thing now to create further residual streams of income. I will share these four economic seasons of my life in detail in the subsequent chapters.

A Simple View of a Successful Life

My beloved wife hinted to me that nobody would be interested to read about the journey through these four economic seasons of my life. She had the right to be sceptical because when I started writing, I, too, was sceptical about my chance of success. However, I strongly feel that that my humble working life punctuated by discoveries, challenges, wonders, and the many lessons learnt may inspire many youngsters especially my grandchildren to follow and live a purposeful, a healthy, and a more fulfilled life. I believe that a good life allows our full potential to blossom, and we can have the financial freedom to give back to the community what we have benefited. It does not matter which profession you embark on. What matter is that you like your job and enjoy what you do, accomplishing as much as you can. There are three things that really matter: what you do, where you do, and whom you do it with. Everyone has a different definition to the meaning of success in life. People think that having wealth and position are necessary metrics for a successful life. But I beg to differ. Having these two metrics may be necessary for security, power, and freedom financially. Depending on these two metrics may appear to be sitting on a stool with two legs according to Ariana Buffington. She thinks that we need another metric embracing four main pillars: well-being, wisdom, wonders, and giving. All these values will be dealt with in the subsequent chapters of this book. My simple definition of success in my life means that I have travelled each of the three stages of life happily, enjoyed what I do, gained valuable experiences, accomplished what I can, allowed my full potential to grow, kept myself healthy, and had the freedom financially to give back to society what I have benefited. I believe that I have achieved these basic feats. I have made full use of opportunities available to learn, to experience, and to grow in each stage of my life. I have earned an honest living and learn not to take life too seriously. Nothing in life is certain, but it is certain that my journey in life will end someday. The destination is not important. Making the journey enjoyable and exciting is a top priority. Contributing to society in many forms is my ultimate goal in life.

The Wonder of Infinity and the Infinite Power of the Mind

I am always attracted to the concept of infinity. What is infinity? How much is infinity? How many is infinity? I do not know the answer. A famous writer in China by the name of Wu Hsin wrote beautifully about this concept.

> 'The infinite has no preferences. It kisses both the darkness and the light equally.'

By the way, Wu Hsin came about 100 years after Confucius, and in Chinese, his name means 'no-mind'. But I believe in the infinite power of the mind! I have passed through seventy-five spring seasons and have witnessed the human power in innovation and invention: from bicycle to motorcycle, from car to aeroplane, from ordinary train to bullet train, from radio to TV, and from telephone to Internet. There is no limitation, and more innovations are on the way like three-dimensional printing and new industry in robotics. A revolution of industrial workforce is emerging. Soon, the new adaptation involving 'cloud computing' will become our daily practice when we use our computers in business and research. And our pocket phone will replace our credit card for purpose of money transaction. It will be harder for credit card thieves to function.

The main purpose of sharing my experiences, discoveries, and lessons learnt in my three stages of life is to encourage young people to make full use of their infinite power of their mind. Do not allow your circumstances to dictate the growth of your potential. Listen to what Stephen R. Convey said,

> 'I am not a product of my circumstances. I am a product of my decisions.'

My attitude towards new things has always be guarded by Virgil Garnett Thomson, who said,

> 'Try a thing you haven't done three times: once, to get over the fear of doing it; twice, to learn how to do it; and a third time, to figure out whether you like it or not.'

I believe that tomorrow will be better if I make use of today's opportunities well. I was involved in daydreaming when I was young, and I also had many dreams. Soon I began to see the difference between the two concepts. You want something but do nothing; that is daydreaming. You take action because you want something; that is having a dream. My name in Chinese means new dream. I have lived up to my name. I have turned many of my dreams into reality with the help of creative visualisation, and it helps me to become who I am. They have brought me everything I could have ever asked for in life, success, talent, happiness, you name it.

During my three stages of life, I have used many successful techniques that have completely changed who I am. I believe I have adopted the policy of what Og Mandino said,

> 'I am here for a purpose and that purpose is to grow into a mountain, not to shrink to a grain of sand. Henceforth will I apply all my efforts to become the highest mountain of all and I will strain my potential until it cries for mercy.'

During my learning stage, I discovered an effective self-study strategy including interaction with others that helped me to learn and remember facts effectively. I also discovered an effective drill strategy that helped me to excel in the sport I love. These simple strategies only need discipline and time to carry out effectively. I believe in the infinite power of the mind. I also believe in meditation and creative visualisation. Regular meditation practice involving a few minutes per session helps to enhance my creative visualisation power and my decision-making processes, and it helps me to focus to accomplish my dreams. Consequently, meditation helps me to be more patient, and it helps me to make good decisions. Meditation releases the intelligence which helps me to be creative and be happy. My experiences may serve as a catalyst for you to experiment this technique to make learning more effective. It may change your approach to your learning life and open up your mind power to achieve your full potential. Later, I realised that I was actually integrating my body, mind, and soul through meditation. Regular meditation helps to harmonise the three parts of my life, helping me to make sound decisions, to be healthy, and to be happy.

My simple self-study strategy and my persistent training drill in basketball skills served as the backbone of my accomplishments in education and sport respectively. These approaches had helped many of my students to achieve their goals in learning and to excel in the sports they loved. All you need is an open mind and the power of intent. Once you are willing to adopt this simple self-study strategy to learn and the persistent drill in game skills, my experiences will lead the way for you to harness the power of your mind, to become an effective learner, and to excel in any of the sports you intend to take up. The purpose of learning life lessons began here. Its implications and applications have wider scope in my later life.

The working stage of my life has provided me opportunities to grow and to accomplish many successes. I want to share with you the steps that I had taken to accomplish what I have. Whatever career or profession you are in, it does not matter. Working life only lasts twenty to thirty years or slightly more or less, if you are lucky. What matter most is your well-being, your resourcefulness, and your happiness. Always make sure that you have enough sleep. Able to keep in good shape and fit will form the very foundation for a happy and healthy retirement. The lifestyle I led may serve as a good example to keep in good shape. Exercise regularly and eat moderately with plenty of fresh fruits, vegetables, and proteins.

During this short working period, find the quickest and easiest way to attract wealth, even if you've never been much of a money magnet. My experiences in using a multiple approaches to attract wealth may serve as a corner stone for you to consider. Learn from many sources how to grow your wealth in preparation for your retirement. At the same time, try to discover what really makes you happy even if you've always felt something is missing. You need a cool and calm mind to make the best decisions in life. Learn to be assertive and not aggressive in your daily life. Practising creative meditation or other spiritual approach can be of great help. Find a partner or soulmate of your life is critical. To make this important decision, you need to follow your heart. Understanding your past can help you make good decision. Whatever job you have taken, get the confidence you've wanted. Look for a job or start your own business that will make you happy. Above all these, career is a choice. No matter how humble a job is, you can make full use of the opportunities available. Master various skills like communication, assertive interaction, painting, writing, and others even you've never found the time or inclination to take it all the way. Importantly, try to make the most out of today, and tomorrow will take care of itself. By keeping your intent and purpose clear, it helps you to take control of your future. My working life experiences as a humble teacher, writer, tutor, business initiator, and investor can offer some food for thought. All works no play can make you a dull person.

Take up a sport and play like a pro, even if you never thought it is your strong point. I continue to play competitive basketball game even when I was over fifty years old. Competition and endurance had always been in my blood since student days. Playing competitive games add a lot of excitements to your life. When I was over fifty years old, I was still involved in international veteran games in basketball. I played in many countries, representing Malaysia. When I started teaching as a graduate teacher, I picked up golf and tennis. Though I did not excel in these two games, I played reasonably well to enjoy the games. Until today at the age of seventy-five, I still play tennis regularly to keep me in shape and healthy. I only play golf occasionally because of time factor. Another important aspect of life is to alleviate your health problems. You are what you eat! This saying is very relevant. If you are careless in your working life, putting too much toxic materials into your body and not eating enough fruits and vegetables plus sufficient proteins to maintain your optimum health, you are preparing to bring suffering and pains in your retirement. My working life experiences can serve as examples for you to start making good decisions and forming good habits to enjoy your working life and prepare to enjoy your retirement. Being healthy in all the three stages of life is the first priority. If you are concerned about the possibilities of being sickly during your retirement, you are not alone.

A Simple Purpose of Life

From my own experience, my career as a mathematics teacher is a stable job for me to make a living. I enjoyed teaching, and it had become part of my purpose of life. I begin to explore possibility of making my career a calling. Does such a thing really exist? I am aware that many of the jobs to which a calling is attached (nursing, childcare, educator, preacher and others) do not pay much. The warm tingling we get from 'making a difference' is often insufficient to compensate for the lack of compensation. I support the normal purpose of education. I am just one of the many people who intend to leave their mark, no matter how small in the grand scheme of things. I spend extraordinary number of hours dedicating to the job, hoping to have some sort of positive impact on the world. In my spare time, my calling becomes a stepping stone, providing me a platform to become a writer and curriculum innovator. I derived more recurring income from my dedication to help students learn effectively than my teaching career. So my teaching career and my extra calling as a writer combined together gave me a better purpose of my life. With the financial strength from my first calling with recurring income, I was able to pursue my dreams. I ventured into something else to get to know myself. I started investing and initiating businesses to gain financial independent. This has activated another purpose of my life in relation to my hidden calling. It took me more than two decades of struggle to realise that I had this hidden calling to help and serving others. To be able to help and serve effectively, I needed confidence and financial strength. I learn to understand myself and put my knowledge into action. Occasionally, I might suffer from high activity disorder because I tried to achieve too many things at the same time. My regular meditation seemed to provide some calming effect and in decision making.

Another purpose of life for me is to attend to many arising moments involving my games, family, career, and callings. Especially in game, I derived many excitements. It helps to build my determination and consistency. I believe that I had adopted an effective approach by practicing every element of everyday life again and again until I could function smoothly. These actions together with ample knowledge activated my feeling of happiness and content. I look back to my career and accomplishments with great satisfaction. Life is full of wonders. I wonder why a person pays $300 million for a painting of a dead person. I do not understand all the wonders, but I appreciate them.

Assertiveness as an Important Social Skill in My Life

When I was in secondary school in Penang, I happened to come across this important social behaviour called assertiveness. When I was approached to lead a group of students who wanted to improve their academic performance, I was given the role of leadership. The first thing for me was to establish the right attitude to be assertive. Many people seem to confuse regarding these two social behaviours: assertiveness and aggressiveness. There is a fine line separating these two social behaviours. Being aggressive means selfishly pushing for what you want at the expense of others. In doing so, you generate a host of negative behaviours that make others become defensive, angry, and even vengeful towards you. This may create hostility, threat, gossip, and other unreasonable demands. Aggressiveness may allow you to get what you want immediately, but you will not have what you need the next time. On the other hand, assertiveness means standing up for your rights while respecting the rights of others. It also means using appropriate expression of your feelings, needs, and opinions while respecting the feelings of others. Being assertive always means communicating what you really want in a clear way while ensuring that you are not being taken advantage of. Shakti Gawain put it this way,

'Assertiveness is not what you do, it's who you are!'

So there is a huge difference being assertive and being aggressive. Being assertive is a way of living where you get the most out of life without others telling you how to do it. It simply means that you do not need to be obnoxious, pushy, or rude to get things done according to your way.

I was lucky that I learnt this social skill early in my life. When I started to conduct tuition sessions to my classmates and neighbouring kids in my secondary school days, I started to learn to be assertive not aggressive because I needed to take care of their feelings. This awareness gave me the transformation to use expressions that encouraged changes especially attitude in students under my care. I learnt to respect their feelings and their rights as I learnt to take charge of my own life. I needed to be honest to myself in what I was doing and teaching. I was calling the shorts and making all the decisions for them. I learnt not to push them too hard and allowed them to develop their learning skills slowly. I believed that I had learnt assertiveness very carefully in my early life. The motivation was there together with incentive and rewards. This social skill was further developed when I became a graduate teacher, deputy principal, and then principal. Many in-service courses on leadership and administration further strengthened my assertiveness as an individual, as a teacher, as an administrator, and as a writer. Unfortunately, the school curriculum does not touch on this social skill called assertiveness. Stephanie Matson has pointed out,

> 'When children are treated with acceptance, they develop self acceptance.'

Students experience pressure both at home and in school, so it may be necessary to teach them to be assertive. They need to know their rights, and they need to be taught. The biggest obstacle to the students' personality development might just be their social skills including assertiveness. Most students are lacking in social and communication skills resulting in them the lack of self-confidence. They are unsure about what to say or how to approach other students; some are big bullies. Some exposure to the skill of assertiveness is essential for their well-being and self-confidence.

When I was the principal, I used to impress on them their basic rights during short school assembly. No one has the right to make them feel guilty, foolish, or ignorant. They do not have to make excuses for every little thing they do. They should be allowed to change their mind and not feel bad about it. They do not have to know everything, and they have the rights to ask questions when they do not understand. They do not have to be perfect in everything. None of us is perfect. The biggest obstacle they face is their social and communication skills before they can become assertive. Perhaps, a move to teach assertiveness should be initiated in the curriculum called living skills. Students should be taught to say 'no' diplomatically when things are detrimental to their personality or social development. Assertiveness in their expressions will form the boundaries where their peers will soon learn to respect. A certain amount of training and practice is necessary to drive home this essential social skill.

Relationship and Happiness

Have you ever ponder what is the most important thing in your life? My life experiences taught me this critical secret of life. After enjoying seventy-five spring seasons, I realise that relationship is most important. Improve your relationship with family members, friends, and colleagues. Always practise consideration, kindness, and helpfulness to them. Don't forget assertiveness while doing these. Show love and kindness whenever necessary. Attitude is critical. Leo Tolstoy once said,

> 'Seize the moments of happiness, love and be love! That is the only reality in the world, all else is folly. It is the only thing we are interested in here.'

The best way to pay for a lovely relationship is to enjoy it. Being assertive especially in communication will be a great asset to develop friendship, trust, and love. Love is more a desire than an emotion. So provide it freely to develop good relationship.

Another important metric to enhance a good life is cultivating good friendship. Everyone is different. Choose your friends wisely. My approach to lasting friendship is simple. Associate with friends who have the same attitude and interest as you. It's important that they can help you to grow and vice versa. Do not forget to show kindness to those whom you do not pick as friends. Elbert Hubbard's wisdom is a good guide.

'A friend is someone who knows all about you and still loves you.'

Having friends not only brings happiness but also is essential for healthy development. A healthy friendship is what we live for and enjoy. Hanging out with friends of common interest brings not only happiness but also necessary for our soul. Having lunch or dinner with close friends can help us relax and find better meaning in our life.

The Key to Normal Growth Is Love

I liked the metaphor the first time I read in the book *The Five Love Languages* by Gary Chapman. He wrote, 'Inside every child is an "emotional tank" waiting to be filled with love. When a child really feels love, he or she will develop normally, but when the love tank is empty, the child will misbehave. Much of the misbehaviour of children is motivated by the cravings of an empty "love tank".' Parents are advised to take note of this important component of relationship if you want your child to grow up normally. The desire for love is natural. Many children suffer from the lacking of love demonstrated by parents because of ignorance. When I was working, I was too busy with all my activities. The mother is always strict and firm. She does tolerate nonsense. I was ignorant of the skills of parenting. My own son is complaining that he grew up with an empty 'love tank' most of the time and now he is reflecting on things affected by the lack. He reminds himself not to repeat the same treatment he is giving his children. Hopefully, his children will grow with their 'love tank' always full.

This is a good realisation for the future generations.

But this emotional desire for love, however, is not simply a childhood phenomenon. Love is a critical desire. This need follows us into adulthood and into marriage. Remember we need love before we fall in love. This emotional desire always resurfaces because it is not only fundamental in nature but also the centre of our emotional desire. All of us need love as long as we live. Material things will not be able to replace this human touch of emotional love. Marriage is designed to meet the intimacy and emotional love.

We know that marriage is important, but it is also elusive. When a couple fails to meet each other's needs, this invisible 'emotional love tank' with its gauge can be empty. It is possible that an empty tank encourages misbehaviours, harsh words, critical spirit, and withdrawal. On the contrary, a full love tank can create a climate that it is possible to discuss differences and resolve conflicts.

I like the metaphorical comparing of our 'emotional love tank' to that of an automobile. Running our marriage on an empty 'love tank' may cost more than to drive our car without petrol. Now I try to fill up my 'emotional love tank' by learning to speak the primary love language of my spouse. I used to meditate deeply and let my subconscious mind explore possible means to learn my spouse's primary love language. Gary Chapman introduced the five love languages: words of affirmation, quality time, receiving gifts, arts of service, and physical touch. Now I know that people behave differently when their emotional love tanks are full. This basic principle applies to all human beings. Knowing all these secrets will help us to enhance the quality of our marriage and our relationship with our loved ones.

A common mistake people make is that we take our spouse for granted after years of marriage. I must admit that I had made this mistake out of ignorance. We had received critical or demanding words and negative comments from our parents as we grew up. Usually, this memory is deep rooted in our subconscious. The tendency of imitation usually emerges as time goes on. Soon using negative words, critical remarks, and sometimes putting your spouse down in front of friends or relatives make their ugly appearance. Our love tank begins to drain and soon physical touch between us disappears. The other languages of love will soon vanish too. Hopefully, this awareness will remind us to refrain from using such critical and damaging words. We need self-control. Words of affirmation encourage appreciation and reconfirm love for each other. It really means a lot to each other's emotional love.

I am always prepared to learn from others. In addition, I used to make use of creative visualisation technique of meditation to learn from a successful person. I believe in deep meditation through Quantum Jumping advocated by Burt Goldman. If a successful person can be imagined, the person exists. Now I try to use my imagination and creative visualisation. The imagination provides me the process of reaching a successful doppelganger. Learn his methods, draw upon his skills and experiences, and find out how he becomes happy, talented, or successful in relationship. Now I read widely to enhance my imaginations. Now I really make an effort to ensure that my spouse and grandchildren have their love tanks full. I had plenty of experiences of negative words from my wife and parents because I was too optimistic and always had big dreams. I was overconfident because of my past successes. I was accused of talking big and being unrealistic in life. Our marriage almost broke down when I became a Christian after my son made the same commitment. The only thing that saved our marriage is the deep love we have for each other. I appreciate her language of love on acts of service and acts of receiving gifts. She is a passionate woman while I am not. We spent a lot of quality time together before trouble started. We were always together. All the negative words and demands will not help in the marriage. The love of Jesus and the creative visualisation during meditations helped me in my decision. She was strong, and we discussed our differences. I told her not to use past mistakes as weapons to suppress others. We managed to resolve our main differences and conflicts. I had made some mistakes saying things that might not be true. But occasionally, she still reminds me of my big dreams and still thinks that I am still talking big in spite of not mixing with others regularly. Hopefully, we will be able to fill our love tanks again. This confirms the importance of words of affirmation leading to other languages of love. Since I have discovered the primary love language of my spouse, I would choose to speak it consistently and regularly. In addition, I would like to extend this radical concept of 'emotional love tanks' to my children and grandchildren. In addition, I had learnt a very critical lesson regarding marriage and relationship. Now I know that most of our marital arguments cannot be resolved. We had spent year after year trying to change each other's mind, but it cannot be done. This is because most of our disagreements are rooted in fundamental differences of lifestyle, personality, and values. I regretted that I had fought over these differences all the years. All we had succeeded in doing is wasting our time and harming our marriage. Now I learn to accept that these differences in beliefs and values are part of our marital relationship. These differences are similar to joint pains, backache, and other ailments as we grow older, and we need to learn to live with them without disrupting our active and happy life. We may not love these problems, but we need to learn to cope with them and avoid situations worsening them. I need to create strategies to improve the situation and learn not to use past mistakes to create and extend these problems.

Since I started to practise meditation in a process known as Quantum Jumping, it helps me not only to take responsibility of the things that are beyond my control but also to help to change them for the better. I like watching fish because it induces peace. Fish move slowly and breathe slowly.

Watching them is like gazing at a calm inner world. I turn to meditation to reach this peaceful stage. Whenever I manage to reach the alpha stage of visualisation in meditation, it becomes an antidote to alleviate sadness, pains, anxiety, depression, fears, hatred, and confusions in my life. My level of happiness seems to increase. I am able to let go of grudges and other things that I cannot change. Even the inflammation and pain on my knee joint because of my regular tennis games seems to decrease. I suspect my frequent meditations must have produced more antibodies to a flu vaccine because I seem to avoid flu most of the time. Before that I used to contact flu whenever the weather changed. *Time* magazine recently reported that meditation brings in many benefits. No reason is given but the report says meditation works. Reaching alpha level in meditation is supposed to help depression, control pain, increase longevity, slow down cancer, invigorate the immune system, and significantly reduce blood pressure. Meditation is used to control weight and sometimes be used to replace Viagra. Medical brain scans suggest that meditation may be rewiring the brain to reduce stress and to slow or prevent pain of chronic diseases like heart conditions, cancer, and infertility. It is believed that meditation at alpha level can serve as a means of transforming our creative visualisation. Our mind is always responsible for change and success. This powerful imagination technique called visualisation can change almost every aspect of our life. I soon realise that visualisation works if I believe and take actions. An experiment was carried out by Shawn Achor, the author of *Happiness Advantage,* involving two groups of people. The first group exercised a finger for four weeks. The second group just imagined doing the finger exercise through visualisation for the same period. The first group found that they increased their finger muscle strength by 53 per cent, whereas the second group managed to increase their muscle strength by 35 per cent. Our finger muscle strength can be improved by visualisation through meditation. It seems that our subconscious or nervous system cannot tell the difference between a real and an imagined event. So it is not wrong to conclude that we can enjoy small improvement in every aspect of our life through visualisation in our meditation.

Since I am aware that most of our marital arguments cannot be resolved, it will be a waste of energy and time to try. What we can do is to have strategies and routines we can use to cope with these differences. It is important for us to refrain from criticising each other and to show contempt in various ways. We can accept complaint. Criticism attacks the person not the behaviours. Name calling, sneering, or mockery can be poisonous form of contempt. It conveys disgust. We should try to avoid indulging in such behaviours. We should avoid using defensiveness as a weapon because defensiveness is really a way of blaming your spouse. Last but not least, we should avoid cutting off our spouse emotionally in the relationship. Just to be aware that relationships often fail because of individual issues, not because of a bad match. We have learnt to resolve difficulties as soon as we can. They do not strengthen relationships, but they cripple them. Some of the things we do to enhance our relationship include doing exciting things together, celebrating each of our success, and showing gratitude. We are aware that it's easy to get lazy when things are getting well. But a little effort can go a long way. A new journey should begin if we know where we are heading. Stop all the unnecessary arguments and learn to know each other's world. Accept differences as part of marital relationship and remember things that make each other happy. Try to avoid using you and I whenever there is a fight. At the end of each day, reunite and talk about how it went. The goal is to overcome stress that can negatively affect the relationship. It takes hard work to make a marital relationship blossom. Remember a good marital relationship has positive effects like increasing success, longevity, health, and happiness.

Family Life

I have a beautiful wife and two good-looking children. We have been married for almost forty-five years. Our initial family life was loaded with heavy responsibilities. My father passed away when I was twenty-four years old. My youngest brother and my youngest sister were only in primary schools. My father, before he breathed his last, told me to see them through life. I agreed. My youngest sister came to stay with me. She finished her HSC and eventually got her honours degree in economics at University of Malaya. My brother was admitted into University of Singapore and obtained his engineering degree. I had to support both of them for six years: two years in form six and four years in the university. In addition, my wife's brothers and a sister were boarding with us while they pursued their degrees. I have great respect for my wife, who is a good home manager. There were actually nine persons living in my house including my two children and a maid during our early marriage life. Getting food on the table was her responsibility. I still remember buying fish, prawns, and vegetables in bulk at the wholesale market early in the morning. The market wholesalers thought that we were running a restaurant. We had to be there very early in the morning. A lot of effort and time were spent to prepare the foods and keep them in our freezer as supply for the week. All of them helped in the preparation. Since both of us were working, we could only do our marketing once a week. My wife worked very hard. She had to work as a nurse and had to cook at home. On top of this heavy responsibility, she was the mother of two kids. However, we survived. Years passed, and my sister, my wife's brothers, and sister were graduated from the university. We are indeed proud of our achievement.

My role is to provide the financial support for the extended family. At that point, money was an amazing, innovating, and motivating catalyst; it pushed me to do astonishing things. I did not neglect my extended family and my responsibilities. Perhaps, it inspired me to greatness, to innovation, and to charity. I lived well. I had purpose. I had passion. I had a father's drive to deliver financially for my extended family. I had a reason to get up every day. I had something to live for, a direction, a focus, a knowledge that every day I would set to succeed. I had to exercise my brain muscle to constantly develop my intellectual assets. I was busy but happy. That's what set me on course and what put me in contact with the interesting, the exciting, and the possible. It is what drove me to be innovative, competitive, and enterprising. The pursuit of the feeling that I had delivered, handsomely for my extended family, is critical to me. It was a challenge to lead an everyday life at the time. I felt I had done something worthwhile. All the experiences were important. All these efforts contributed to my happiness.

Retirement Life

The retirement stage of life has more to offer. I enjoy the most in this stage of my life. This is partly because of the sound decisions I had made during my working life. I worked hard, learnt new skills, and involved in extra hobbies like writing and investing to develop my full potential and to create wealth. I worked hard and enjoyed the journey of my working life. I took on extra responsibilities by helping my brothers, sisters, and nephews (including those from my wife's family) financially and teaching them self study strategy to succeed in their academic pursuits. The fruit of success is in front of my eyes. I see them grow and become successful and useful citizens of society. I really feel the sense of satisfaction and achievement. I really reap what I sow. Today, I am benefiting from their generosities and appreciating their gratitude.

Personally, I am equally successful. My belief in the infinite power of the mind has helped me in developing new skills in writing and investing. In a short span of my twenty-three years of working life, I had written and published more than two dozens of mathematics textbooks, guidebooks, and revision books. We had a family trust account to cater for our extra income and to make investments when the time is right. All these publications had brought me great financial rewards. The extra income annually enabled us to make investments in properties, businesses, and equities. I was also in a position to initiate new business like publication and importing and assembling computers as a wholesaler. All these long term investments put me in good position for a great retirement.

At the age of fifty-one, I embarked on a new adventure. I strongly believe in the infinite power of the mind. I left Kuala Lumpur to search for more knowledge and information. I enrolled at the University of Queensland to pursue my doctoral study. I was rewarded a Ph.D. after three and half years of intensive research. During that period, I had published a few more textbooks including pure mathematics and applied mathematics for sixth forms. I am still writing in my retirement. My belief in the power of the mind is growing stronger. I write about everything from learning aids to motivational books. With a strong foundation of multiple streams of income - a pension from the government, rentals from my investment properties, dividends from my equities and other sources such as royalties - I become financially independent. Our family trusted account gives us financial security. I am one of the lucky people who discovered a few secrets of life earlier. I spent years cultivating my self-study strategy and building up new knowledge and started investing for my retirement very early. I experienced school life, college life, and university life before I started teaching. Now I had experienced research life in a well-known university. All these experiences gave me an advantage in writing and investing. I continue my quest for more knowledge. I have just enrolled as a student in Quantum Jumping and personal development programmes. This will keep me busy in learning for many years. What more do I ask for in life! In the past, I thought I was clever, so I wanted to change the world. Today, I am wise, so I am changing and equipping myself for more knowledge. I realise that the horizon is always just as far away no matter how far I travel. It is not until I turn around and look back over the distance I have come to appreciate the progress I have made. I will keep setting new goals every year. It is more important that I set aside time to stop reflect and appreciate where I have been. My goals can become empty pursuits of achievement that not only add little to my experience of joy but can actually reduce it. Over the years I have better understanding of goals, and the process of making them have transformed significantly. Perhaps they will continue to transform. One of the realisations is that most of my goals came from a focus on what I perceived to be missing or not having enough in my life. Most of them were accomplishment based. Consequently, my sense of self-worth became directly tied to how many goals I accomplished or didn't accomplish. Some of the goals ended up doing more harm than good because they kept me stuck in the belief that my well-being was something to get rather than something based on more profound awareness of who I really am and what life is really for. It is more important that setting goals that will serve me instead of enslave me. I need to explore the prerequisite that any goal I set must be a stepping stone to my ultimate goal of my life. They must not be distractions or vain pursuit of my personality. The ultimate goal of my life is to live moment by moment in a state of appreciation of what is and the awareness of the essential truth of who I am and what is life for. I now know that I am not here to change life but to contribute my part to it. I need to make an appointment with myself where I can have some quite time for reflection and writing. All these experiences will be discussed in detail in the subsequent chapters.

Family Achievements

My wife bought a piece of land of about a quarter of an acre at Chapel Hill in Brisbane, Queensland, and built us a beautiful home for my two children and me. My two children joined the high school here and went on to complete their university education in Brisbane. My daughter graduated with first-class honours in applied science, and now she is a senior manager credit of a big corporation, Global Credit Funds at Colonial First State Global Asset Management. Her present responsibility involves analysis and monitoring of new and credit exposures and acts as the back up to the head of credit research. She is considered a highly skilled credit analyst with over a decade experience. She is the fixed income and credit team's responsible investment champion. Since 2008, she has overseen the consideration of environment, social, and governance (ESG) risks factored in the credit research process. She represents the team on the ESG committee and is part of the stranded assets working group sub-committee looking into the risk associated with potential stranded carbon intensive assets. She had served a portfolio manager, Colonial First State Global Asset Management, managing nearly 1.8 billion in Australia and New Zealand fixed interest portfolios. Her wide range of experiences includes the following: quantitative analyst (1997-2001), portfolio manager (2001-2003), credit analyst (2003-2009), and now manager credit (2009-present). My son graduated with distinction in computer science and an honours second class upper degree in electronic engineering. Both of them were awarded Commonwealth Scholarship to do their doctoral studies because of their outstanding results. My son took up an appointment with IBM at the Silicon Valley, California, USA. Later he joined Freddie Mate, a US company, as a junior director. Later, he started his own business, and now he is involved in investment. I have four grandchildren now. I can look back with satisfaction regarding all the achievements we have accomplished.

My active life goes on. I still keep myself busy with writing, investing, and researching. I play tennis like a pro and enjoy every minute of the game. My tennis partners are mostly retired university professors, lecturers, and senior corporate executives. We play the game quite seriously try to win all the time. My life in my new beautiful home in Brisbane became a routine. Every morning we usually enjoy a morning walk up the hill near my home. I play tennis regularly either in the morning or in the evening. All these activities keep me in good shape. I am always an action man. I remember what William James once said,

> 'To change one's life; starts immediately. Do it flamboyantly. No exceptions.'

Another wise saying by Mark Twain came to my notice. Mark Twain uttered,

> 'Twenty years from now you will be more disappointed by the things you didn't do than by the ones you did so. So throw off the bowlines. Sail away from the safe harbour. Catch the trade winds in your sails. Explore, Dream, Discover.'

When I landed in Brisbane, I immediately set out to achieve my goal. The objective was clear as revealed in my deep meditation when I arrived. I wanted to improve my writing skills and to enhance my knowledge. Straight away I enrolled at the University of Queensland. I put up a proposal for my research which concerns renewal of mathematics curriculum. I was delighted that the university accepted my proposal and waded all fees. I did not ask for a scholarship because I was already a wealthy man. Every morning when I arrived at the university library, I began my day with the usual ritual as I did when I was a school boy in Penang. My creative visualising technique during meditation gave me an inner peace and kept my focus intact. My search for information kept me busy for almost three and half years. Finally, I was rewarded with a Ph.D. During this period, I also managed to publish a few more textbooks and guidebooks. Besides my research, my interest in equities also kept me busy. I researched into value companies I wanted to invest.

I have the advantage of two dimensions of strengthening my brain to improve my physical, spiritual, and emotional health. My regular practice in meditation helps in my subconscious visualisation and improve my ideas creation needed for my study and writing. When I became a Christian, I also practised spiritual exercises such as prayer. Through the practice of short prayers uttered by fellow Christians during gatherings and my own prayers, I became more optimistic in my life. I believe all these mental activities help to improve my relationship with friends, increase my happiness, improve my immune system, and help me to become a healthier person. I am also aware that my belief in religion is always a relative truth because others do not share the same belief. I have to show respect for others who do not share the same relative truth. There is a difference between relative truth and absolute truth. Believing in the stories from a Holy Book is classified as a relative truth. Only the believers do but others do not. There are things that everyone who practice them believes that they are truth such as Yoga Exercise improves health. Meditation and Prayer enhance spirituality. These activities are absolute truths for those who practice them. To many of us who meditate and pray, who share the same absolute truth of experiencing less stress, struggle and more capable of peak performance.

I am lucky to stumble upon the wisdom of Abraham Hicks, who wrote that one of the biggest things keeping us away from our ideal vision is that we do not know what this ideal vision is. I used to argue with my wife over issues regarding my children and other petty things. Taking on the wisdom of Hicks, I realised I have to let go the need to be right. I learnt to calm down my emotions. And I ask myself mentally. I obviously do not want the arguments. So what do I want? It becomes clear that I need harmony more than the need to be right. My work is simply to determine what I want. My short practice in meditation and in prayer helps to build the vision of life I need. According to Abraham Hicks,

> 'The most valuable skill that you could ever develop is the skill you want - to be adept at quickly evaluating all situations and then quickly coming to the conclusion of

what you want most - and then giving undivided attention to that.'

Do I have a purpose in life? I did not know initially. What are the things I used to talk about? What are the things I used to think about? What I have been talking and thinking perhaps gave me a clue to my life's purpose. I loved to teach, and I enjoyed seeing my students doing well in their studies. I got excited when I played basketball. I always wanted to be a better player. I love all the excitements in the game. I loved writing and usually felt very satisfied when the finished products stood in front of me. Now I know what pushes the button of my soul! What are the things that excite me! I went through seventy-five years without realising the time. Time does not stand still. Most of my working life, I could do all day without any regard to what time was. I was always busy learning, teaching, playing, writing, reviewing, and attending to my two children's needs. There were so many things that needed my attention. I really lived a full working life. Just like most parents, I went through pain and pleasure in bring up my two children. The same experience I had with my brothers and sisters under my care. Even my relatives under my care provided both pain and pleasure. The pain usually came when they misbehaved and unruly. The pleasure came when I saw them achieved what they set up to do and became successful. To me there is a balance between pain and pleasure. Why do we want children? The answer lies on one word, 'Love'. I love what my life is dedicated to work and family. I spend my money only on things that I value. Most of my earning went to maintain my car, food, house upkeep, books, and sports equipment. Keeping healthy and fit comes first in the family. I had three golf sets: one for me, one for my son, and one for daughter. Anything related to my children's educational needs, I was ready to spend. Most magnificent parents know that to bring up children, there will be pain and there will be pleasure. This gives us a little purpose of life. I have a conviction, and I am prepared to bleed a little, sweat a little, and cry a little. I work extra hours by staying up late. I recognise that my success doesn't belong to me alone. It belongs to all the people who are inspired by the contagiousness.

I used to ask myself whether I have lived a magnificent life? If I am to compare my life with those who have lived magnificent lives which are concentrated in a small village called work, very close to the neighbouring areas called imagination, visualisation, meditation, persistence, consistency, discipline, curiosity, love, and determination, then I am almost there. Just like most magnificent people, I never stop learning. For me learning is life and life is learning. I am aware that in order to live the life I love and love the life I live, I have to be willing to step on the other side of normal. I share my experiences so that you may follow this philosophy. What do you want to learn about? What do you love about? Even in my retirement, I am still busy. There are so many things to learn especially with the boom of technology and the Internet. Now that my children had left us to start their own families, I have a new responsibility to make the rest of my life the best of my life. I do not want to rest on my laurels. I still want to achieve things which I dream about. I will only stop dreaming the day the Lord decides.

Finally, the only thing we should be worrying about is our choices: choosing yourself and choosing to be happy. I learn to let go the unhappy events of the past and move forward. Remember, whatever things that hurt me but do not kill me really help to make me stronger. Most of us inherited the politeness of saying yes most of the time. I too realise that 'no' is sometimes the hardest word to say. Now I realise that it's the most necessary. I personally have the experiences of saying 'yes' to the wrong things such as overwhelming requests, bad relationship, and time consuming obligations. I was too naive and could not summon the power to turn them down. After all the experiences, I learn to be assertive and explain the situation involving role exchange. What will the person who makes the request do if I am to make the same request? A polite answer 'no' usually does not hurt if spoken amiably. I begin to take this power back and a well-placed 'no' can not only save my time and trouble and it can save my life. Now I know I can say no to anything that is hurting me. I will say no to social standard that does not suit me. I will also say no to people who drain my creativity and expression. Any belief that appears not true to me, I will also say no. According to James and Claudia,

> 'It's one thing to say no, it's another thing to have the "Power of No". When you do, you will have a stronger sense of what is good for you and the people around you, and you will have a deeper understanding of who you are.

And ultimately, you'll be free to say a truly powerful 'yes' in your life - one that opens the door to opportunities, abundance and love.'

How I Manage My Time

Timing in life is important. I know I cannot borrow time. And to be at the right place at the right time is critical to my success in life. I was lucky to be at the right place when I got married. I was also at the right time when parents were paying great attention to their children's education. With these advantages, I learnt to manage my time to maximise my extra income so that I could help many people under my care. When I was teaching in Petaling Jaya, a city next to Kuala Lumpur, I was always very busy because of my involvement in group tuition, weekend tuition classes, part-time lecturing, teaching Further Education Classes (FEC), and playing my games regularly. Later, I was engaged in writing mathematics textbooks and guidebooks. So the most important thing I had to do was to manage my time well. I planned my time and tracked it well. Every hour was important. Otherwise, I would be thinking of opportunity lost in earning some extra money. I kept a time log book. I wrote down a timetable for the week. My core duties were clear. Monday to Friday, I had to be in school from 7.20 a.m. to 2 p.m. Saturday and Sunday, I was engaged in tuition classes from 8 a.m. to 11.30 a.m. Most of the evenings from 5 p.m. to 7 p.m., I played tennis or basketball except two nights: Tuesday and Thursday, when I had to teach FEC from 7 p.m. to 9 p.m. After teaching FEC for a few years, the classes were closed down by the Ministry of Education. I moved to lecture part-time at the Tunku Abdul Rahman College. I was involved in teaching applied mathematics for two days. I had to start earlier from 4.30 p.m. to 6.30 p.m. instead. Once this opportunity passed, I started looking for other part-time job elsewhere. When part-time lecturing job opened at Mara College, I took it, helping Malay students preparing for overseas universities. All these duties had a fixed time in my time log. I wrote down what I did each day. Every hour I had was accounted for including travelling time. Most of the evening, from 5 p.m.

onwards, I would be involved training my students playing basketball or I played tennis. These hours were usually out of bound. What left were the afternoon hours from 2 to 5 p.m. I would use two of the afternoons for small group tuition. The rest were hours left for me to develop my core competency that is my writing. This planning helped to maximise my planned activities and productivities. I enjoyed teaching and playing games, and I was motivated to write. I was good in these three activities, and they made me happy. The rewards gave me further incentive to do better. Even when I became principal of the school, I still spent as much time as possible on these activities and outsourced minor things to others. I did not allow other things to get in the way. I believe most successful people spend time on the things that they are good at and they can do their best. They will normally leave the less important things to others. Perhaps this was the secret that delivered results over the long haul. I was not only an effective teacher and administer but also a successful curriculum developer. On my weekend, each morning was used to provide tuition classes. I could only plan my weekend based on the time available after my tuition. Family outing usually took place in the afternoon. My wife used to plan outing, and she used to let me know earlier so that I could enjoy the anticipation. I was a very happy man although I was busy all the time. This clearly demonstrates that we are happier when we are really busy. I have no time for mind-wondering which is supposed to make me unhappy. I also had no time to watch TV for long period, which might depress me. I discovered that mastering a skill like writing or play a sport is stressful initially but eventually makes me happier in the long term. I put in more efforts, and my signature strengths in writing and sport make me happier and more successful. A good lesson for all who want to enjoy a productive life is to keep a time log and keep busy with meaningful activities. A busy man is usually a productive man. One thing leads to another. When you are busy, you become productive, you become successful, you enjoy your life, and you become happier. Not only these, you value your time and learn to use it wisely. So the conclusion is that it is not success that brings happiness but working happily and productivity will bring success.

C H A P T E R   T W O

INTRODUCTION TO FINANCIAL SECURITY

Nobody teaches me about money. I receive no formal education in this most critical of all life skill. In fact, our school curriculum should include this critical skill. I started my working life rather late. I went to university at the age of twenty-six and graduated at twenty-nine. After graduation, I had a debt of about four thousand Malaysian dollars which I borrowed to finish my science degree. I had to retire as a teacher at the age of fifty-five, compulsory retirement in Malaysia during my time of service. So I knew I did not have much time as a teacher to secure my financial security. I realise early that if I do this wrong and end up short of funds, then my quality of life in retirement will go down the drain. By the time, I have past my working years, so there's not much I can do about it. I do not get a second chance to build my retirement savings. I started planning early and took action. I am aware that by acknowledging the fact that my financial abundance is in my own hands. By adopting this attitude, I have placed the power under my control. Life does not simply happen to me. I have to make life happen for myself. I have to be confident in myself and my abilities. I am aware that if I have low self-esteem, I can't fulfil my dream of financial abundance and I can't come up with solutions that will help me overcome challenges. I choose to believe in myself, and when people ask for my service, I will ask for a reward that matches my skill set and experiences. I begin to realise that people around me will notice my confidence and soon I will be attracting the money

I deserve. I simply go after my dream. I do not ask myself the question of making more money than I deserve. I ask myself how my service can help others. I begin to shift my mindset from chasing after money to making a difference in some one's life through my service. This paradigm shift is my key to attract more money as I serve people and help them to succeed in education. This attitude of serving others increases my financial abundance vibration. I simply follow the natural laws of attraction. If I want support, I will provide support first. If I need help, I will provide help first. I will not do unto others what I do not want others to do unto me. I realise that when I am in harmony with my soul's purpose, what I am here to be and do, things get easier. I have revealed to myself what I want to be, to do, to create, or to give according to my educational level and training. I have spent almost three decades preparing myself to be an educator. My life is precious and unrepeatable. I have defined my dream, and I can see my future. I begin to reorient my thinking so that I can really explore possibilities by setting my sights on what I really want in life. I seek financial stability so that I can live in harmony with the laws of the universe. The way I shape each day creates a pattern that becomes a way of life. This repeated patterns become my lifestyle. My dream of financial abundance is defined, and I have to determine whether that dream is really right for me. Not whether I am worthy of the dream, but rather, whether the dream is worthy of me.

I am aware that nobody will care more about my finances than myself. So it is critical for me to embrace immediately. I simply can't just find somebody smart and hand my money responsibilities off to him. I know very early that the quicker I take control of the ultimate responsibility with my money, the quicker I will start building my legitimate fortune. I can't ever give up that responsibility. I have to be the learned captain here, the captain of my money ship. I realise that there is no magic bullet or short cut to my financial security. I didn't become a basketball star in my state by taking short cuts. I had to work harder than the next guy, learn more than him, and focus with more intensity than the next guy to achieve my goals. If I want to invest successfully, I have to do the same thing. I can't get by on one hot tip after another. I know I have to do my homework and due diligence. When I find a strategy that works, I will keep repeating it. This applies to investment too. There are no short cuts to creating linear or residual incomes. Sound investments require knowledge and experience. Developing the discipline and consistency is my first step towards financial security.

When I started teaching, my first financial goal was to repay my loan. This was my first financial planning. I had to put aside $200 per month, and it took me twenty months to settle my loan from my second brother-in-law without interest. I am still eternally grateful to him. More importantly, I had created a good financial habit. My next financial planning was to purchase my first car and first property. I needed $2,000 and about $5,000 as down payments for a car and a house, respectively. I started planning immediately when I moved from Kuantan, where I spent my first two years of teaching, to Petaling Jaya, the city where I lived for almost twenty-three years. I knew I had to start planning immediately before I got married because my time asset diminished each day. I knew I couldn't buy time or borrow time. I only had about twenty-five years of working life as a teacher. By having a financial plan to buy my first car and my first property, I knew I had a better chance of success if I planned way ahead. It also enabled me to adjust my plan and rebound from errors. I had to be resourceful. I started reading into this issue very early. I started reading books on multiple streams of income. I just could not depend on my salary. I would have retired a poor man with a small pension to see me through my retirement. I was always thinking how to become financially successful! Besides reading from stories of successful people, I absorbed attitudes from my parents, from the media, and from the examples of successful friends. All these ideas and information I learnt were haphazard and many were actually wrong. Most of the books were boring and not practical or relevant to me. I was confused and frustrated. I have limiting perceptions about myself that create doubt about my possibilities. I try to understand myself and being aware that I am a spiritual being having human experiences. The truth slowly emerges as I move towards my dream. Knowing the truth that I have absolutely unlimited creative capabilities is critical. I must not limit them with my own thinking and understanding. Once I can change my thinking, I hold the power to create whatever I want to. Once I have come to see myself as the architect of my own financial life, one that requires my passion, persistence, and a belief in myself, I actually realise that I am worthy of having my dream come true. But I knew money is the most important subject in my entire life. I had a heavy responsibility. Many people depended on me because I am the first graduate from my family. I read that life's enjoyment and life's greatest disappointment usually spring from our decisions about money. My peace of mind without anxiety depended on getting my finances under control. Without financial security, I knew my family and my relationship with those who depended on me would be affected. I needed to understand money, how to earn it, and how to keep some of it for growth. In moment of uncertainty, I meditated and used my creative visualisation to help me in creating multiple streams of income besides my salary. My future, my relationship, and my happiness depended on how I do it. So money to me at that time was a game, a very important game. Just like my game basketball. How did I excel in my game? I remember I put in a lot of extra efforts. I dribbled. I learnt to control the ball. I practised shooting and various essential skills almost every day to excel. I could apply the same strategies in the game of money making and keeping some of it for growth and investment. A physician George David said,

> 'Wealth is when small efforts produce big results. Poverty is when big efforts produce small result.'

The following sections will show you some of the strategies I used successfully to create many streams of income. You too can follow my example playing the money game by creating your own streams of income. I started my formal working life in the 1970s. I was just like any of you, dreaming of becoming financially independent. My salary as a teacher was terribly inadequate. The Malaysian Government did not value our service, and schoolteachers at that time were poorly paid. I was forced to use all my resources available to help my extended family to survive. I cannot follow my ideal belief of getting a good education, getting a good job as a teacher, and getting a decent income and live contently. I tried to say the right things, to be a good parent and a good citizen, and to live a good life and enjoy it. I could not do those things. I was struggling and I had to survive. First, I had learnt to love being poor when I was young. I knew if I wanted to get rich, I had to take my chances. I have a good weapon. I have an honours degree in mathematics. The subject was in big demand when I started teaching in the city. It's similar to a military campaign. When you go on the attack, you concentrate your forces on a narrow front where you have an advantage. Making money is competitive too. I gave myself an edge by concentrating on students preparing for School Certificate (SC) and Higher School Certificate (HSC). At that time I was a sixth-form mathematics teacher in an established school. I knew I am a good and enthusiastic teacher. Within a few years, I had established a name for myself. At that time, my immediate goal is to earn enough for my extended family to survive. I needed transport, and my extended family needed food and a roof over their heads.

I was giving tuition when I was a secondary school student. I enjoyed teaching and helping others. So it's natural that I started home tuition for small groups to get some extra income. During weekends I conducted tuition classes for sixth-form students preparing for HSC at a tuition centre. During the school holidays, I had special tuition lessons for some rich parents' kids preparing for British universities. I loved what I was doing and enjoyed the extra income. Other opportunities appeared once in a while. I took them as I went along. For a few years, I taught in FEC for working people who wanted to sit for HSC. Because of the shortage of mathematics lecturer, I also lectured mathematics part-time at Tunku Abdul Rahman College and Mara College for a couple of years. I also served as a mathematics education lecturer at the Curriculum Development Centre in Kuala Lumpur for key teacher trainers in modern mathematics. Whenever there was an opportunity for me to make some extra money, I was involved. All these efforts only produced little rewards financially. All these experiences anchored well for me as a mathematics curriculum developer and writer later on. One thing led to another. The power of money could do wonders. I knew very early that getting rich required original approach. Sooner than later, I realise that the path to wealth no longer travels through streams of linear income. I needed streams of residual income. I took my chance to write my first mathematics textbook. At first I was rather sceptical about my effort. I knew if there is no risk there is no gain. I was prepared and not afraid of failure. After my first success, I became more adventurous. Consequently, I had written more than twenty mathematics textbooks and guidebooks to my credit. A big secret of my potential is revealed. I really enjoy writing.

I was fortunate I didn't have much money when I was young. And I found that I enjoyed poverty without forming expensive habits. When money started to flow into our family trusted account, our saving grew and grew. Being poor before, I did not cultivate any bad spending habit. Initially, I did not know what to do with the money which kept flowing into my trusted account yearly. My wife is a good money manager. Together we started investing in properties, equities, and joint ventures. By the time I took my optional retirement at the age of fifty-one, I had established many streams of recurring income. I had built my financial security, and my distant goal was to be a successful writer and an investor. I wanted to retire happily with financial security.

How I Create Lifelong Streams of Income

Nowadays a very few families can survive on less than two streams of income. I was in that situation when I started teaching at La Salle High School in Petaling Jaya, Selangor, after my transfer from Technical Institute, Kuantan, Pahang. I spent two years teaching applied mathematics and addition mathematics at the Technical Institute in Kuantan. When I got married after a year of teaching in my new school, I inherited an extended family. I rented a double-storey terrace house very close to the University of Malaya. My youngest sister came to stay with us. She was sitting for her HSC. She needed special tuition in principal mathematics and English from me. My wife's younger sister and two younger brothers were also lodging with us. Two of them were just admitted into University of Malaya and another was preparing for his HSC. He also needed my guidance in mathematics. I had another responsibility. My youngest brother was admitted into University of Singapore for an Engineering Course. When my father passed away, I promised him that I would look into his education. Soon my daughter was born. I needed a maid to care for her. My new extended family could not survive on our two meagre salaries. Necessity is the mother of innovation. I had no choice but to create other streams of income for our survival. I had to work my butt off then. I would like to share my experiences, mistakes, and all. I had no choice but to get my finances in order. Although money is an 'off-limits' conversation, I took the risk in sharing. Many people especially my friends did not like it. I had to create parallel careers for my financial security. I was lucky to be aware that there are two different types of income streams: linear (active) and residual (passive). Within a few years of working, I had created two different streams of income. They were usually not equal. Some of my income streams were considered linear and others were residual. In my twenty-three years as a graduate teacher, I had created a few linear streams and some residual streams of income. What is the difference between these two different streams? If you are paid only once for each hour of work, then the type of income you get is linear. The salary I earned is linear. The extra money I got from tutoring and the pay cheques from my part-time lecturing were linear income. Getting linear income requires hard work and is time consuming. During my quiet moment, I was telling myself that I did not want to work this way throughout my life. I had to change the way of creating income. I had to work smart to create residual streams of recurring income. With residual income, I needed to work hard once and it unleashed a steady flow of income for months or even years. I turned to my writing skills. I motivated myself to take the chance. Getting rich requires me to take a more original approach. I had the required mathematics knowledge. I only need the gut to take a small step and start. I should not be afraid what might turn out. At that time, there were only three things that really matter: what I do, where I do it, and whom I do it with. I remember after three years of teaching, I experimented with my first mathematics textbook, additional mathematics for forms four and five. I was not confident. Anyhow, I persevered and tried my best. A good thing I experienced is that I enjoyed writing. It laid the foundation for my writing career. I had found a parallel career as a writer. After one success, I started to write my second textbook, applied mathematics for sixth forms. My second success drove me to write more books. In the span of about fifteen years, I had written more than twenty mathematics textbooks and guidebooks to provide financial security for my future. This venture soon became my second parallel career creating residual income for many years. This success enables me to accumulate enough money for investment purposes.

After a few years of hard work, I had many sources of income, both linear and residual. They kept flowing into our trusted bank account. I invested into properties by putting down reasonable down payments. Soon, rental income started to flow into my trusted account. I had another source of residual income. With so much money flowing into my trusted bank account, my wife started to invest into value stocks. Another source of residual income in the form of dividends started to flow. Later, I went into business on a joint-ventured basis. All these investments have provided me with lifelong streams of residual income. Although I had created so many streams of income, I disciplined myself to take care where my money were spent and how much were saved. I will share with you how I have managed to create all these streams of income during my working days and how I have used my savings to grow my wealth. So I need to be conscious that requires honesty. I know that busy people are usually productive people. So I wanted to be one of them. Even in my retirement, I am still busy growing my wealth so that I can constantly give away to those who are less fortunate than me. I have another dream in my retirement. This new dream is to bring my level of prosperity to the next level so that I can plan bigger project for my community. My generosity of spirit reminds me to give back part of my fortune to the community. The projects I have in mind are facilities for sports like tennis courts and basketball courts for the underprivileged.

Providing Mathematics Tuition and Lecturing Part-Time as a Source of Linear Income

When I started teaching as a graduate teacher, my salary was not enough to maintain my extended family. I had to find other streams of income for our survival. During my secondary school days, I had been giving tuition to some of my neighbours' children and two of my classmates in mathematics and science. I enjoyed teaching them. That experience provided me with an immediate solution to create another stream of linear income. My special subject is mathematics especially applied mathematics. When I started teaching in Kuantan, I was a specialist teacher for applied and pure mathematics. When I was transferred from Kuantan to Petaling Jaya, I was the only mathematics graduate teacher in the school. I served as senior mathematics teacher for sixth forms in the school. My discovery in relation to the approach of humanising the teaching of applied mathematics became well known to my sixth-form students. This information began to spread to other sixth-form students in other schools in Kuala Lumpur and Petaling Jaya. When I started tuition classes for pure and applied mathematics for HSC and additional mathematics for SC at a tuition centre in Petaling Jaya during the weekends, the classes were crowded with students. The extra income I got was a great relief for my extended family financial well-being. My responsibility was heavy, and with this extra income, I was still struggling to make ends meet. To get extra income to enable me to save for raining days, I taught FEC at the Methodist Boys School, Kuala Lumpur, during the nights. For a few years, I taught applied mathematics for four hours a week. Every hour I was paid fifteen Malaysian dollars by the Education Department, Selangor. I had an extra 240 Malaysian dollars per month, and this was added to my saving. During most school holidays, I was approached by some rich parents who were planning to send their children to British universities for engineering courses. They wanted their kids to have a strong foundation in mathematics before they left for their A level in England. I provided them with intensive mathematics tuition. I had to turn some of the parents down because of my time constraint. They were prepared to pay any amount I specified. To them money was never a problem compared to the amount they were prepared to spend in England. I was considerate and charged only fifty Malaysian dollars per hour of intensive tuition. At that time, the amount was considered very high because government rate was only fifteen Malaysian dollars an hour. Many of my students went on to become leaders of our society. One of my ex students is now the CEO of a big corporation. Most rich parents know the value of education. They invest in their children's education so that their wealth will be preserved. To enhance my financial position, I was also involved in part-time lecturing at the Mara College and Tunku Abdul Rahman College for a few hours per week. I also served as a teacher trainer when there was a shortage of lecturers. The government started Regional Training Centres and in-service courses for mathematics teachers. Most of the classes were conducted during the school holidays. Most of these opportunities only lasted a few years until the colleges got their own academic staff. I was at the right place at the right time when mathematics graduates were in big demand. These opportunities created other streams of linear income for a few years. With all these extra streams of linear income, I was able to put aside any surplus for raining days and for investments.

Writing Mathematics Textbooks as a Source of Residual Income

I knew when I started teaching that I could not just depend on my salary and other linear streams of income to have my financial security when I retired. For all my linear streams of income, I was paid for every hour of effort I put in. And when I did not show up, neither did my paycheque. It dawned on me to create other streams of income preferably residual type. Teaching was my passion at the time. I did not know other passion yet because I did not start anything besides teaching. But how am I going to find out? So I kept writing down possible things I could do besides teaching. First in the list was writing, selling insurance, housing agent, stock investment, property investment, direct sale agent for Amway, and many others. I began to filter them, and the most relevant to me at that point of time was writing. My end goal is take my struggle with money out of my life's equation so as to allow me to spend more time on things that really matter to me. I have these three important things in mind: experiences, growth, and contribution. Before I could embark on this mission, I had to take a small first step in writing as my mean goal. I read about famous writers making a fortune because their books sell like hot cake. Royalty is a good form of income. Remember President Obama makes an average of $72,000 per month through his famous book the *Audacity of Hope*. I wanted to be one of them. I started to look at the works of some of the mathematics writers especially textbook writers. Most of the mathematics textbooks used in the schools were imported and not very suitable for local situations. I had never written any book! How do I start? I had my own speaking voice when I taught mathematics. So my writing voice should not sound like anyone else's either. I was determined to begin. First, I took a chapter of coordinate geometry from an established writer. I wanted to create my own writing voice. I focused on the main ideas and the theories involved. I tried to rewrite these ideas and theories in my own expressions. I wanted the presentation to be similar to what I delivered them in class. I also tried to relate these ideas and applications of the theories to students' daily experiences. In other words, I was trying to humanise the teaching of the topic so that the ideas sound relevant to their lives. I tried to remove expressions that were not mine from the chapter. I wrote and rewrote until I was comfortable with the presentation and expression. Here I had an advantage. I tried out the materials in my own class to assess the response from my students. It took me a long time to develop my natural and distinctive style of presentation. I also tried out questions behind every section of the chapter in class to ensure that they were relevant to the theories and their applications. A lot of effort was made to humanise most of the mathematics concepts and made them relevant to their everyday experiences. It took me a year to hone my skill and style until my first book was ready for publication. It took me one complete year teaching the subject and writing it. My first additional mathematics textbook for form four and form five was ready after my fifth year of teaching. The book was submitted to both the Ministries of Education in Singapore and Malaysia for approval as standard textbook. It was accepted by both countries and used as standard mathematics textbook for form four and form five. The market is not big because the number of students doing additional mathematics in both countries was small at the time. This was my first success as a writer. The following year I experienced my first royalty from both countries. I had created my first residual or recurring income. The textbook was used for almost twelve to fifteen years before I had to rewrite it and improve it. Imagine I had been receiving royalties for my first textbook for so many years. When the ministry asked for a new book to be written, of course I had to compete with other writers to have a good share of the pie. The first taste of honey was sweet, and that gave me great motivation to write my next mathematics textbook. During my first two years of teaching applied mathematics at the Technical Institute, I discovered the technique of humanising its concepts. This gave me great advantage to write my second textbook. I followed the same procedure because I was involved in the teaching of pure and applied mathematics in the school. It took me two years to get ready the applied mathematics textbook. It was a great success, and the book became popular in most of the schools. The standard textbook imported from England was finally replaced by a local book. I did not stop there. It took me another year to produce the pure mathematics textbook and another year to write the statistics textbook for the sixth form. The advantage was that I was involved in the teaching of the subjects in the school. These textbooks were equally successful. So I had created another three streams of similar residual income. Altogether these four streams of income kept flowing in for many years. Even when I took my optional retirement, royalties kept flowing into our family trusted account.

I was actually a very busy man when I was teaching. I seldom took any holidays. I worked seven days a week including giving tuition classes during the weekends. I did some part-time teaching and lecturing whenever opportunities presented to me. All these opportunities gave me the chance to promote myself and my writing voice. They also provided extra income to complement my salary and gave me some saving for investment. I did not neglect my health. I played my games, basketball and tennis and later golf. I kept myself physically fit most of the time. Being a competitive sportsman, I had to keep fit most of the time. I played for a basketball team in a club, and my service was required all the time because of my skills. I had never fallen sick for the period I was teaching. When I took my optional retirement, the Education Department was in shock that I did not have any sick leave recorded. I was able to work extraordinarily hard seven days a week because of my super physical condition.

I did not rest on the laurels of these achievements. I had found my writing voice in my own style. My voice in my teaching style was well known. Students showed great confidence in my teaching style. At one year, I was teaching applied mathematics to an upper sixth class, and a new mathematics graduate from England was teaching them pure mathematics. The students told him that they had great confidence in my teaching than his. The teacher replied that it was because all the textbooks were written by Mr Wong. I was a very confident and competent teacher partly because I put in a lot of effort in writing the textbooks. I knew the content in and out. I did not require a textbook when I teach. I knew where to simplify a concept and when to shorten the lesson. I also understood most of the students' problems in concepts acquisition. I did not teach modern mathematics from form one to form five in school. But I was involved in teachers' retraining when the subject was introduced in Malaysian schools. I knew the syllabus well and the philosophy behind introducing the subject. I started to write elementary modern mathematics textbooks for form one to form five in the late 1980s. This provided me an opportunity to go along and refining my writing voice and style. I experimented with the concept of humanising the teaching of elementary mathematics early. There were many questions I would ask myself and I would provide the answers. First, I would like to make my approach simple and interesting as I explored my path to success. I wanted to teach students exactly what to do, with a step by-step process, in a forthright, no-nonsense voice. I became comfortable creating a writing voice that was self-effacing so that I could step back a bit and let the process of logic took over. I would gravitate towards short and medium sentences to make my style simple to read and comprehend. I was willing to write and rewrite until I was satisfied the final product was the best I could produce. It took me five solid years to complete the series. The series was adopted by many schools specified by the Ministry of Education. Once they were completed, I started to write guidebooks and revision courses to help students preparing for Lower School Certificate of Education, SC of Education, and HSC of Education. The thousands of hours I spent in writing were rewarded. Royalties started to flow into my family trusted bank account year after year. The cheques kept flowing for many years as long as the books were used. Money kept flowing and flowing into our family trusted account. When I was doing my doctoral study at the University of Queensland, the raging river of residual income still flowed to my bank account, year after year. Even today, I am still receiving small royalties for guidebooks and revision courses written by me years ago. All these extra income enabled me to save and had the power to do what I want. It dawned on me that I needed to let the money work for me. I started my exploration in investment opportunities.

    All these extra efforts and experiences tell me that true greatness and success would take a lot more than being a few steps ahead of the peck. If you want to be the Michael Jordan of your profession, it would take a lifetime of dedication. In case you do not know. Michael Jordan was a great basketball player for the Chicago Bull, USA. I know most of us do not need to be the Michael Jordan of anything in their life to have life-changing success. We only need to acquire a small, measurable amount better in the important things in our life. I would like to encourage you to follow the footsteps I had taken when I was working. If I want to pass an examination that will give me a promotion or moving to the next level, then I will stick to my study timetable and I will not be distracted by my silly TV show or other side interest. By disciplining myself, I will be better prepared to pass the test. Another example is that if I want to lose weight, I will make it a habit to have one less can of Coca-Cola or one less sugary snack a day and take a few more steps in walking each day, and I will set in motion a metamorphosis. If I want to have more money in my saving account, I will take a small step to have a few part-time jobs other than my regular one. To succeed in life, discipline is the key. I will always try to write something, try to sell something, be a broker agent, or be anything that interest me like promoting insurance, sale agent for house, and others. If I want to make money in the stock market, I will try to have one less loser each month and replace with one more winner; soon I will transform my portfolio of shares. I do not need to be Warren Buffett to achieve my investment goals. By simply making a few changes in my way I pick stocks, the extra results can quickly pick up. I am not impressed by some people who are preoccupied with getting rich quick that they forget the biggest fortunes are made slowly and steadily. I adopted the policy of investing for the long term. I am aware that investing in stocks is not like placing a bet on number 19 on the roulette wheel, but instead, it is buying a tangible piece of a business. I always remember that if I buy the right business, I will make a lot of money for my retirement. I will buy any wonderful company at a fair price and hold it for the future. I will share with you my strategy I adopted when I was facing failure initially. I encourage you to take action and know when to change. Do not be afraid of failure! I experienced many failures on my way to success. I did not give up. I consider the period of failure the training ground for planting the seeds of my success. Failures and success come and go. Each failure usually becomes a critical lesson telling me that my approach is wrong. So I try to create more successes than failures. Consider all these as normal and start to build opportunities for streams of consistent linear and residual incomes.

INVESTING IN PROPERTIES AS A STREAM OF RESIDUAL INCOME

I read about the secret of the wealthy people regarding the creation streams of residual income. They have more money as well as more time freedom. Their streams are mostly residual incomes, and they have time to spend on anything they want. They may not appear to be earning, but their residual incomes actually grow in tandem with their investments. Professional people like doctors and dentists do not earn residual income unless they also invest. They can only see fixed number of patients a day. Teachers and lecturers can only teach at one institution at a time. And they have to be there for every one of them. Linear income is usually capped.

Realising the limiting power of my linear income, I started to create another stream of residual income by investing into properties. I bought my first property during my fourth year of teaching after renting a house for almost three years. The timing was right. With as little as $5,000 as down payment and a bank loan, I purchased my first double-storey terrace house for about 32,000 Malaysian dollars. I did not have to pay rent any more. I started to pay instalment for my house. After a few years, my saving from my salary, income from tuition classes, and my royalties began to grow. I decided to upgrade my house. I put down payment for a corner double storey terrace house for $72,000. The construction of the house took almost two years to complete. Before I shifted into my new house, I sold my first house for almost $140,000. I made a handsome profit. I started looking for commercial properties to invest. I bought my first shop using partly my profit and a government loan at 4 per cent interest. The shop was rented out for about $2,000, and my monthly instalment to the government was about $800. So I had a net residual income of almost $1,200. This was great. I started to look for a second shop to invest. When the shop next to my current shop was available, I bought it immediately with the help of my third brother-in-law. The shop cost about $200,000. The bank gave me a loan of about $100,000 because of my salary scale as a teacher was rather low. The others came from my saving from royalties, initial help from my third sister, and profit from the sale of my first house. My monthly instalment to the bank was about $1,400. The second shop was also rented out for $2,000. I had another residual income of almost $600. All these residual income began to flow into our family trusted account months after months. I realise that cash flow is the most important word of money. Another important word in investing is leverage. I am aware that leverage is power and that power can work in my favour or against me. Since leverage is a power to me, I must make sure that I do not abuse it. Most people fear it and never venture to use it. This actually explains why most people do not become rich because they fear the power of leverage. Many others want to be rich but fail to become rich because they abuse the power of leverage. Our saving began to grow exponentially from my tuition money, my royalties, and now my rentals. I should have been more adventurous and should have bought more properties. But I did not because I do not believe that I should put all my eggs in one basket. In case of any property bubble burst, I would not be terribly affected. I also intended to invest in others like stocks and businesses. I also had in mind relatives who are in needs. I am always ready to give them a helping hand. So having cash in hand is always an advantage when opportunity to help others or any good investment crops up.

Dividends of Stocks as another Stream of Residual Income and Growth

I started to read into stocks during my free time. My wife was very interested in stocks. She started investing before I got interested. I was influenced by some of my university friends who were very active in trading stocks. They advised me to invest into value stocks that pay good dividends consistently. They told me that the easiest way to retire rich is to invest in dividend stocks. This will create another stream of continuous residual income. According to them, great businesses reward their shareholders in three ways: one, with dividends; two, with share buy-backs; and third, with growth. This was a good way to put my money to work for me. I started doing my own research and at the same time started to gather information from established investors. In addition, I learnt to use information from social media to parse out positive and negative trending information to enhance a higher probability of success in investments. All these knowledge provide the leverage to find profitable investments. My main focus is to pick value stocks for long-term holding. First, these stocks provided me with a regular cash return in the form of dividends, another form of residual income. I was fascinated by a study which showed that investors earned almost 394 per cent on stocks from 1991 to 2010 and that 43 per cent of that return came from dividends. To me, it was a huge chunk of return. I started correctly by buying value stocks with special focus on dividends. I looked into companies whose net profit kept increasing in tandem with their dividends. The second thing I started to look into businesses that reward shareholders by buying back their own shares. This is when a business takes its profit and buys back its own stock in the open market thus reducing its number of shares. A friend of mine tries to explain to me that when a company reduces its share counts, it's like cutting a pie into eight slices instead of twelve slices. I will get a much bigger piece of pie. Likewise, as the company's share counts fall, each remaining share is worth more. He explains further that share buy-backs are also great from a tax perspective. I have to pay tax on some cash dividends unless the dividends are fully franked. I do not have to pay taxes when a company uses cash to buy back shares, even though a share repurchase makes my share more valuable. In another words, a share purchase is like a non-cash dividend that is not taxable until I sell my shares of the company. A good example of the power of dividend reveals that a value company like IBM started 2013 with a market cap of about $213.9 billion. During the year, IBM paid out $22.9 billion in dividends and share buy-backs. That is roughly 10.7 per cent cash yield for the year, based on the market value at the start of the year. It is estimated that the yield for 2014 will be about 13.6 per cent. The buy-backs by IBM will increase the value of the stock. The rest is like a non-cash dividend that is untaxable until you sell the stock. There is also growth for the company. This will give us a complete picture of how much cash a business is returning to shareholders, we need to factor in buy-backs. This provides a little bit of guide to buy elite, high-yielding stocks like IBM or Apple for good investment. There are other aspects in identifying value stocks. A detailed discussion will be dealt with later. Here I have created not only another residual stream of income but another source of growth for my capital. If you intend to grow your saving, this type of investment may suit you as an employee. My experience tells me that stocks at present are still the best house in the financial-asset neighbourhood. According to Stansberry Associates Investment Research, in the United States, companies with the largest buy-back programmes have outperformed the broader market by 20 per cent since 2008. The companies include Apple ($32 billion), IBM ($19.5 billion), ExxonMobil (13.2 billion), and Pfizer (10.9 billion), where the figures in the bracket are values of buy-backs.

I started in stocks investment halfway through my working career. Initially, I did not have the necessary information and knowledge regarding the market. I used to buy stocks on the recommendations of friends. Consequently for the first few years, I did badly and lost some money. I began to analyse my mistakes in investments so that I would not make the same mistakes again. Eventually, I succeeded in developing my own strategies. Towards the end of my working career, I started to cut back my tuition engagements and part-time lecturing because my royalties and rental income had grown exponentially. Financially, I was more confident then. I started to read more about equities investment. I read about Warren Buffett, Bill Spetrino, Jim Rogers, Sean Hyman, and many other great investors. Finally, I decided to follow the style of Bill Spetrino and Sean Hyman concentrating on value stocks. Within a few years, I began to see results in terms of dividends and stocks growth. Many of the stocks in my portfolio are considered value stocks because their profits keep increasing, dividends are consistent, and these companies have plenty of cash as retained profits. Many of the value companies with plenty of cash from their retained profit started to buy back their own shares. Whenever I came across these buy back companies, I added more shares on to my holdings. I did that for many years, and the results were unbelievable. I got back all my losses for the first few years. Before I left for my doctoral study in Queensland, Australia, I had already made a significant sum to give me financial security. I held some of the good stocks like banks and telecommunication companies for a long period. I only sold them when I left Malaysia. In investment, there is no short cut, no press button, and no crystal ball. To be successful, a lot of perspiration and hard work in terms of research have to be done. I used to concentrate on value stocks with good dividends and potential growth. The dividends keep flowing and the prices of some of the stocks have double, triple, and even quadrupled. I will share with you many of my strategies of investment in later part of this chapter.

Joint Venture as Another Source of Residual Income

I am aware that every business I invest, there is always a risk factor. I focus on due diligence before I venture into any business. After I had completed all the textbooks from form one to form six, I went into joint venture with two partners to form a company called Hexagon Publication. The two partners were active, and they managed the company. I was an invincible partner because I was a government servant. My name was not included in the partnership. A relative of mine is one of the partners, and he had my share. This was built on trust. The initial capital involved was not big, and I took the risk. I started writing teaching and learning aids including revision courses from form one to form six for the company. I benefited by getting 10 per cent royalties on all my works sold in the markets. The company was doing well initially and was growing very fast for the first five to six years. The two partners running the company could not see eye to eye. They were on constant conflict. Soon the company ran into cash flow problem because of its fast expansion. The two partners did not have capital to rescue the company. I did not want to pump in my money to rescue the company because my name was not included. At the end, the company collapsed. What I benefited from the set-up of the company was in the form of royalties and rentals since the company made use of the premise of one of my shops. This taught me an important lesson in relation to picking stocks. Always look for companies which have more cash than debt, that is, good cash flow.

The flow of cash into my trusted account through tuition, part-time lecturing, rentals, and royalties began to accumulate. I did not want to buy more properties. The reason is obvious. I did not want to put all my cash into one or two baskets only. My creative visualisation told me that I should try to be an entrepreneur. In the '80s, the use of computer was picking up in Malaysia. Most of the computers from the United States and the West were rather expensive. Most Malaysian could not afford to pay for the high prices. We went into joint venture with a closed relative. My wife and her partner managed to import parts from Taiwan and assembled them in Malaysia. At the initial stage, the new company was short of fund because the partner was a new computer graduate from England. He did not have much saving. My wife had some cash available because of my royalties and rentals from my two shops. She was courageous to approach the bank for credit facilities. She even used my Volvo 940 car to take a bank manager to dinner for giving her the credit facilities. At that time, I was already the deputy principal of the school. We had the advantage because we had two adjacent shops to do the assembling. My wife and her partner became a wholesaler distributing computers to all dealers and shops throughout Malaysia. The business picked up and grew and grew. After many years of profiting, my wife's business partner left for Australia. The wholesale business was left to my wife and her sister to manage. She had her strengths and weaknesses. From my observations, her strengths were her honesty, sincerity, and straightforwardness. She was very caring for her brothers and sisters. She worried that her partner's new business might not be successful in Australia so she kept part of his share in the company for him. Her younger sister was a mother of two kids, and at the time, she was not working because she had to take care of the two kids. The recession set in, and her husband was retrenched from his engineering job. He started to be a dealer selling computers. Relationship between my wife's partner and her brother-in-law became sour because of personality differences. They could not see eye to eye in many business deal and other things. My wife's weaknesses were obvious. She lacked confidence, and she did not know how to manage the business. She was straightforward and did not have much business sense. The wholesale business was divided into three major shares. She held one-third, the partner who left for Australia still held one third, and one-third of the company was awarded to her younger sister practically free. The husband and wife team was given the monopoly to run and control the company. Initially, my wife was given a salary in par with her younger sister. But her sister objected to the deal because my wife was not a graduate. Later on, my wife rejected the deal and did not take up the job. The husband and wife team did well. They drew reasonable salaries, and they managed the company well. My wife did not hold any position in the company. She was the one who obtained credit facilities from the bank for the company. She only served as a financial provider, and she got some interest for lending my money to the company. Actually, she lost control of a good business she partly inherited. With all the financial backing from us and the credit from the bank, the company grew and grew and became a multimillion dollar business. The younger sister and her husband were the real beneficiaries of the business. They worked hard and worked smart. We provided the shops and facilities for the company to grow. The rental for the two shops was stagnant for many years. We did not complain because we owed one-third of the company. They upgraded their house from double-storey terrace house to a bungalow. The company also paid for him to study for his master's degree in business administration. When we left for Australia, the company was at its peak. My wife wanted to withdraw from the company, and she also allotted one-third of the business partner's share to her mother. The company was rich in cash, and they used the company's profit to pay off my wife's one-third of the share. We got a good share of the profit. Consequently, my wife's younger sister and husband had the major share of the company. They kept running the company well and more profits flowed into their saving. They became rich through the entrepreneurship. I offered my congratulation because of my generosity of spirit. I do not envy people becoming successful because they are hard working. They also left for Australia when their two kids required university education.

My wife's business partner started the same computer assembling business in Sydney. The business became very successful in Australia, and eventually, he went into Internet, software businesses, and infrastructure for Internet. The company now is traded in Australian share market. It is one of the 100 biggest companies in Australia. The company alone makes him a rich man. In Malaysia, the sale of cheap computers began to decline. Sensing that the cycle of cheap computers from Taiwan was over, my wife's sister and her husband closed down the company in the '90s with plenty of cash in the bank. Although we did not have a lion's share of the profit, we were grateful for what we got from this entrepreneurship. The cash generated was actually our surplus. We channelled most of it into value stocks in Australia. We have created another stream of residual income. We were able to purchase a big piece of land in Brisbane and built our own home. Until today, all the residual incomes are still flowing into our trust account.

I would like to share some secrets related to the success story of our business partner. He worked his way from the bottom to the top. Even when he was a small boy, he was very interested in business. He used to organise trips for the locals and made some profits from the trips. He sold utensils in the night market and made some good profits. In most of his business ventures, he didn't have a master plan. He simply thought of better ways of doing business and things. From my observation, there are a few secrets of doing things that are different from others. All these have contributed to his business success in a shorter period of time than anyone else.

First, he was not afraid of failure. He worked as a programmer at the university for two years, and he started his software business in Petaling Jaya. In fact, his first venture into software business in the early '80s was a failure because the timing was not right. Computers were not widely used in Malaysia at the initial stage. He was not afraid to be proven wrong. He was a competitor. He did not hold stupidly to his original belief once it was discredited. He had the unique ability to lead the troops in one direction. Once proven wrong, he would make his immediate about-turn and lead the charge in the opposite direction. He was quick to cut his business short because the idea was not working. He was right not to waste valuable time trying to make a wrong a right. Through my own experience, I notice that many smart people have a hard time with this idea of changing course resulting in valuable time wasted.

He started another business, jointed ventured with my wife, assembling computers from parts imported from Taiwan. In the '80s, computers were expensive and most Malaysians could not afford. The timing was right and the business prospered.

Another observation regarding business deal, he did an outstanding job. He was able to explain what was in it for the other guy. A very good thing about him was that he did not talk about himself, his wants, and his needs at all. He used to talk about the benefits for the guy on the other side of the table. Many of the dealers were convinced to do business with him. Like everyone, the guy on the other side of the table is selfish. Most of the guys doing business do not care what is for you. He was able to convince them that he would make them more successful in what they do, so he got most of the deals. As a result, his wholesale business started to grow.

Another observation in his business deal was that he praised and constructively criticised people equally. If a dealer screwed up, he would call him out. When dealers did well, he praised them with incentives. It was mutual benefits. I also noticed that he was friendly with rivals. He even gave away some of the company's secrets. At first I did not understand the move. I was sure his rivals did not understand either. After spending time with them, his competitors often wanted to be his partner. This move helped to grow his business and also his profits. Very often, when his rival's business folded, the employees tried to get job. He ended up with the best talents in his importing business. His insight revealed that he did not mind giving some of his secrets away because he knew they would not be able to execute the way he did. He was able to scout for talents, and he hired people smarter than him. He was brilliant but not very organised. So he hired people who were smart and systematic to run his business. When he expanded his business, he hired the best guys he could find. His employees were well rewarded with good incentives.

Finally and most importantly, it was not only money. Money was only one scoreboard of his success. A lot of it was about fun and about coming up with business idea and seeing it worked. After all the success, he left the business for my wife and her sister to continue. I was a government servant, and I could not be involved in the business. The business grew and lasted for many years. My wife's business partner left for Australia, a totally new environment. He started a new industry, and in a short period of time, he found his success again. This time it is a much bigger scale involving Internet business and infrastructures. He must have made use of his secrets to do things over and over again.

There are many other qualities exhibited by him. He is able to make any business person doing business with him feeling at ease. He will seek his thought and opinion without making any judgement. He knows that most people do not feel comfortable being judged. Although he is successful, he does not show his ego. He is always very humble, and he does not speak much. He is also a good listener. He uses to ask questions to encourage businessmen to give him their feedbacks. His contagious smile and his posture give people confident and feel at ease. All these add to his business assets, and as a result, he becomes very successful. In simple language, he has a millionaire mindset. First, he believes that he has the right to be wealthy. He wants to make a difference in the world by creating something of value. He sees the world through the eyes of abundance, freedom, and opportunities. Second, he spends as much time as possible studying the finances as he earns. Most of us do not bother until a bill crops up. Third, he is not held back by his limiting beliefs. He does allow his limiting beliefs to slow him down from achieving his goals and dreams. Being proactive, he utilises his resources effectively to become wealthy.

If you aspire to be a successful businessman, whatever business ideas come to your head write them down. If you want to be an entrepreneur and want to broaden your idea spectrum, you should try to cultivate these habits that make people like you. His breakthrough goal is to be a multimillionaire so that he can have all the freedom to choose where he retires, where he lives in his retirement, and how he gives back to society. Remember, Warren Buffett is preparing to give away 85 per cent of his wealth to society. I believe that he is going to do the same. If your intention is to bless others, you will be blessed. He has great respect for his parents and other members of the family.

Advantages of Residual Income over Linear Income

What percentage of my income is residual? I did not calculate but the percentage is above 90 per cent. If we want to retire with financial security, we must start to create as many residual streams of income as possible while we are working. I suggest you follow some of my footsteps, one step at a time. With residual income, you work hard once and it unleashes a steady stream of income year after year. Just like my case, I get paid over and over again for the same effort. I think it's nice to be compensated hundreds of times for every hour of my efforts. You can do the same thing with your creativity. Writing books is only one of the ways to create residual income. Song writers and song recordings are possible ways of creating residual income. Insurance sale can also generate residual income. I read about the inventor of Duracell battery. He presented his idea to many companies, but he was turned down every time. Finally, a Duracell Company saw his genius and it agreed to pay him just a few cents for every pack of battery using his idea. Now he is earning millions in terms of the residual cents add up per year. He invested many hours to create this concept. The effort was only once, and now he is getting paid without him doing much. He does not have to be there anymore. He has created a stream of residual income that keeps flowing year after year.

There are many other exciting ways of creating residual income. You must have heard of Warren Buffett, the smartest stock picker in history. He is worth tens of billions. He started investing in value stocks and others. He gave me a good starting point. Instead, I made use of the algorithm expounded by Bill Spetrino and Sean Hyman. Bill was a community college professor in accounting. He started investing into value stocks with an initial sum of $10,000. He preferred to invest in companies with plenty of cash and little debt. He looked at the numbers in the quarterly account of the companies. His choice of stocks was based on their profits, dividends, and earnings per share (EPS). Another factor is their potential for growth and uniqueness. These are the types of companies most billionaires are looking for long-term investment. Bill claims that he uses the billionaire's extra sensory perception (ESP) strategy to identify stocks which billionaires will soon follow. I was attracted by his approach when I got interested in stocks especially in retirement. He buys these stocks before billionaires even know that they are going to buy. He seems to understand billionaires' mindsets by reading widely about them. He claims that he knows Warren Buffett, George Soros, and other great investors more than their wives. His extraordinary ability to pick stocks before billionaires know they are going to invest. This uncanny ability helps him to grow his $10,000 into a few millions. This enables him to retire as a teacher at the age of forty-two. His monthly residual income total in seven figure cheques keep flowing in. He is now the editor of the magazine, *Dividend Machine,* and he has a few thousands followers who are benefiting from his picks of stocks. After researching into his style of investing, I follow some of his footsteps. I invested into value stocks which pay dividends consistently. I managed to create a good residual income with cheques flowing in month after month. This extra income together with my monthly pension, royalties, and rentals provide my family with financial security. I do not follow Warren Buffett style because his style of holding for life does not suit my temperament. He could identify potential growth companies and hold them for decades. Just like Bill, I buy value stocks which pay good dividends. I sell them whenever their profits start to decline or their dividends slow down. I have all the time freedom to do anything I want because most of my streams of income are residual now.

Remember that if you only depend on your salary and work hard for many years to ensure your family financial security, you are living only in the illusion of security. What happen if the company closes and you get laid off? You are not secure. You need to create additional streams of income. I encourage you to follow some of my footsteps. Start your own home-based business or a part-time job to create another stream of income in your life as a safety net in case any of your streams dry up. Foods and services can be good businesses. But these types are usually hard work. I have nothing against the hard work. I went through hard work myself. If you need to start that way to save some money for future investment, give it a trial for a few years. Try to think of residual or recurring stream of income that continues to flow whether you are there or not. Just like my royalties from books, rentals from my shops, and dividends from my stocks, you need to create your own streams of income to suit your talents and interest. So when you start working in your chosen career, do not procrastinate. Use your creative visualisation and take action. Working life is always short. The earlier you prepare for your retirement, the safer is your financial security. There are thousands of ways to create linear and residual incomes. Do what I do! I avoid debt and always live beneath my means so that I can put aside part of my income for investments. The few strategies I adopted are just a tip of the iceberg. If you are smart, start to shift your income streams from linear to residual. This will give you the time freedom to do what you want when you want. Read widely and start gathering information as early as possible. Knowledge and action are essential to ensure your financial freedom and a comfortable retirement. Start now by creating on at least one new residual stream every two years of your working life. In my case, after years of hard work, I have created many streams of income forwarded to my trusted bank account year after year. I do not stop writing. I still enjoy writing. Hopefully, this book will provide another good stream of residual income for the rest of my retirement and for my grandchildren college education. After this book, I have already thought of another book to write so as to keep my mind active. The books I have in mind are known as *Nothing Venture Nothing Gain* and *Everything You Can Conceive Is Possible*. I have set another goal and hopefully create another stream of residual income. I am inviting you to walk with me in the journey of life as a brother of prosperity and a brother of possibility.

Prosperity will give the power to enjoy what you want, to become who you want to be, to live where you want, to give to whoever you want, and to inspire those come into contact with you. All the freedom of choice will only come if you start creating streams of residual income while you are working.

From my own experiences, there are three things in my life that really matter. As stated before, the first thing is what I do, the second thing is where I do it, and the last thing is whom I do it with. Money was involved in all these things but not necessarily the way you think. When you are rich, you can do a lot of things that look like fun. But from my own experiences, many of the things people do after becoming wealthy do not turn out to be of much fun. The experience of other rich people I know, these things are often not so much fun after all. Let me tell you a story. A friend of mine made a fortune in book business and in publication. He figured out to distribute his books to the dealers and how to get writers to produce the books. He made his fortune in his early fifties. He sold his business and made a lot of money. He did not have to work the rest of his life. But what he is going to do? He took up golf. He was under the sun almost every day. He played in almost every course in countries like Thailand, China, America, Europe, and elsewhere. He forced himself to play with a few of his friends. He pretended that he enjoyed playing. He tried to fill the time he had. It was exciting and fun for a while, but he got sick of it. He wanted to get back to his book business and publications. That is what he is really like doing and play golf during the weekend. You see building a fortune is more fun than having one. This teaches me a great lesson. I do not want to abandon what I enjoy doing. I continue to learn, to write, to do research, to invest, and to play the game tennis I love. I want to continue the journey that I enjoy.

INVESTMENT LIFE DURING RETIREMENT

I used to ask myself why I need to write and invest during my yearning days? I need a clear answer. While I was walking one day, my creative visualisation provided me with two very good reasons. First, I need to keep myself occupied, so writing and investment will provide me with plenty of research to do. I love to do research, and the process will keep my mental ability intact. There are plenty of information to gather and a lot of reading regarding the current economics. This reading habit will enhance my idea muscles and help in my writing. It appears to kill two birds with a single stone. Second, by investing correctly, I will have a vehicle to complement my income besides my returns from other asset classes and enjoy some luxuries whenever there is surplus. To achieve this goal, I need a very clear plan. For any strategy to be successful, you must have a plan for implementing it. This is true for sports and especially in investing, to ensure consistent success in result. My objective, besides complementing and enhancing my income, is to provide gifting to my children and grandchildren. Actually, my spending needs are well taken care of by my other investments with their residual streams of income. So the principle of the more the merrier applies. I will have more to give away to my relatives who are not doing well and to contribute to society whenever necessary. I also realise that investment in stocks involves risk. So I need to construct a portfolio of about ten stocks that has a balance of risk and rewards. I need to go through the process of risk management periodically to ensure my portfolio matches my risk profile. I must know the direction I am going; otherwise, I will end up somewhere else. My return expectation is small because my needs are intact, and I need not have to speculate. From the beginning, I adopt a disciplined approach and I will evaluate my plan and implementation periodically. Research and information will help me to make tactical changes when necessary. I concentrate on value and dividend stocks for the start. I do not want to simply pick any stock for my investment. I do not want to throw darts and hope to strike the right stock. I would prefer to follow the footstep of well-known investors like Bill Spetrino, Sean Hyman, Warren Buffett, and others.

For five days a week, after our morning breakfast, I will be at my computer doing my regular research into companies I am interested in investing and also do some writing. My wife shares the same interest and passion in investing. She has her own portfolio, and I have mine. She is in effect a keener investor than me. We seldom interfere in each other's investments. Our belief in the infinite power of the mind enables us to make sound decisions regarding investing. The question we face is very obvious. Do we take trading and investment as a hobby or as a business? We did not know at that point of time. So I began to use my little knowledge to find out the truth. We know that a hobby is normally defined as an activity not engaged in for profit. But if profit can come from a hobby is an extra bonus. This sounds good. But in most cases, if a person treats trading or investment as a hobby, there is a high probability of losing money. I strongly agree that stock trading is a performance-based discipline and it's a unique kind of business. We need to arm ourselves with all the necessary information and knowledge. We need to prepare ourselves mentally to be ready to take the next step, transforming our investment or trading from a hobby level to a business enterprise.

I am a fan of an old phrase by Leonardo:

'Simplicity is the ultimate form of sophistication.'

Simplicity in trading must be guided by adequate information or knowledge of the fundamental of a company. In Taoist philosophy, there are two types of knowledge that contribute to the achievement of a goal and knowledge that does not. To me the only knowledge worth pursuing is the one which serves my purpose. Just like the self-study strategy I pursued and advocated to others because I am goal oriented. I use the simple supply and demand analysis. I am lucky that I stumbled upon some simple secrets very early in my investment career. I like companies that pay good dividends. A dividend is a periodic distribution made by a company to its shareholders. The distribution is usually made from current year profits. There are also companies that use accumulated profits from prior years to pay extra dividends. In some countries, dividends may also carry certain tax advantages. I am also aware that high dividend is not a necessary feature of a high-performing company. Usually, when deciding whether to pay a dividend, companies first assess their future cash needs. They may need cash to replenish plant and equipment or embark on new growth initiatives. So it is not a bad thing that a company pays low dividend but reinvesting the cash in its business growth. How do I make a decision to invest in a company based on its dividend payout? I usually think of the available alternatives such as leaving the cash with the company or reinvest it elsewhere. In the case of a high growth company, I think I am in a better position if the company reinvest my dividend cash as the return is greater than a bank deposit or another lesser-performing company. This tells me that a high-performing company with a low dividend is not a bad thing! I am also aware that for poorly performing companies the opposite is likely. A low dividend is a poor investment as the cash is probably better off elsewhere. So before making an investment decision, I need to consider all aspects of a company not just the percentage of dividend payout. I must not focus just on dividend in isolation. Dividends are an important part of my investment, and I keep an eye out especially for those companies performing well in all areas. Research has shown that from 2010 to 2015, dividend-paying companies achieve a total return that is more than double the market average. If I had bought all the dividend paying stocks in the American market in the last five years, I would have achieved an average total return of 79 per cent compared with the market's 48.5 per cent total return. The risk is also there. About 16 per cent of dividend-paying companies lost at least half of their values. Nevertheless, the odds are clearly far better. This secret gives me a good choice by putting the odds in my favour.

Another secret in investment soon becomes clear to me. The idea of investing into companies that sell habit-forming or even additive products came into my investment radar. This idea is not popular and people do not like to mention it. My research into the statistics involved this habit forming companies reveals that most of them outperform other ordinary stocks over a long period of time. Companies selling soda drinks, fast food, candy, cigarettes, drugs, and alcohol are doing very well in terms of profits. Companies in the United States like McDonalds, Coca-Cola, Pepsi-Cola, Hershey Foods, Toolsie Roll, Big Red, Abbot Labs, Merck, Philip Morris, and others are benefiting from selling their habit-forming products. All of them sustain sales growth and healthy margin in terms of profits and giving generous dividends. When they hit upon the right recipes or the right mix of whatever it takes to make good products, they don't have to make large, ongoing investments in their businesses. Their cost of research and development is usually small. So a large percentage of their profits can be sent to the shareholders as dividends. Warren Buffett invested heavily into this simple idea. I too take advantage of this unpopular method of investment. A good example is the coffee chain Starbucks success story.

From 1995 to 2006, the stock advanced almost 2,000 per cent. I was lucky that I stumbled into this mode of investment and harvested a good return. Another company Sam Adams, which produces quality beer, gained 1,000 per cent from 2003 to 2013. So it is a good idea to invest in quality businesses that sell habit-forming products. My experiences tell me that investing in this type of companies is a safe sleep-at-night way to build wealth in common stocks. With the emerging middle class in India and China, it is worthwhile considering investing into habit-forming business reaching these countries. Remember not to rush into buying these quality stocks when their values are too high. Follow the advice that I hold close to my heart when investing and trading. There are many methods of investment which I experimented. They are mentioned later in my explorations. Only try out methods that you feel comfortable and confident. I was lucky that I stumbled into these five keys in trading and investment that provided me consistent profits.

First, I focused on the methods of picking stocks. I followed a clear and concise method of investment based on the fundamental of a company. I like companies whose revenue keeps increasing, whose profit rises, and who are very generous in terms of dividends. But most companies do not exhibit these combinations well. I start to look and identify companies with brand names, attributes of their products, and the strength of distribution system. In America, companies like Coca-Cola, Gillette, and Hershey come under such category. They have enormous competitive advantage, erecting a protective moat around their economic castles. These companies produce high returns when measured against company's asset base and require little additional capital. Even Warren Buffett started as a value investor just like David Dodd and Benjamin Graham. He bought stocks whose stock market capitalisation was a fraction of their net assets. He figured out by investing in great businesses that can compound his earning for decades. Buffett's approach in investing stock like Coca-Cola is a good example. It is based on capital efficiency. He bought about 60 per cent of Cokes in 1987-1989 because it was a safe stock. He did not try to roll die. He only bought sure thing. He knew Coke's business model well. It was incredibly capital efficient. And judging by its previous results and its growth, it was not hard for him to figure out. Later, other investors would bit the shares to a stupid level. At one time, Coke was traded for more than fifty times its PE ratio by 1998, for example. But Buffett never sold his stocks. It didn't matter to him how overvalued the shares were, as long as the company kept raising its dividend. About two decades later on, Coke's annual dividend was about 50 per cent the buying price Buffett paid for. In 1993, Buffett wrote about his Coke investment and his approach stating clearly the benefit of buying stable, capital efficient companies with the intention of holding them forever so their compounding returns would make a fortune. On the strength of this information, I started to list down companies which satisfy these conditions. I will wait for the opportunity to buy them at the right price. Once acquired, these stocks will be extremely long-lived. I will even advise my children's children not to sell these type of stocks. This will set the family's wealth on the path of compounding.

I have another method of selecting stocks based on the concept of insiders' trading, which is illegal. But during open periods directors are allowed to increase their holdings. This is perfectly legal. So I channelled my efforts into looking for companies where their directors keep increasing their holdings. This gives me an indication that the company is turning around as their directors are gaining confidence. The probability of being wrong is less when directors of a value company begin to add extra shares to their portfolio. Another method that serves as a guide to buy is looking for value companies buying back their own shares using their extra profits to reduce the number of shares in the market. I follow these specific methods that help me to understand when to buy and when to sell a stock. Most of my trading or investments are based on numbers, performances, and balance sheets. My analytical tools are simple, and I avoid complicated one. I do not worry about picking the winners of the year. I focus on making as much money as I possibly can from stocks paying good dividends. This gives me an edge. It turbocharges my returns when these stocks are soaring and protect me during market downturns. I avoid stocks with high dividends when prices are falling. My priority is to pick stocks that are high in quality and will steadily rise in value over time. One excellent indicator is their earning. The number of EPS in each quarter is critical. Earning is the driving force behind a company's success or failure. There is a difference between revenue and earnings or net profit. Revenue is the amount of money a business brings in and earning is what the company keeps. Earnings show me that a business is making money. The longer and more consistently a company shows that it can grow earnings, the more confidence I have that it will continue to do so. Undoubtedly, the stock price will eventually follow suit. There is a difference between revenue growth and earnings growth. The former is not earnings and the company may lose money in spite of revenue growth. I need to adhere to the principle of buying low, sell high, and don't get distracted by the headlines in the interim. It's about selectivity. When I know a company's value, I do not worry about what the analysts think a stock is worth. Knowing a company's worth is important because eventually the company's intrinsic value will be reflected in the stock price.

I also focus on discipline. Once I establish a method, I need to have the discipline to follow through with that method. It is that discipline that allows me to make consistent profits in my investment and trading. Should I make a mistake, it should be on the side of discipline. I adopt this formula for success by consistently follow and apply a proven method.

I also need to be realistic. I do not believe all the noise that I read and hear on how to become wealthy overnight carrying low or zero risk. Once I have a method, I follow it with discipline. I know my return will be according to the capital I have in the market. I know that if I want more profit, then I have to undertake more risks. It's that simple. I learn not to get greedy, and I soon understand the investment race is won by investing and trading slow and steady. I avoid being overconfident. I read with caution that over 80 per cent of traders lose money. I do not want to be one of them. So I am determined not to follow their missteps of being greedy and overconfident. By following this precaution, perhaps I try to avoid unnecessary risks that may cloud my judgement and make me lose money. Many traders talk about momentum trading. Momentum trading is basically buying when a stock is rising. It is the idea of buy high and sell higher. It works sometimes. I do not believe because it does not work for long. It is based on the illusion that if a stock price is rising, the company must be doing well. To me stock price only shows how everybody thinks a company is performing. Earnings show how a company has actually performed. I have made up my mind not to follow the crowd.

To succeed as an investor, I need to practise patience. Patience is the great quality of a good investor. In trading and investment, it's very common to get the feeling that I have missed the train and lost an opportunity to make money. It's at this moment that I may get into a hurry and try to rush the next trade. I try to avoid taking short cut on my method and start taking stocks of lesser and lesser quality, and this inevitably ends up overtrading or over investment. I am fortunate to realise that there is no reason to worry about missing the next opportunity because there is another one right around the corner. When I miss a bus, I always remember there is another bus which will leave after ten or twenty minutes. I learn to wait for it and follow my plan. I will take time to evaluate my plan and analyse market conditions before enter a trade. Perhaps in trade, one needs patience to deal with different situations: point and time of entry, how to manage the trade, and waiting for the set target. One needs to respect market conditions and take what the market offers. I learn never try to outsmart the market. I also learn to establish a cool mindset by avoiding impulse and revenge trading or investment. I will never force a trade or investment. If I have to squint at a chart or method, it means that the trade is not there, I try to move to the next trade or investment.

Every day I try to gain confidence. Confident traders or investors rely on their own judgement and not what others are saying. I learn to take full responsibility for my own decisions. One of the elements of success in trading or investment requires us to trust and follow our own plan. There will be losers and winners in our trading. I used to cultivate the habit of analysing all closed trades, winners or losers. I always try to identify what works for me and what not to help me funnel in the right direction. This is a useful method of personal trading introspection.

I need to control my emotions. All of us are affected by our emotional swings and emotional stresses. All these emotions will affect our trading or investment decisions. I learn early that if I trade with my emotion, I will not be able to trade clearly and rationally. Since separating emotions from trading is not totally possible, I need to take control of them. It is well known that money outlasts hate, love, greed, and anything you can think of. The most effective way to control emotional trading or investment is to follow your plan and method with great discipline.

Finally, I need risk management. I stumbled upon this concept early to avoid any big loss in case a mistake is made. A good rule of thumb is never risk any more than 4 or 5 per cent on any stock of my portfolio. Any stock I buy, I am only ready to lose not more than 20 per cent of its value. This is capital-preservation which will ensure longevity in trading and investment. The story of the tortoise and the hare will ensure slow and steady wins the race. So developing healthy trading habits is as important as your trading strategy and personal plan. Having the right approach and self-discipline is what makes a trader or investor successful.

Another important factor is to maintain a positive trading attitude which will help in money management and risk management skills. I do not allow a negative trading mentality to alter my thinking and mindset. I am lucky to learn earlier that trading attitude is more important than market knowledge and even my experience. Remember that it is more important how I react to the market and not the market will do to me.

I am wondering why so high a percentage of traders are doing badly. Perhaps, they become a gambler than a trader. They may not trade on the probabilities but the potential profits. For beginners initially, it's best trade small position sizes based on our account. I do not risk my whole account. I always trade based on a plan and not emotion. I always enter a trade with an edge that can be defined or quantifiable facts. I do not trade with entries that are opinions. I use extensive research on what works and what does not. I do not trade in ignorance. I make risk management my top priority and profits secondary. I do not trade in a way that can lead to financial ruin. Discipline and focus are important. I always follow my winning strategies instead of changing trade due to winning or losing streaks. I always trade in the present moment and do not get biased due to old wins or losses.

There are many other things to look for when investing. One important thing we should look into value companies that reduce their outstanding shares by buying back their own stock. They usually outperform the market. A company is considered valued if it is financially sound and uses its own profits to buy back its own stock. I want to share this experience. Do not be deceived. If a company borrows money to buy back its own stock, the judgement is a 'no'. But there are exceptional circumstances where companies are doing well and had plenty of cash for expansion. They may borrow to buy back their shares because of cheap capital available and the stock is undervalued. I learn to look well into the matter. I make sure that I am not affected by imaginary fear. I always look at the numbers: profit, cash available, debts, and revenue growth. This provides food for thought before investing. If you intend to use the notion of share buy-backs as a strategy to trade a stock, you need to be aware of many other possibilities. You need to know the real story why a company buys back its own share. First, it is possible that the company has largely exhausted investment opportunities that would generate a positive net value. Second, the stock is trading below its intrinsic value. Third, it is possible that the tax on dividends is so high compared to the capital gains tax that it makes sense to boost the share price by buy back its shares. Press releases emphasise that buy-back return value to shareholders. This is usually exploited by analysts to spot a stock to write up and the company managers like to tout their focus on shareholders returns. But we need to be careful. Many managers often have their own reasons to buy back their own shares. Management's compensation is often based on share price performance or earning metrics like EPS which buy-backs are designed to boost. Higher share price usually increases the value of a company's options. Most managers are big shareholders, and they have direct access to the treasury. Their own interest is usually their priority instead of the companies' business growth. So it is always possible that share buy-backs become a standard (and often abused) signal to the market that the company's stock is undervalued and that management takes care of the shareholders. Both these statements might be correct in isolation based on the fundamentals and management practices. Nonetheless, a buy-back should not convince you that either is true. We should not overlook occasions where top managers are fired for wrong acquisitions resulting in big losses. These are cases where *Wall Street* quarterbacks are sharp to point out that these losses would have been better paid as dividends to shareholders. My experience reminds me to always aware of two possible perspectives when a company buys back its own shares. Especially in technological stock, its product line can easily become absolute. So a company buys back its shares to boost its product line or move them into new businesses with long-term potential. Another factor involves borrowing at high interest rates to buy back its own shares. This action usually spells doom. Always look for value companies which make acquisitions for the company to grow and pay dividends for the next generation.

  The ultimate goal in trading and investing is to make profit. My wife seems to be ahead of me in investment and trading. She learns all the technical aspects to help her picking and selling stocks. I love simplicity. Any simple strategy that serves the purpose must be repeated and refined to become the strategy. The goal is to make as few mistakes in picking stocks as possible. Occasionally, I seek her help before picking a stock using her technical skills. We have been in the game for almost forty years and have acquired enough experiences to manage risks. I remember that our initial journey in investing was marred with losses. This is part and parcel of the game. We had paid to learn. After years of losing in my stock trades, now I have adopted the 'Trailing Stop Strategy' as part of my golden rules in investing and trading. The first golden rule is not to lose money. I have about ten to twelve stocks in my portfolio. These stocks are picked normally based on their quarter-to-quarter performance that is their fundamentals. After years of investing, I have discovered a strange phenomenon. I found a simple principle to make profit in trading. I call it 'honey attraction strategy'. If there is honey, there are ants. This simple attraction strategy usually works as long as the company's profit keeps flowing in. When the quarter profit of a company keeps increasing, good sentiment is usually created. Soon many investors and punters will come to notice the company's increasing profit, the share price is bound to rise as a reflection of its value. I have to be knowledgeable and understand the business the company is involving in. Any sign indicating the cycle of the business is over, I must be prepared to abandon ship. It is impossible to pick all winners all the time. There are times when I pick the wrong stocks. A single good quarter result does not add value to a stock. Just like a swallow does not make a summer in a cold winter. A good advice came from the best investor, Warren Buffett, who said,

> 'Be fearful when others are greedy and be greedy when others are fearful.'

After years of experience in investment, I begin to trust my own research, and I avoid all the noises of the market. Whenever the market is over exuberant and even taxi drivers are talking about the share market, I know it's time to come out of the market and take holidays. I will wait patiently for the next cycle.

Position Sizing and Risk Management

No matter how attracting a stock may be, I always limit each recommended position to no more than 5 per cent of my entire portfolio. This simple strategy is to safeguard and protect from any catastrophic loss. This strategy together with trailing loss of not more than 20 per cent for each stock will ensure that any wrong choice of stock will be contained. There is no perfect strategy that will ensure profit in investment or trading. One of simple strategies to beat the market is by using supply and demand analysis. Stocks can easily be classified into two general categories: value stocks and others. Using my simplicity method, I would classify value stocks as companies that consistently performing well during all cycles of economics. Especially in a bull cycle, its profit keeps increasing and its dividend also rises annually. In a bear cycle, its profit is still reasonably consistent and dividend is still maintained or slightly less. In any major recession, its profit is still there but less. The critical thing to consider is the point of entry for any value stock. This needs patience and due diligence. When stock prices are high, avoid touching them. In any major correction, the prices of these value stocks will fall but not so drastically as others. It provides opportunity to accumulate these value stocks. Once I keep to this basic principle of investing, the share prices will always fluctuate, and I am not concerned. These stocks will weather any downturns. Maybe it's time to pick more of these value stocks during a downturn. These dividend stocks will always perform better than the overall market in any downturn. The dividends keep paying me income, even when stock prices are falling. I will not recommend that you sell these value stocks when their prices are falling and go for cash. Cash pays little when interest rate is so low. Study after study has proven that only way to build wealth over the long term is to stay invested. And the smartest way to invest is with safe, high-quality, dividend-paying stocks.

I stumble upon this algorithm when I read the investment history of Bill Spetrino. He worked for $7.50 an hour as an accountant and later as a teacher in a community college. He used this algorithm buying only value stocks and held them over reasonably long periods. He started with only $10,000 and added more and more money as he worked into these value stocks. About twenty years he did all these investments; money keeps showing up in his mailbox, and his investment accounts like clockwork, month in, month out, only the cheques getting bigger and bigger. He retired at the age of forty-two. Now he is able to spend the majority of his time with his family going to baseball games and fishing, instead of sitting in an office slaving away.

After reading Bill's success, I did the same thing when I was working, and even now I am still investing in value stocks. I do not believe what most people claim that they can move out of the market during downturns and get back in just before a market run-up. They claim that by doing this simple feat, they can make more money. But Bill strongly disagrees. Trying to jump out of the market in anticipation of a downturn and back in when prices start to climb is market timing, and it doesn't work for ever. According to Bill, none of the successful and great investors used market timing rigidly. Not one. On the strength of this advice, I know investing in value stocks, I do not use timing. I do not worry about the day-to-day fluctuations of a stock's price. I do not get involved in cheering with the bulls and crying with the bears. What I care is making money consistently by investing in good-quality companies that pay dividends consistently, regardless of what is happening with their stock prices. I am living the life I always wanted, on my own terms, without anxiety or fear. I have absolute financial security. This is like putting on an 'autopilot system' that will all but make sure your future prosperity. I would like to share Bill's and my own experience with you. Following this simple principle, anyone can get rich.

Everyone knows that successful investing consists of buying low and selling high. My experience in the market for almost forty years tells me that the truth is no one knows that a particular stock is at the top. Nobody has the proven ability to time the market correctly. For example, in Australia, for the last two decades, when was the best time to sell stocks like Woolworths or Commonwealth Bank? We bought Commonwealth Bank in the '90s from $5.50 to $9.50 and sold at $11.50. We thought the price was at its top. But today, Commonwealth Bank is valued more than $90.00 with so much dividends being given through the years. For the last five or six years, when was the best time to sell TPM? The company went as low as nine cents and now is over $9.00. Nobody knows! As the investing giant, Jesse Livermore once said,

'The big money is not in the buying or selling, but in the sitting.'

Twenty years ago, if I had identified outstanding Australian business like Woolworths or Commonwealth Bank and I had held on to these stocks until today, I really would have made big money. Even six or seven years ago, if I had identified value stock like TPM at ten or twenty cents and held on to it until today, I would be laughing all the way to the bank. The trouble with us is that we do not have the patience. We are too eager to take profit, and we miss the full potential. So if we are serious to build wealth, a better strategy is to focus on identifying outstanding businesses and wait for the right timing to buy them for a long haul. Companies having outstanding patents like most drug companies are usually preferred for long-term investment. They are value stocks. A patent is a legal monopoly that crushes competition and guarantees profit. Apple is a typical example holding patent on its products. Most of the companies holding patent on their products are value companies. All the technical analyses do not apply to these value stocks. I always remind my wife not to repeat the same mistakes using technical analyses to decide buying and selling value stocks. I became aware that wealthy people own valuable assets. People like most of us, belong to the middle class, we simply rely on our salaries. This awakening tells me that depending on our salary we will never become rich. And one of the most important attributes of good investors and entrepreneurs is the ability to see the next big trends in businesses. This instinctive ability comes with knowledge and reading. Talking to business people and well connection with innovations will give us a huge and obvious advantage. In the 1980s and 1990s, I sensed that publications and social media trend was beginning. And everything including setting, TV, cars, and electronic devices would be connected to the computer and the Internet. I got into companies dealing with Internet years ago when the trends were new, and these ideas and others helped me make a bit of money. I invested into these ideas earlier, and many of the companies went on to help me to make great gains in recent years.

My wife uses technical analysis such as moving average convergence and a bunch of others to decide picking and selling stocks. Although I am a mathematics graduate, I do not like this type of approach based on crowd theory. When the crowd moves in a certain direction, the stock price follows. To me, this kind of stock price movements is not sustainable. I cannot count on this type of stocks to deliver returns. I understand the concept of moving averages, the strength of its price, and others. But I am only interested to use such technical analysis for entry purpose. I want companies that have substance in terms of cash, dividends, earning, and revenue growth. I want my stocks that will deliver gains now and in the future. If the stocks I have picked based on these criterions and they are not performing well now, I am not that concerned because they have solid, fundamental reasons to grow in the future. I learn to be patient and collect dividends first. Ultimately, the share price of each stock will adjust according to its earning and its real value. A big portion of my stocks is in this category, and they will provide me with consistent income to enjoy my retirement. I also venture into potential growth stocks which can provide huge gains if the choice is right. I used to restrict only a small percent of my capital in this category of stocks. The risk is always there if my judgement is faulty.

A Big Secret in Investing

Businesses are created by people, managed by people, and owned by people. They are just like people. Each one is unique. No two companies are exactly alike. And some businesses are vastly better than others. For comparison purposes, I will focus on comparing companies in the same sector. The difference in profitability means everything. For my investment purpose, I will focus on companies that earn money for the shareholders and ignore companies that always require shareholders' support to survive. Most profitable companies in a sector normally spend on things that matter and nothing on anything else. These superior companies usually have competitive advantages over their peers. My attention should be focused on the identification of these value companies with potential growth for investment. Although there is no 'one-size-fits-all' metric for determining these superior companies, there are certain measures of quality that help me quickly to find truly value stocks. In general, I notice that companies that consistently trounce their peers in the most relevant metrics have some of the following characteristics:

1. Companies have a strong brand name.
2. Companies have products or services that are difficult or not plausible to replicate.
3. Companies have products in high demand that are resistant to recession.
4. Companies have extremely focused niche and no viable competition.
5. Companies have expertise in 'dirty' or 'unattractive' businesses.

If you can identify a company that satisfies two or three of the above characteristics, that company is worth investing for a long haul. There are other factors to be considered. After all, if one company can make two or three times the profit of its closer peers selling the same basic goods or service, it must be doing something right. In order to discover other superior companies in other sectors, plenty of hard work and research have to follow. You can find some of these great companies, but it is harder to figure out what price to pay for them. We do not want to overpay. We have to depend on our valuation multiple. A simple judgement is usually made using annual EPS and the market stock price. If the PE ratio exceeds the average of the sector, the valued price may be considered high. This approach is rather unsound and can be misleading. Another possible approach is using the main metric comparing enterprise value (EV) to free cash flow (FCF) over the previous four quarters. EV is the amount of money it would cost to buy a company's outstanding shares and repay its debt. FCF is the amount of money left over after a company pays its bills and makes the necessary investments in infrastructure and equipment. It is essentially the money left over for the shareholders. As a rule of thumb, an EV/FCF of less than ten is cheap. But bear in mind most of the value companies are never cheap. Some may have their EV/FCF exceeding twenty. So a good moment to buy these value stocks is when they dip back below twenty. This strategy may turn out to be extremely profitable in the long haul when we buy them at the dip to the valuation level. Patience is the key word. Wait for the right time to enter and hold them for a reasonable period to benefit from your investments. According to Fulton J. Sheen,

> 'Patience is power. Patience is not an absence of action; rather it is "timing" it waits on the right time to act, for the right principles and in the right way.'

We know that fundamental analysis is critical, but without knowing optimal entry and exit points, it falls short. It would be great if we can follow institutional investors who use complex technical analysis to establish a system to guide them in investing. We too can create a trading system based on our knowledge on fundamental analysis, sentimental analysis, and some reliable technical analysis mentioned above. Our success will not be based on anything more than random luck. Besides, we need to monitor market sentiment and manage our portfolio sizes to different risk attributes. A great rule of thumb is to try to balance our portfolio with positions that are short in stocks that have been underperforming the market and long that have been outperforming. Our decisions are based on fundamental analysis. We may not achieve the standard of institutional investors, but at least we have considered fundamental, technical, and sentimental analyses before we invest.

No one knows when the stock price has peak. So I hold on to a stock as long as I can to benefit fully. To my own experience, a value company which keeps increasing its annual dividend and its profit keeps rising and its growth potential is still intact, I will hold on to such a company. Unless I am sure that the economy is turning from good to bad; otherwise, there is no reason to sell such a value and potential stock. A 20 per cent trailing stop strategy will help to ensure that I keep whatever profit accumulated before any market collapses. Now I am aware that there is nothing lucky about getting rich and holding great companies.

TECHNOLOGY STOCKS FOR THE FUTURE

There has never been a better time than *now* to invest in technology. If we are to think about it, there is not a single sector of the economy that is not impacted by technology. There is no doubt that the role of technology in our everyday life will only increase in the coming years. Just try to remember what life was like without a cellphone or iPhone, and we will get an idea of how reliant our society has become. Look at the market now; technology is prevalent in nearly every aspect of our daily lives. Everywhere we turn, we'll see impressive technology, from the smart phone in your pocket to TV we can hang from our wall. Ten or fifteen years ago, no one would have dreamt of anything like this was possible. And now a more stunning technology has unleashed: robot-driven vehicles.

In the yesteryears, we knew that Warren Buffett, the greatest investor of all times, was snubbing technology stocks. But now, this great investor is putting his investment into technology companies worth billions. This may serve as a strong indicator for us to start picking up stocks in this field so that we may not miss the train. For information sake, in the last five years, the NASDAQ-100 Technology Sector has outperformed every major sector in the American market. Even Bill Gates is optimistic regarding technology industry. He boldly predicts that this industry will be bigger than the computer industry! What companies we should be looking at? Perhaps plenty of research should be focused on companies producing robots and other automatic devices for industries. We are about to witness the technological changes in the workforce. Do not forget telecommunication and Internet exploration. This provides food for thought. As the saying goes, as with most opportunities, time is of the essence.

From 2005 onwards, some big companies began to start centres to provide 'cloud computing' which will save companies billions of dollars in software update. This revolutionary change in information storage will change our future usage of computer softwares. This new technology will wipe off many billions of dollars from software providers. We just have to tap into the cloud and obtain all the necessary softwares we require. We can assess any computing information and systems through the cloud. IBM has started to build a super-power 'cloud computing centre' for China costing a few billion dollars. This super-computing centre will provide all computers used in China with all the information and systems required to do business and research.

This revolutionary IT arms race is now in progress in many countries. For investors who get into successful companies providing 'cloud computing' would be like in the 1990s, when investors bought into companies like Microsoft, Apple, IBM, Intel, and others. Many of the investors made a few thousands per cent gains. The ability to identify potential companies into this new revolution will make many times the money you are going to invest. My experience tells me to start looking out for companies which has potential in providing 'cloud computing' facilities.

Trading and Investing Golden Rules

Successful investors like Peter Lynch, Warren Buffett, and Jim Rogers have their own system of investing. They all know that there is no such thing as a perfect system. Each has trust and confidence in his own system develop through the process. The incorrect assumption is that good investors or traders are good at everything they do. They do not jump from one strategy to another. They follow their own system. Sean Hyman uses a different system known as his Biblical Money Code to amass millions. He draws on the wisdom of King Solomon, the Apostle Paul, and Jesus of Nazareth. He started as a pastor earning $15,000 a year to give away $50,000 a year now, more than an average household income. To him it is a blessing to be able to bless others. Many people think that money is the root of all evil. No, it is the love of money that is the root of all evils. The love of money is the cancerous evil that can destroy our life. Here the love of money refers to greed, and it can take down any investor who aspires wealth instantly without due diligence. On the other hand, Sean chooses to become prosperous so that he can bless others. He claims that he always look well into the matter before investing. So we should not be blinded by the love of money. Even Warren Buffett promises to give away 85 per cent of his wealth. Sean Hyman helped his father to invest his $40,000 retirement saving to almost $396,000 so that he could retire comfortably and had the freedom to give away. Sean Hyman makes use of fundamental analysis, sentimental analysis, and technical analysis to ensure that he looks well into the matter before he picks his stocks. Sean claims that he has access to a secret calendar used by *Wall Street* insiders to consistently make money during every economic cycle. This calendar has the exact date to buy and sell certain stocks. Most of these successful investors are focused, and they look well into their investments. They also have extra information and knowledge common people like us do not have. A good thing is that many are very generous philanthropists. They are far from being lovers of money. They use investment as a righteous way of making money to gain prosperity and have the freedom to live the life they want. They have discovered a system that works for them, and they keep repeating it over and over again. They adhere to their own rules and guidelines. However, if the love of money forces us to hide it without investing, it can be equally stupid. Inflation diminishes the value of our money over time. The fear of loss is in fact more destructive. For me, I choose to invest in equities to grow my saving. I choose to look well into my investments. I have spent a lot of my time looking for guidelines and come out with the following rules to follow to maximise my profits. With these guides I will be able to improve my ability in investment. Hopefully, I will have plenty of money to live the life I always want and be able to bless others.

Rule One

Expect to lose when you enter a trade or investment, but define the limit you are willing to lose. I have adopted a trailing stop strategy to cut loss if a stock I have picked falls about 20 per cent, I will immediately instruct my broker selling the stock. I have strictly adhered to this strategy. There is no ifs or buts business. This strategy will ensure that big losses are avoided. Take for example, if I pick a stock at $10.00 and if the stock's price rises to $20.00, my trailing stop will now moves to $16.00, 20 per cent below the new price. I will sell immediately if the stock falls to $16.00 or slightly less. To make this strategy effective, I must not hold too many stocks. Ten or twelve are the maximum. On the other hand, if the stock falls from $10.00 to $8.00, I will immediately sell to avoid a big loss. This has become my first risk management golden rule. Now a computer programme is available for trailing stocks. I am in the process of adopting this programme.

Rule Two

If I am lucky that I pick a good stock that keeps on rising, I will let the winner run until it reaches its peak and starts to fall. A trend is a good friend. Once a trend is identified, I will allow it to progress until it wears itself out. Then a 15 per cent trailing stop will apply. A trailing stop is a predetermined price at which I will exit a stock holding. It literally stops from a good profit to a loss. It's calculated as a percentage below a stock's highest recent price. As an example, if I buy a stock at $1 per share, I use a 15 per cent trailing stop. If the stock rises to $4, I will sell the stock if it falls 15 per cent to $3.40. The beauty of this strategy is that it allows me to stay long during the uptrend. I have a predetermined strategy for exiting plan for exiting position when the trend turns lower. We had a good experience in one stock which rose over 3000 per cent. We bought large quantities at very low price. We sold partly the stock using the trailing stop and harvested a fortune. This experience has given us a very useful lesson to allow a rising stock to flow without being too eager to take profit. During our initial stage of investing, we looked too closely at taking profit, resulting in selling all the good flowers and keeping the rotten one without knowing the philosophy of risk management. We were amateurs then. Amateurs look at immediate profit first while professionals look at risk.

These two strategies appear to reward me in my investing and trading. For example, if I pick ten stocks and five of them suffer losses, I can only lose 20 per cent of my capital or less in each stock. If the other five stocks go for their run, the profit can be huge. The important thing is that the sum of the winning profit must be bigger than the total loss. The example I quoted above in one stock gave us a big profit.

During my initial stage of investment, I had committed a big mistake by selling my winners too soon and kept my losers too long. This is a common mistake most traders and investors make. Logically, we should be motivated to prune the losers and let the winners run. But in the battle of these two contrary motivations, we let the irrational one influence us more. Do you want to know the psychological reason? Most of us focus on our winners because winning generates the feel-good chemical dopamine deep in our brain. Paying attention on our winners makes us feel good, and so our winners become our darlings and our losers are the 'stepchildren'.

The chemical dopamine provides us the sense of motivation, and we are motivated to do things that tend to boost it. It is a powerful drug. Selling a winner creates a flow of dopamine, and we feel good. It can be addictive, and we keep on repeating selling winners without let them run. It becomes a habit. Do you know why? Selling a winner because of feeling good is a habit rooted in the basal ganglia, an area of the brain we have virtually no conscious control over. Keeping a loser is usually based on hope. The hope that the loser can one day recover and generate another delayed feel-good experience. This 'hopamine' encourages us to keep our losers in the portfolio. Perhaps our anticipation of a positive result generates more dopamine than the actual winning. It keeps us hopeful of a turnaround in our portfolio slackers. Another possibility of such irrational act is the joy of denial because we do not want to face any loss. The focus on loss causes dopamine to plummet, making us feel bleak and hopeless. So it's easy for us to shift our attention away from our loss as long as possible. The consequence can be devastating. Now I make sure that I do not get trapped. I will follow my first two golden rules to avoid any catastrophe in investment and allow my winners run to maximise my profit.

Rule Three

Never be swept away by exciting stories created by analysts, traders, brokers, well-known friends, and the general public. Constructing an investment portfolio out of public thinking is like building a skyscraper out of marshmallows. The bigger your portfolio the riskier you are in. Just like a skyscraper, the higher it goes, the squishier it gets. Information from these people is not solid. Instead, they are combinations of theory, interpretation, guesswork, spin, hunch, and imaginary fears. Understand the business you are going to invest. I will not invest in a business I do not understand. Once I know a company's quarter profit keeps rising, I will keep a close watch. I will wait for the appropriate time to start investing. I had suffered great losses for picking a stock at very high price. Now I learn never to chase a stock no matter how good the profit is. I had been 'the bigger fool' before. Timing is always critical in investing. When a good stock starts falling in its price, I learn not to jump in. I had caught a fallen knife before. I learn to be patient, waiting for the price to pick up first followed by rising profit. It's safer to earn a few cents less than to be caught in long period of bear market. Investing in trend too late can easily make you one of the greater fools. Knowledge in the fundamentals of a company is critical. Companies with plenty of cash and profit never have trouble. Years of experiences in investment teaches me not to be bullied by good salespeople. The market is never short of cranks, charlatans, and salesmen.

I was told that trends are one of the most important concepts in all trading. What is a trend? It is simply a series of price movements in one general direction. Some trends go up and some go down. When a stock is in a big, multiyear up trend, I should keep my trade on the 'long side' - the bullish side. This will ensure that I am trading with the trend, not against it. This approach will ensure that I benefit from the tailwind to my trade, not a headwind. I need to discipline myself not to panic out of the stock when it suffers a small correction. I invest with an open mind. I do not depend on others that may lead me to take foolish action.

This is the secret that separates average investors from the best of the world. Knowing when to sell and when not to sell during an uptrend is always tricky. Many novice investors like me initially get excited about a small profit and sell before the biggest gain. They also 'panic sell' when the market pulls back in a natural correction, only to watch shares rebound to new highs. My experience tells me now to look at the big picture, and since the awareness prevails, I manage to avoid missing the train of any big gain. What is this big picture? A big trend in stocks shows a series of 'higher highs' and 'higher lows'. Each peak is above the previous high and each low stops short of the previous low. This is a typical bull market trend. Once we understand the big picture, we will not be affected by the reading of gloomy headlines and panicking selling during a natural correction. The best place to make money is still follow the long side of the market. Watching the big picture helps to identify the big trend and stick to it. My experience tells me that it is never my thinking that makes big money, but it is always the sitting. But I keep to my protective stop losses under rule one and rule two intact.

On the other hand, if the price of a stock keeps falling, we may be tempted to buy because the stock is cheap now. We need to be aware that we may be catching a 'falling knife' or a 'falling safe'. In any downtrend, even the value stocks are not spared. Experiences tell me that by jumping in while the price is falling, my money may be in trouble. I have got into risky trades many times. A better alternative is to practise patience and allow the 'falling safe' to slam into the ground first. Sometimes, the price of the stock may move sideways for a period of time. This period may last a year or two. I will wait for the market to form a bottom ground first and allow the prices to move a bit higher before buying. It's then time to walk over and pick up the money. When a stock starts to rise despite all the bad news still circulating, I know it is 'acting well', signalling a bullish-up trend. It tells us that the trend has changed. When these tiny glimmers appear, we know the market free fall is over. Now it is time to jump in and pick up the stock. Patience is the key to invest during any downturn.

Rule Four

I usually follow a simple strategy when I pick stocks. I usually buy a stock with a PE below ten and a debt-to-equity ratio below fifty. This is one of the suggestions given by a famous investor, Mr Graham. This will help to minimise valuation risk. A company with a consistent dividend growth and growing earnings is a good indication for long-term investment. Companies with good profit margin and plenty of free cash flow (FCF) are my top picks. This will avoid balance sheet risk where companies can't pay their debts. Once I have identified a company with strong dividend and growing earnings, then I will look at its price. I look for a cheap price because I do not want to overpay its value. A little bit of patience is needed and wait for the right price at the right time. Simple is better than being smart in investing. I always caution myself not to overestimate the limits of my knowledge. I remind myself of many things which I do not know. Knowing what you do not know is much more useful in business than being brilliant. I know very early that to be a successful investor, I need a combination of gumption and patience and get ready to pounce when opportunity presents itself. It is waiting that helps me as an investor. Many people just can't stand to wait for the right time. When the market is at the peak, many people are impatient and they join the crowd. They have exhausted all their funds. When a big correction comes, opportunity for making money suddenly presents itself. Unfortunately, these impatient investors are now on the sideline. If you do not inherit this deferred gratification gene, you have to work very hard to overcome that.

Rule Five

I learn to never buy a stock based on price. When I started investing, my problem is that I used to evaluate a stock simply based on its price. It is a lousy way to invest. Now I learn a much smarter, safer, and frankly more profitable way to evaluate a stock based on its business. Looking for a good deal and timing is important. Now I usually make sure that I do not overpay for a stock. I want to make sure that the company is worth much more than is currently reflected in the stock price. To ensure this, I need to look at the business, its balance sheet, and earnings. I need to determine what factors will propel the company forward and what factors would keep it from growing. I need to assess what real market value the stock price should be. Finally, I determine what is the highest price I can pay for the stock and still receive my 6 per cent or 8 per cent annual return. So I do not require any technical indicators to help me picking a stock because it is based on logic and numbers rather than historical prices and momentum. Remember, a stock can be priced cheaply by historical measures but still be basically worthless because if there is no way to assess its value.

Rule Six

Although insider trading is illegal, but there is an exception when insider trading is perfectly legal. During open period, directors and senior executives are allowed to buy their own company's shares. The only problem investors encounter is the difficulty of detecting this type of scenarios. Once this situation is detected, we can use three secret signals to successful insider trading.

The first indicator is when the company's lawyers who are usually non investors start buying the company's shares. This is clear signal that they must have seen something really great regarding the company's performance. This provides a strong signal for us to follow and buy the stock.

The second indicator is when you see a cluster of senior management staff including directors buying their own stock at the same time. This sends a strong signal that something good is coming out of the company's performance. It's time to follow.

The third indicator is when members of the management staff who have seldom buy stock start to jump in buying the company's shares. When it is raining bargains, I will use buckets, not thimbles, to scoop up stocks for my portfolio. But when the bargains are few and far between, I need to be choosy. I will act only when it makes sense to do so. This strongly indicates that exceptional performance or good news is on the way. With these signals in place, you can seldom be wrong to buy the stock.

Besides these six rules, there is another most advanced skill you can develop as an investor. It is simply the emotional disciplines to be incredibly patient. Most investors who do their own due diligence know what businesses they want to buy. If you really want to succeed and make plenty of money as an investor, you must start developing the ability to wait until you get the rarest of opportunities to buy the businesses at the right price. The waiting can be very long and you need to have the patience. In his younger days, Warren Buffett wanted to buy the business GEICO, a company where his mentor made a fortune. He waited and waited for almost thirty-four years until he got the right opportunity to buy the company at a very cheap price. After one or two decades, he made 400 times the amount he invested. I learn from his example, and I can do the same if I can develop the quality of being patient. I started to keep a list of value companies and follow their annual report and the companies' progress in good time as well as bad times. I always keep aside enough funds and wait until the market gives me a great opportunity to buy the stocks cheaply. I believe I can also make 100-400 times the amount I am going to invest. Do I have the discipline and the patience? If I can, I believe I can easily become a very successful investor! Actually, I achieved this excellent result a few times already and hoping to have more.

With these six rules in mind, once I buy a stock, I never have to worry about the stock's price again. If I buy and the stock goes up, great. I am making money. I will not take profit immediately. I will wait for the share to run its course. If I buy and the stock goes down, great! I can buy more at an even better price. I am calm because I have done my research to know there is a real value there, and I know that value will eventually be reflected in the stock price. I want to own more of a good company. I do not chase after any stock if the price keeps rising. I do not believe in buying high and trying to sell higher. I do not believe in momentum trading! For good company, I buy low and buying lower if need be. So timing is not always right for every investment. In order to sleep well, my portfolio is concentrated on conservative value stocks and less on aggressive and international stocks. It is easily say than done. Many a time we make mistake by faulty analysis. So do not forget to apply the trailing stop strategy to avoid big loss.

Knowledge and Information Key to Investment

There are many ways to invest depending on our objective and the stage of life we are in. For me, at my retirement stage, I prefer to follow the strategy adopted by Bill Spetrino. I like his mantra:

> 'Keep your investments boring, and the rest of your life fun and exciting.'

This strategy will ensure safety, consistent income, and dividends. These boring companies that pass Bill's rigorous multistep vetting process must have a number of key characteristics: having brand name, possessing a pristine balance sheet, and having cash stash to help them survive and thrive in difficult market. In addition, they are in an industry where they hold strong competitive advantage. Most of these multinational companies are dealing with consumer goods, pharmaceuticals, retail, banking, and technology. Plenty of research is required to spot these companies satisfying most of Bill's standard requirements. Once the companies are spotted, patience is required to find a suitable entry to each stock. These companies are further classified by Bill Spetrino into three types: the conservative portfolio, the aggressive portfolio, and the international portfolio.

All investors know that chasing after high-growth stocks may be fun, but it may deliver the same thrill as striking a jackpot in Las Vegas when you stumble upon a winner. The probability of losing money is equally high. As an investor especially during retirement, this 'exciting investment opportunities' that promise 'incredible heart-pounding growth' should be avoided at all cost. Bill has a good advice. This is not an acceptable fate for people retirement nest eggs.

Experiences have taught me to arm myself with information and knowledge by reading widely before I venture into equity investment. Many successful stories of great investors serve as stepping stone for me to emulate. I learn from successful investors by imitating how they made their money. I read as much as I could about their strategies. I tried out by 'modelling' their behaviours to see what worked. Surprisingly, what these legends did with their money is significantly different from what I learnt in school. The theories from books and what is taught in school didn't work out so well in the real world. These legends are rich, and most professors are not. I realise that we can't beat the lessons of real-world experiences. These are some of the obsessions practised by these great investors.

The first principle is not to lose money in investing. So to most of them, defence is many times more important than offence. All of them are very focused on the downside at all times. This seems to agree with my goal in investing, that is, never let a small loss turn into a big loss. So the golden rules of investing is critical, especially the trailing loss approach adopted by me.

The second principle helping them making money is risk a little to make a lot. With a stop loss of 20 per cent, the downside risk is capped and the upside potential can be 50 per cent or more. This strategy provides a great reward-to-risk ratio. This thinking is critical to my investments. I follow this diligently because the path to make money is to make downside risk as small as possible and make upside gain as much as possible. So stop losses is necessary to control downside risk.

The third principle to make money is to anticipate even with little information. Now I realise that many brilliant people are terrible investors. Most of them are unable to make decisions with limited information. By the time full information emerges, everyone else knows it and they do not have an edge. The ability to anticipate with little information comes with experiences. When everything about a stock looks great, there is practically no upside left. When the picture of a stock looks cloudy and everyone is scared, anticipation counts. These legions invested first before everyone had all the information. Their ability to anticipate helps them to make a lot of money.

Timing of buying a stock is critical. Many stocks related to the medical world can bring in great profit. For example, in 1920, investors bought into companies linked to the discovery of Penicillin made a great fortune. Today scientists are working on drugs to cure cancer, Alzheimer's disease, and drug addiction. A component of the drug comes from the blood of the giant keyhole limpet or sea snail. This Keyhole Limpet Hemocyanin (**KLH**) - a magic molecule - is normally extracted from these giant sea snails. It seems that usually when the blood is extracted from the sea snail, the creature dies. Not many of these giant keyhole limpets are left off the coast of California. A company is culturing these sea snails and has acquired the know-how in extracting its blood without killing the sea snails. This technique is patented. As an investor, such knowledge is critical. Since the alternate way of producing synthetic KLH is not feasible. As *Popular Science* reports: 'KLH is too big and complicated to synthesise.' The scarcity of these sea snails has driven up the price of KLH. It was reported that each gram of KLH is sold at very high price. As soon as the company is listed, your guess is as good as mine. Profit may come in terms of a few hundred or thousands times. This type of information is not restricted to the medical world.

Information regarding technological developments can also bring great success. Technical companies like IBM, Apple, and Microsoft all experience the boom. Currently, many biotech companies are experiencing boom time. A little bit of focus in researching into some value biotech companies can help to ensure good profit. Knowledge and information will serve as a corner stone for investment success. A new metal graphene made from carbon has been discovered. This new metal is much stronger, has much better conductivity, and is thinner. This will revolutionise our phone, TV, computer, cars, aeroplane and speed up everything we use. I start looking up for companies which will manufacture this new product. I also keep looking out for new technological companies specialise in robotics and telecommunications. Productivity will increase and cost of manufacturing will come down. Today, there is an arms race in IT technology involving 'cloud computing'. IBM is helping China to build a gigantic 'Cloud Computing Centre' costing billions of dollars. Many countries around the world are doing the same revolutionary process, concentrating in providing 'cloud computing' centres to provide information and software systems for businesses, researches, and individual uses. The ability to identify companies doing this type of centres for cloud computing will bring great profit in investments. With a good timing and information, I believe our investing journey will be well rewarded.

This little secret I discovered some time ago reveals the critical things not only in investment but also in the games I enjoy. I play golf quite regularly besides basketball and tennis. Whenever I play golf, I always keep these few critical things in mind. First, I do not swing too hard and always keep the eyes on the ball while keeping the head still. Second, I do not take big risks. Following these few critical things in mind and discipline to follow them, I eventually become a good golfer. This is almost similar to investment. Finding that one critical thing can bring you a bit of peace and clarity. Most investors get bogged down by too much noise and advice, and most of it is not helpful. So it's important that when you feel bogged down and overwhelmed, just return to the critical things like the golden rules. Chances are you'll come out ahead.

There are two important common secrets most successful investors share. All of them have a system, but none of them has the same system. This tells us that there is no such thing as a perfect system. They have confidence and trust in their system when especially during time when it makes them look stupid. The experience of Warren Buffett during the tech bubble reveals a good story. He was labelled as old and out of touch because he did not invest into tech companies. He ignored it. He had trust and confidence in his system when it made him look stupid. As long as my system works, I will stay with my system. There will be time when things are not going as well as I like. Over time, if the system works, my confidence and trust will be enhanced. Another secret is that most successful investors avoid large losses. So the principle of buy-and-hold method should not be rigidly adhered to. When a mistake is made, always be prepared to cut loss. If you make a loss of 50 per cent, then it takes a 100 per cent profit just to break even. On the other hand, if you have a 10 per cent loss, it only takes 11 per cent profit to get back even. So you need a system that you have trust and confidence.

At this moment, May 2015, the bull market is still intact. For the last four or five years, we had seen occasional pullbacks of 3 per cent or 4 per cent. And last October 2014, the S&P 500 dropped almost 7 per cent. So for a long time investors have not experience a 10 per cent or 15 per cent correction. We note that prior to 2011, the stock market used to suffer through one or two correction of this magnitude every year. We need to understand that corrections are necessary for a long-term bull market. They are necessary for the market to work off overbought conditions, eliminate the complacency of some investors, squeeze some excessive stock prices, and provide some bases for the market to launch another rally. It appears that the market is overdue for one. We anticipate the market to reach its all time high at the end of April 2015. The possibility of a 10 or 15 per cent correction is on the way. The financial sector is usually the leader of the market. A strong indication of this possibility is given by the trending decline of most financial stocks. The S&P 500 has been making higher highs and higher lows all the time. But the moving average convergence divergence is moving lower lows. All these indicate a bearish pattern. Once the index breaks the boundary line, a 10 per cent correction is always possible. What precaution people will take? For me, I think it's time to get defensive. I will sell most of my stocks except those with good dividends and those in commodity sector. It's a good time to start raising cash to get ready for a big correction. Investing with information and knowledge will always give us an edge.

STRATEGIES TO FIND BEST GROWING STOCKS

Every investor loves growing stocks because of their potential to help them make big money. First, we need to know the factors that define growth stocks. In simple term, a growth stock has monopoly or patented products which will grow in demand because of big market. Its revenue keeps rising exponentially, and its profit follows. An easy way to understand growth stocks is to examine the common traits of past growth stocks like IBM, Apple, Microsoft, and others and look at the historical aspects just before they made the major price move. And just as importantly, they flashed similar signals as they eventually top and began to decline. The difficulty is in the identification of these growth stocks. You will not be wrong if you focus on companies with high-earning growth and companies with new, innovative products or service. Any form of accelerating earning growth is a strong indication.

Another glaring indication is that institution investors start to buy heavily. So a logical way to invest in growth stocks is to buy them when the market is on the uptrend. Most growth stocks have their own cycle, and once they reach the top, they too will face a decline. The cycles will repeat. So it will be wise to take defensive action as the downtrend emerges. Another indication for decline is when institution investor start to sell the stocks. It is perhaps time to get out and sit on the sideline. This type of information will help to preserve your profit gained during the uptrend.

Technically, we can use a screener to help us detecting this type of stocks. Many investors use the fundamental screener 'FinViz.com' to help them identify these growth stocks. I tend to use practical method by following the big money, growth stock investors such as institutions and hedge funds. I used to follow Bill Spetrino's billionaire ESP strategy. They provide the leadership that has been proven over the years to be highly effective. But their reports of their holdings and their purchases are usually stale because of time lapse. However, you will discover that what they hold regarding growth stocks provide great investment ideas.

Another source of growth stocks comes from experts from each sector of the stocks. Many well-known analysts and fund managers also provide valuable information regarding these stocks.

Finally, I rely on my own experiences to sport some of these growth stocks by analysing their growth potential over the years. Drug companies with their patents of monopoly are potential stocks for growth. Sporting them early can turn a few thousand dollars into a fortune. Remember that no amount of academic study or book reading will provide this critical skill. This talent is much sort after, and it normally takes years of experience. Some investors use advisory such as 'Weathpire's Consensus Picks' to help them locate these stocks.

I am lucky that I stumbled on Bill Spetrino's ESP Approach of picking growth stocks before the billionaires come in. The first thing in picking value stocks is to look at the numbers. If the company's cash is much more than its debt, the stock is worth investing for long term. The second thing to look for is the history if the company's EPS. If the EPS is growing at a good rate each year, the company is worth investing. Another thing to look at is the history of its dividends. If the dividend is increasing year after year, the company is a good candidate for long-term investment. I follow these basic rules with the suggestions mentioned above to help me picking stocks to invest. I also look for companies that consistently trounce their peers in the same sector in the most relevant metrics mentioned below. A company with strong brand name has advantage. A company whose products or services that are difficult or not plausible to replicate also has advantage. Look for companies that have products in high demand that are resistant to recession. A company which has an extremely focused niche and no viable competition is also a good candidate for long-term investment. Finally, look for companies which have expertise in 'dirty' or 'unattractive' businesses. They are usually very profitable. In my research, if I find a company that satisfies two or three of the metrics mentioned, I would have placed the stock in my investment radar waiting for the right time to invest for long term. Patience, experience, and due diligence are essential elements for successful investors to sport growth companies for long-term investment.

The Demon Fear and Greed in Trading and Investments

All of us are lured by the notion of making big money and making it fast when we start to invest and trade in stocks. Greed is a great motivation for becoming involved in trading. Although there is nothing wrong with that because many things would not be accomplished without some element of greed to provide the incentive. But demon greed often overreaches reality and the limits of our account and ability, producing more risk than we can handle. Then another demon, fear, often takes over and prevents us from capitalising on potential opportunities when they appear. Clearly, it depends on the market situation at the point of time. For example, during a bull market rally, greed tells us to buy into the stock market; fear tells us the market is overbought and due for sharp correction. How do we manage and conquer these two demons: greed and fear. Many advices are given by experienced traders, and their wisdom can be distilled into a simple phrase: plan to win but expect to lose.

Whatever strategies we have can be useful. Set up our strategies to win on account of our style, size of our account, and the condition of the market. Everyone knows that the stock markets can be a little perverse at times, not unfolding as expected. All of us are aware that panic is not a good environment for sound trading decisions. Here are some approaches we can take to reduce the effects of greed and fear on our trading.

First, when I am a beginner, I start by trading small. If ever I get into trouble because of a wrong decision, the loss is bearable. I avoid the risk exposure by taking positions that are too large for my account. I do not allow the demon fear to become an acquaintance too early in my investment or trading.

Second, I learn to expect to lose when I enter a trade but define the limit I am willing to lose. I swear to be firm and committed by not waffling if the point is reached.

Third, by the same token, what amount of profit is enough to satisfy me in a given trade? The trading adage is 'let the profits run'. Taking a profit may be the case or reduce the size of my position can give me confidence and alleviate greed or fear concerns.

Fourth, I try to trade with a shorter time horizon. It may not be an intraday affair. A short-term perspective in the market environment provides quick feedback about my analysis and can reduce the time I am exposed to the vagaries of the marketplace.

Fifth, I try only to trade with the amount of money I can afford without affecting my lifestyle. By doing so, I may be able to reduce the demons greed and fear in decision-making.

Whenever there is a drastic correction or a market crisis, there is also opportunity for making money. You need to be cool and calm. I try to observe these rules that help me make some money. First, be patient and wait for the prices to stop falling. Second, when the situation starts to correct, use a tight stop. Third, when I start to invest, I keep my position size small first, and finally, allow the trade a few chances to work out before investing further.

Finally, I try to balance between being a little greedy and a little fear. A little respect for what the stock market can do will help us to reduce the demons fear and greed. When I trade, I must feel comfortable as my plan dictates. Otherwise, I will keep my cash for opportunities later on.

A small suggestion that combined fundamentals and a simple chart showing the movement of the price of a stock can help a beginner to invest safely. I look for quality of companies. For me to invest for long or medium term, capital efficiency of a company matters. Companies like See's Candy and Hershey are classified as capital efficiency that allows them to pay larger than normal percentage of earning via dividends. They exhibit such quality of a noticeable lack of capital expenditures or required additional capitals. Once you have identified a capital efficient stock with good fundamentals such as revenue increases, EPS increases, good dividend, and cash more than debt, yet, in the short term, other factors come into play that are not explained by the former. Sentiment is one of them. The emotional reactions of investors and traders, together with news and events, have an influence on the price movement. Bear in mind that in the realm of finance we live in a world where fear and greed dominate our decisions, and it's usually at the wrong moments. Learn to examine the emotion and psychology of the players in the market through the lens of technical when emotion runs fast through the market. Looking at the volume and level of movement usually gives an indication of commitment and participation. All these observations require consistent, persistent, and plenty of research experiences to master before you can spot the right time to enter your trade or investment. Other more sophisticated technical analysis can be added as you progress. Alternatively, I used to look for trends and patterns that repeat over and over again. Human behaviour never changes because of fear and greed, so I look for the same patterns arise at different moments in time and anticipate the next move. At the end of the day, if I combine technical with a good sense of fundamental analysis, it is a great way to gain a market edge. There are many ways to skin a cat. So is the stock market. Investors have to develop their own strategies or follow well established strategies to have an edge in trading and investment.

Four Common Mistaken Beliefs Traders and Investors Make

Most beginners think that the markets are easy. My past experiences tell me that this assumption is always mistaken. All the knowledge and skills we read from successful traders and investors cannot be easily translated into profits. The only easy thing about the market is losing your trading capital. We are so used to cookbooks teaching us how to prepare a delicious meal. But if you have never cooked a meal, your food may not turn out as described in the cookbook. The same philosophy applies to the stock markets. If we think it's easy to make money in the market, we are wrong. Perhaps we are naive, and because we have some success in other things, this may not apply.

Many people seem to think that trading in the market can replace their income especially those who just lost their jobs. By putting in efforts like attending seminars and conferences and reading into ideas of successful traders, they think they can be successful in the stock markets. Unconsciously, they put themselves under great pressure to make every trade a winner. Nobody needs that hanging over them. Do yourself a favour by finding another job instead of plunging yourself into the markets under such circumstances.

Most people think that they do need someone's help in trading. This common mistaken belief is especially prevalent among the intellectuals. Remember data is not information. Information is not knowledge, and knowledge is not wisdom in trading. The ability to interpret data for information requires experiences and time. Besides doing due diligence in any trade, much information is required and guidance is needed to process the information to become valuable knowledge to help investing wisely. Getting the right mentors with vast experiences and knowledge can reduce mistakes in decision-making. I do not put too much trust on some brokers and advisors. Many are charlatans who do not have your interest at heart. They would probably fleece my pockets. I usually try to look out for traders or investors of common interest. I never assume I know. I ask questions and build relationship. I make my learning journey in the market graciously.

Another mistaken belief is that you must always trade. Just as a doctor and-patient's case, more patients translate into more profits. But in trading, this may not be the case. When situation is not favourable, do not take any position. Wait patiently for the right time and the right price before you take a position. Do your own due diligence. Review the trade metrics and examine the fundamentals before making any decision. Is the stock undervalue or overvalue? Is the stock a value one? Is the sentiment right? Is the timing right? To be a successful trader or investor, I know I need more time, money, and discipline than others. I learn to humble myself as humility is a prerequisite for knowledge. I learn to use knowledge wisely before I invest. So I need to roll up my sleeve because the hours will be long and the work is mentally taxing. Overtime, I'll learn to respect the varied nuances of the financial market while finding my niche. I will learn every strategy I can and apply only those strategies that have been proven winners consistently.

Another common mistake most of us make is cutting a winning trade or an investment short because we are too eager to take profit. I had experienced this phenomenon a few times in my investment and trading. A lack of patience usually results in a conflict of our mind and thought. One part of the mind told me that a profit was better than any loss. Another part of the mind told me that it felt sorry for taking the stock out of the investment. The market continues and the stock price keeps rising. The consequence is that I feel miserable for closing the trade too early. So which part of the mind is right? Is it the one telling me to get out and take the profit or the one now scolding me for doing what it told me to get out? Obviously, neither is right. Now I realise that being fused in my thought like what I had done, believing them to be true and accurate and acting on them, can influence my investment and trading. This conflicting thought can make me feel sad about my action, and it's never constructive. I need to follow my golden rules with discipline. I need the weapon called mindfulness. It is one of the best ways to address accepting our thoughts uncritically. I learn to let go of insistent thoughts and emotion. Being mindful teaches me to free myself to choose more valued investment actions. I now place more attention to what matters and follow my trailing stop discipline. By uncritically accepting my thought and mind and follow my strategy reduces my stress and fear, and I now focus hard when the price of a stock goes for a run. Plenty of practice is required to attain mindfulness as a weapon to overcome these conflicting of thoughts.

A Good Strategy to Make Big Money in Stock

Increasing one's wealth a few times might sound absurd. But it's possible in the business of finding and tapping the world's gold, copper, oil, diamond, and uranium deposit. More than any other sector, natural resources can produce tremendous gain. This sector is comparable or even better than the technological sector. It can take years to find the right set-up to achieve these types of gain. Familiarity with the natural resource market's cyclicality is an advantage. History tells us that natural resources go through huge cycles of boom and bust. Consider the case of uranium from 2000 to 2008. Uranium is a natural resource whose chief use is fuelling nuclear power reactors. There were excess production of uranium in the 1990s, and the price of uranium was depressed. Low price of uranium meant no one was investing in new uranium deposits. There simply wasn't any money in it. In 2003, for example, it cost $20 per pound to mine uranium, but they were selling it for only $15. Miners were losing money. Many mines closed down. It was grim, a classic bust period for years. After that the demand for cheap uranium increased. But the lack of investment in new uranium projects meant supply was limited. The law of supply and demand applies. Eventually, the price of uranium climbed to $140 per pound, almost ten times higher than that of 2003. The price of many uranium stocks skyrocketed. Mega uranium went from $0.04 in September 2003 to $7.41 in April 2007. A massive increase of 18,425 per cent takes place. It's not just uranium. This massive increase happens all the time in natural resources: oil, natural gas, and nickel. Platinum and silver, you name it.

This unique approach known as CHU Strategy was adopted successfully by Dr Steve Sjuggerud at Stansberry and Associates on many occasions. C stands for Cheap; that is, a stock is considered cheap at the point of time. H stands for Hated; that is, there is great fear for the stock to go burst and many investors are abandoning the particular stock out of fear. U stands of uptrend; that is, the particular stock has just begun its uptrend. A sound knowledge of the particular stock is important. I have applied this strategy successfully to a particular stock. When the two companies merged, the agreed price was about sixty cents. Confidence on the particular stock was lacking at that point of time because its profit was declining quarterly. But the new company after merging had a great potential. Its quarterly results began to improve. We spotted the stock by looking at the numbers and took advantage of the imaginary fear propagated by the media. The share price of the new company began to decline, and within a few months its price had dropped to as low as nine cents. So this stock fulfilled our strategy C because it was very cheap. Many investors were desperately tried to get out for this particular stock because of their past experience with another same type of company listed in the market that went burst. This fulfilled the strategy H because the stock was 'hated' by most people. The share price was flat for sometimes because of imaginary fear. We did plenty of research into the company's background, cash flow, current performance, and other numbers. To our surprise, the company at that point of time was financially sound and business was beginning to pick up. The first half year financial report indicated that the company was doing well and followed by another half year of good performance. The uptrend U began. The share price went to nineteen cents and over twenty cents. This fulfilled our U strategy, and we went in a very big way. We kept on purchasing and accumulated a big slice of the stock. Months and years past, this stock never looked back. It went on to reach $7 within a few precious years. It is now over $9 per share. We were lucky to hold this stock, and it gave us peace of mind in our retirement. We also sold most of the shares too early, resulting in loss of potential. History repeats itself, and we made the same mistake for not letting the price run. The company began to grow, first organically and later into acquisition of other related companies. Now it is one of the first 100 top companies in Australia. Our consolation is that we still hold a reasonable number of shares to give us peace of mind for our retirement.

I have used this strategy to a few other natural resource stocks, and we are equally successful, although the quantum profit is not that dramatic. A key word of caution for people trying to use this CHU strategy is patience and timing. A stock may fulfil the basic C, H, and U, but the timing is critical. Another important factor to look at is the numbers in the quarterly account. Is the company financially sound? Is the debt bigger than its cash? Is the business relevant and viable? The U can also be misleading because there are always unscrupulous people pushed it up to sell. You may end up holding the unwanted baby. So you need to look well into the matter before you invest. Get to know the potential of the business and the economic situations. For natural resources stocks, we need to follow the cycles. We buy the stocks when nobody wants them. Going against the crowd may make us feel sick in our gut. But this is usually a sign that we are doing the right thing. When the crowd wakes up to the bottom times that follow the bust, they will bid up the shares to incredible heights. Take 2008 credit crisis, resource stocks were coming off one of the world bear markets in their history. Resource stocks fell more than 80 per cent during this tough period. This was the time no one wanted to do with natural resources. In 2009, those who bought elite silver company Silver Wheaton harvested 345 per cent within one and half years. Those who bought junior miner ATAC Resource benefited 597 per cent profit. Many other resource stocks exhibited a similar rise in profit. Remember numbers seldom lie! All these awakening awareness will help in your decision-making.

GUILLOTINE AND SANDPAPER PHASES

The economic cycles keep repeating every ten or twelve years. A big correction can usually takes place in a matter of months. This phase, like the price of oil collapses in 2014 and beginning of 2015, is known as the 'guillotine'. The price falls off the cliff. It happens the market suffers a sharp sell-off in a short time. Recovery normally takes time. The period when the price of a particular asset begins to move sideways for a considerable period is known as 'sandpaper phase'. This phase can last for months or as long as two years. For most investors, this is the most frustrating sandpaper phase. Experience teaches us to be patience. Big profit will follow for those who are experienced and can wait patiently for the upturn before jumping in. A good example is the giant aluminium company Alcoa, which suffered a guillotine drop of almost 50 per cent in 2011. Instead of rebounding, the company went through the sandpaper phase for almost two years from 2012 to 2014. The upturn occurred after that, and the stock went on to gain almost 80 per cent in a year. Another example is the airline industries. From April to the end of 2012, the industries suffer a guillotine phase, and from 2012 to 2013, the industries went through the sandpaper phase. Then the recovery happens, and the assets go on a bull run until now 2015.

My experience tells me that a similar correlation is happening to oil price in 2014 and 2015. The guillotine phase is in progress. Gasoline price per barrel has dropped from over $100 to just $45 in a few months. I expect the price to move sideways for months in this sandpaper phase. Investors who have the experience and patience will make their fortune when the recovery sets in. I am waiting for the upturn and start investing in oil related value companies. I think you should do the same for your financial security.

Three Possible Factors Affecting Investors Making Bad Decisions

We are all aware that investing with our hard-earned money is a serious business. Most of us try our level best to use all the necessary prudence and knowledge to achieve our objective. We all want success, and we want a comfortable retirement. We are reminded that data is not information, information is not knowledge, and knowledge is not wisdom. The ability to interpret data can offer us valuable information. We need time, practice, experience, and learning to acquire the necessary skills. If we have the ability to use information correctly to benefit us, then the information become knowledge to us. If we have the ability to use knowledge to benefit and improve the life of our loved ones and others, then it help us to gain wisdom.

There are three psychological factors that can affect us into making bad decision in investment. These three factors include *availability bias, aversion loss,* and *probability neglect* may influence us into poor decision making.

Availability Bias

All of us have the tendency to make our investment decision based on our past success in a certain event or stock. We seem to assume that if a certain event has happened before, then the incident will happen again. This tendency will be available or can happen in the future. This past experience is deep in our subconscious mind. Its influence is always significant, and we long to repeat the same success in spite of the new probability and logic against it. It is important that this awareness can help us in our decision making.

On the other hand, our experience of loss in certain event or stock can also influence us significantly in our decision-making. This emotional failure can cloud our logical thinking and hide all new reality of the event resulting in poor decision-making and missing an opportunity. This factor of making bad decision is known as *availability bias*. Be aware of this setback before you, too, are affected by this factor. With this new information and knowledge, it is always advisable to put all data and facts on the table before you make an investment decision. Having somebody with the necessary knowledge to discuss or consult before investing in a particular stock may help us to avoid this psychological factor.

Loss Aversion

All of us in the game of investment have suffered a certain amount of loss. This experience of loss can have a greater impact than that of gain. This is unconsciously affecting us in general not minding in any gain as long as we do not suffer any loss. This emotional feeling usually makes it difficult for us to bounce back from any loss. This emotional setback in the form of negative feeling, disappointment, frustration, pain, or even humiliation has a significant effect in our attempt of taking risk, which may result in a big gain. This *loss aversion* operates mostly on a subconscious level even without us knowing it. The ability to examine this factor if you have suffered a heavy loss will help in your future investment. Do not allow this factor to become a liability in your future investment.

Mindfulness is one of the best ways to address accepting our thoughts uncritically. Practising mindfulness can help us let go of insistent thoughts and even strong emotion. It can help to free our mind to choose more valued trading actions. We become more focus instead of thinking of past losses. We pay attention on what matters for the investment and take action accordingly. Learn the mistakes and follow your strategy with discipline. I usually avoid businesses that require huge amounts of capital investment before they can earn a penny of revenue. I will prefer businesses that require little capital to maintain and grow. Ultimately, profit is the only driving force in any business.

Probability Neglect

Our tendency to become emotional during high pressure situation or any scenario where there is weighty consequence to every course of action is always there. This applies to any investment decision. We tend to be emotionally rattled instead of logically analysing the data available, using the information in front of us, and applying the knowledge gathered. Emotion and greed takes over all the level-headed thinking. Consequently, we make a poor choice without considering all the probability factors. The probability neglect factor prevents us from looking at all the available pieces of information. Instead, we only see the pieces of evidences that reinforce the worst case of the scenario. This investment attitude always tends to repeat because of our past experience of success or loss. Especially when we had suffered significant loss, we have the great tendency not to repeat or do it again. This past experience also makes it difficult for us to make logical decision. These are normal human behaviours. Knowing this factor can be of great help in appropriately dealing with our losses or gains as they come in investments. The philosophy of looking well into the matter can come in handy including probability factor.

LIFE EXPECTANCY OF A BULL MARKET

Many investors believe that a bull market in stocks like what we are experiencing now (2009-2015) in many countries such as the United States, Malaysia, and others has a life expectancy similar to that of human. It is true that like a human life, the lives of some bull markets in stocks are longer than others. But unlike a human life, there is no maximum number of years built into the DNA of the market. All of us agree that a bull market in stocks has a 'life cycle' showing a pattern from bottom to top, from beginning to end. And there are markers we can see along the way to judge where we are in it. It needs to be pointed out that there is no maximum number of days or years in a bull market in stock. This extra information serves as 'one up' for us as we invest along. Victor Sperandeo wrote a great book called *Trader Vic - Methods of a Wall Street Master* in the 1990s. The book has plenty of good ideas, but one idea he put forward was flaw. He believed that the life expectancy of a bull market was similar to that of a human being. But from our observations, we notice that there is no such thing as a maximum number of years for a bull market in stocks. In the 1990s, the bull market for stocks kept going up and up, defying all odds, defying all life expectancies, and defying all historic measures of value. Investors who believed strongly in Trader Vic's market expectancy would have missed one of the greatest booms in stocks in market history. Now we know that there is definitely a life cycle to bull markets, but we cannot put a number of days or years on each of them. A bull market ends when it ends. It truly is over once all the markets have been hit. Referring to the current bull market we are experiencing, to me, it does not increase the odds of a correction tomorrow. Just like gamblers on a mini baccarat table seeing a row of bankers for eighteen times in a row. What is the probability of the occurrence of a player in the next game? The chance is still 50/50. So in comparison with the bull market in stocks, the chance of its continuation is still there. To me, what clearly matters is where we are based on the usual markers in the life cycle of this bull market as I write now. After almost 1,000 days of running, I know we are closer to the end than the beginning. But I know there is still upside potential from hereafter looking at the economic situations. This extra information provides you with an advantage or 'one up' when someone tells you that a 10 per cent or 20 per cent correction is coming next week or next month. You can nod your head in agreement knowing that there is no life cycle expectancy in years or months for a bull market in stocks.

One thing is crystal clear that when a bull market goes on for many years like what we are experiencing now, May 2015, we know that the market is due for a correction. We have seen the market increasing at incredible rates with very few downward trends over an extended period of time. While investors are happy to see the bull market last so long, it's important to remember that it won't last forever. Looking at the numbers in their account reports of many stocks, you will see that many of them are overvalued. This fact alone tells that a market correction is imminent. What is a market correction? To understand what is a market correction is it's important that you realise that the market is incredibly volatile. Several factors are contributing to how well or how badly the market is doing at any time. You notice that economic data, calm geopolitical conditions, and incredible corporate profits have caused the prices of stock to skyrocket over the last few years. The quantitative easing has also played an important role. These sentiments influence investors to cause the prices to inflate incredibly quickly, in which case, stock prices become higher than their actual value. We can see this in many markets in the world especially America. To level things out, every once in a while we see a market correction. This happens at a point of time when stocks go on a steady downward trend and lose at least 10 per cent of their value. Each stock tends to lose according to its inflated value until an equilibrium value is reached. Stocks with very good fundamentals tend to lose less in sympathy with the correction. If you need to protect yourself from great losses, it's time to take note of the red flags, telling you that a correction is on the way. The first red flag to take note is the long duration of the bull market. As they say, what goes up must come down! This reigns true with the stock market. When stock values have risen exponentially, seemingly breaking records every now and then. This momentum is great for investors. These high valuations can't last forever. This is another red flag. Historically, we notice that stocks have been sold for more than what the underlying asset is worth. This is simply how the market works. However, stock values will plateau, and their growths do not match the fast pace of their prices. Then market correction is imminent. To protect your investments so as not to lose money, you can find alternative investment in gold and silver. Their prices are normally inversely proportional to stock prices. So they may provide a decent return for your investment. Another approach is that when you sense the exuberant of the market, it's time to cash out and take holidays.

Time for Holidays from Stocks

Trading and investing can become an addiction. The bull market or the bear market never last more than ten years with some exceptions. The cycles will repeat. A simple strategy to make plenty of money is to be able to anticipate when to get out of the market and sit on your cash waiting patiently for the next opportunity. In 1989, Jim Rogers told author John Train, 'When the market is getting too hot to handle, it's time to take all your money and put it in treasury bills or a money-market fund. Just sit back, take holidays, and have fun.' He added, 'Then something will come along where you know it is right. Take all your money out of the money market fund, put it in whatever it happens to be, and stay with it for three or four or ten years, whatever it is. You'll know when to sell again because you will know more than anybody else. Take your money out, put it back in the money-market fund, and wait for the next thing to come along. When it does, you'll make a lot of money.' According to Warren Buffett,

> 'Your default position should always be short term instruments. And when you see anything intelligent to do, you should do it. The best way to minimize risks, is to think.'

These great investors know human weakness very well. Most of us in the middle class cannot follow such simple strategy of sitting in cash and investing only when circumstances are ideal. When the market correction occurs in every cycle, most of the stock price will drop 10 per cent, 20 per cent, or even 50 per cent depending on the situations. Many good and value counters follow suit because of the sentiments and plenty of imaginary fear. This type of situation provides opportunity for these billionaires to pour down their cash to scoop up these value stocks. They will hold them for years, and history tells us that they laugh all the way to their banks. For the ordinary investors and traders like us, nobody wants to do it. Nobody wants to be patient. Everybody wants to buy and sell quickly and hoping of making a fortune overnight. The results are usually not that favourable. It becomes obvious that the average investor's impatience is another easy way for these great minds or billionaires to accumulate their wealth over time. History reveals that the ordinary investors' impatience and ignorance indirectly helping these billionaires to become richer. History will always repeat and the exploitation continues. Hopefully, after you have read this book, you can move away from the crowd and follow the footsteps of the rich.

Four Dumb Mistakes Most Investors Make

Wall Street is little bit similar to my school carnival. The purpose of a school carnival is to raise fund. So the more games and stores a carnival has will attract more participants. More participants will generate more funds for the school. *Wall Street* is in the business of selling stocks, bonds, and others. This is big business generating billions of dollars in fees. Where the money come from? Who make the money? The money comes from customers like you and me who are investing. The banks come up with all types of securities, and we are encouraged to buy every piece of crap they come up with. We know a big percentage of the investors will not make money! Are you going to be one of them! So it's important that you know what stocks you are buying. Who are selling you the idea of buying them? In my school, we used to have carnival day once a year. We sell all types of foods and games to raise fund for the school. One of the easiest ways to raise money without much investment in a school carnival is a game called tubs of fun. A store can accommodate many tubs, and many participants can be involved in this simple carnival game simultaneously. A participant will win a prize if he or she can make a softball stay in the plastic tub. The price is normally quite attractive like a watch or something else to attract the crowd. It appears easy, but it's not. The ball is too bouncy and the plastic tub is too hard. Our past experiences tell us that it is quite impossible to prevent the softball from bouncing out of the tub. The player has the illusion that he is throwing a softball into a container. A student running the store will let you take a practice throw. First, he drops a softball in the tub and the ball stays because he is standing right next to the tub. Then the player is invited to try. When the player's ball lands on the softball in the tub, it stays. Physics tells us that when the player's softball lands on the other ball in the tub, most of the energy is absorbed and it does not rebound but stays in the tub. It gives the participant the confidence but an illusion that he can easily win a prize by paying a few dollars for a try. But when a participant plays for real money, he is throwing the softball into an empty tub. Most people are not aware, and they never figure out the trick.

A friend of mine who is a basketball player came to the carnival for fun. He had $50 in his pocket. He thought that he could easily win the prize. He bought a few coupons each costing $2. He kept trying to land the softball in the tub, but he did not succeed. He bought some more coupons until all the money were gone. He did not quit. He borrowed some more money from a friend and tried again. He still did not succeed until all the money was gone again. But hey, it's carnival game. Everybody knows that you are not supposed to win. Right? Well, not everyone who plays the game. A few of them won if they can figure out the trick!

A big percentage of investors of stocks are in this situation. First, they are ignorant of the game they are playing. They do not know that most carnival games are rigged. Many of the stocks in the market are the same as the games in a carnival. Not all investors make money. In fact, many of them lose their shirts. The bankers come up with all types of security, and they encourage us to buy. They are the sure winners, and their profits come from the fees we contribute. When you buy stocks, ask who is selling them or who has sold you the idea of purchasing them. Before you buy any stock, know the business you are in. Look into the numbers of the companies' accounts before you buy them. It's easy to get dazzled by promises of big profit. It's even easier to get sucked in when the promises are accompanied by slick brochures and fast talk with a lot of words we don't understand. My experience tells me that when I do not understand the business, I do not buy the stock. This practice saves me a lot of loss and even time wasted.

The second mistake investors like us usually make is that we tend to pursue easy financial gain. It takes me a long time to learn that easy financial gain is one of the worst things that can happen to us. The author of the book *Life Lessons from the Lottery* said that the lives of lottery winners are usually wreck within about five years of winning. They get tons of money they did not earn. They did not know how to manage the money. They were not prepared for that. More appears to be bad when you are not prepared. Although aspiring to easy financial gain might be normal, but it is also self-destructive. As investors, we can also make the same mistake by buying risky stocks or options on hot tips from friends. This way of pursuing fast and easy gain can easily ruin your savings. Be aware that you do not see the stock market as a lottery. Look well into the matter by buying pieces of world-class businesses that you can hold for decades.

Another big mistake for most investors like us is giving in to a bias towards action. Most investors cannot sit still. And that's too bad. I remember what the seventeenth-century mathematician and scientist Blaise Pascal said,

> 'All men's miseries derive from not being able to sit in a quiet room alone.'

We used to think that that we have to do something all the time. But in investment, this is not true. In fact, doing nothing can be beneficial in investment. Do not look for attention by taking big risk. Taking a big risk is more likely to make you feel a swaggering gambler, someone who is not afraid to risk it all on a roll of the dice. Fear is the dominant emotion in the market at all time. The fear of being left out can lead to greed. That type of fear drives us to constantly seek action in trading or investing.

The final mistake most investors made is not knowing how far they are going to go in investing, just like my basketball friend playing the carnival game. He should have walked away quietly after losing a few tries. In investment, we can also make crazy decisions especially when speculating on financial gain. We listen to others because we do not trust ourselves. When we invest in stocks, we do not decide how much we are prepared to lose in each stock. We only think of financial gain. The tubs of fun player did not decide beforehand how he would behave after losing a few games.

Another common mistake investors or traders made is trading in someone's shadow. They make decisions using someone else's analysis without developing their own assumptions. They feel powerless especially if their strategies go against them and they lose money. We all know it's important to learn from successful investors or traders, but there is a difference between learning from them and relying on them. I follow my own strategy. I do not become someone else's investment shadow. By focusing on fundamental analysis to make decision, I have control of my investment decisions. I feel empowered as I make decisions based on my own assumptions. By doing so, I soon develop the amazing ability to help me to be a reflective individual and become aware of my own strengths and weaknesses. All these awareness help me to work through any of my strengths and weaknesses quickly in order to trade or invest profitably over the long term. Many of the guidelines written in this book will help you in your planning and investing.

A question I would like to ask you. What will you do if the market falls or a big correction takes place? I can't answer the question for you. Different people will do different things. I can tell you what I will do. I have confident in most of my value stocks. I have done enough research to know what stocks I want to buy and which one to avoid. I always put aside some ready cash for this type of situation which happens very often. When market falls, I will buy what I like, same as I do when milk powder or Milo go on sale at the super market. I love it when my money can buy two tins instead of one only. I love equity returns, too, so I really like to buy stocks at bargaining prices. Uncertainty is constant in the market. We have no control of the stock prices, interest rates, and news. We need a system of consistency in behaviours and actions. We must be in control of ourselves.

Buy a good stock when it is cheap, hated during a major correction. Buy only when the price of the stock begins to turn upwards. I always believe the contrarian concept of going against the crowd. A good indication of such move is when directors of the company start to increase their holdings. It is a good CHU strategy discussed earlier. When a stock we pick is a mistake, cut loss and retreat. Learn a lesson and do not make the same mistake. Learn the game and know it well before you invest again.

Properties as Alternative Investment

Another strategy of investment comes from Mr Robert Kiyosaki. Read his books entitled *Rich Dad Poor Dad* and *Retire Young Retire Rich*. When I started teaching at the age of almost thirty and after buying my first house as a basic necessity for my family, I started saving to buy my first investment property. This basic instinct to invest in property came from my father. He explained that once you have the down payment for a property especially commercial property, the subsequent instalments will come from the rentals. Look for property that can be rented out easily. This principle was instilled in me by my parents when I was only a child. My father, while supporting a large family, was able to use the principle of leverage to buy his rubber small holding of about thirty acres. He just had enough down payment to start with and the subsequent instalments were provided by the produce of the small holding. He did that leverage skilfully, and within a few years, he owned the small holding that became our family property.

I was lucky to be at the right place at the right time. I never dream that I will be teaching in Petaling Jaya, a city next to Kuala Lumpur. My girlfriend was a nursing student at the University Hospital in Kuala Lumpur. Our courtship started when I was doing my honours year in mathematics. She had just started her nursing course. After graduation, I taught for two year at Technical Institute, Kuantan, Pahang, a town about 160 kilometres away from Petaling Jaya. For two years, I spent most of my weekends in Petaling Jaya with some of my ex-basket players from the university team. They rented a house as their bachelor mess. Besides seeing my girlfriend, I enjoyed playing basketball with them. We played under the team named 'Old Folks'. We were the champion team in the Petaling District.

After two years in Kuantan, I managed to get a transfer to a La Salle High School in Petaling Jaya. The school had just started six forms, and it needed an applied and pure mathematics teacher. My presence served the purpose. The brother director at the time was Brother Lawrence, the founder of the school. I was a diligent and hardworking teacher there. My contribution to the growth of the school was recognised. I moved up the ladder of positions from a teacher to deputy principal and then principal.

My first year of teaching at the new school, I rented a room in section 17, Happy Garden. During my second year, my girlfriend graduated and we rented a house. My youngest sister who had just finished her form five joined us to continue her sixth form in Petaling Jaya. We were not married. We were life partner all the same. We never had a marriage ceremony. Both of us do not believe in such formality. Our love for each other is enough. We bought a small Japanese car costing RM7000. I came out with six thousands, and she contributed one thousand. We did not have much saving initially. Our salaries were just enough for us to live. Teaching in a rich city like Petaling Jaya offered plenty of opportunities to earn extra income. I started to offer group tuition to form-six students taking HSC examination. I was able to have some saving after a year or two.

Timing was right, and house prices was about to soar. With a few thousands at hand, we managed to purchase our first residential property for merely 32,000 Malaysian dollars. After a few years, we managed to save enough money as down payment to upgrade our house. With a government loan, we bought a second house with a big compound as our new home. By then we already had two kids.

Within the few years of our working life, the price of property leaped two to three times. We sold our first house for almost one hundred and fifty thousand Malaysian dollars. After paying back our bank loan, we still had money to buy our first investment property a shop lot with the help of my government loan at 4 per cent interest. I was already a writer. Many of my textbooks were used in schools. Royalties started to flow in. My wife gave up nursing, and we started a publication company. A partner and my wife were also involved in importing parts of computer from Taiwan to be assembled in Malaysia. Businesses were good and growing. We were able to put aside more than 25 per cent of our combined income as saving because we lived beneath our means. We were never in debts except a loan from the government. Before I turn forty years old, we had already accumulated enough for us to invest in high-dividend growing stocks. For the first ten years of my working life, I avoided investment in stocks because I did not have the time to do my research. I was too busy with my extra activities such as writing and giving extra tuitions during the weekends. My decision not to involve in trading stock initially was correct. Property investment is the preference.

When another shop lot was put up for sale, I took the opportunity to buy it by borrowing a small down payment from my third brother-in-law. My little saving and help from a relative plus a bank loan secured my second investment property. I did my mathematics correctly. Each month rentals were more than enough to cover my instalments to the bank and the government. The investment was necessary because we needed a place to assemble computers for our business venture. When I retired, I had two shop lots all paid up. This gave me confidence to retire at the age of fifty one. I believe this strategy is available to all young men and women who are at working stage of their life. It takes courage and planning to start investing early in your working life. Remember, time and tide waits for no man. Working life is short. Take action as early as possible if you want to retire with financial security. I do my homework regarding leverage, and it works brilliantly for me. I believe every working man or woman can do it. Just focus on increasing your income by building a career and at the same time get a part-time business of your own and live beneath your means. When you are young, do not fall into the trap that a lot of people fall into buying a big and perfect house. I do not believe that we should go crazy into debt to buy such a house. Do not do it. I don't believe of getting into big debt. I will just focus, instead, on living within my means. I will buy a small house or a small apartment first. I will live there for five or more years before I can afford to update to a better house. By dedicating myself not to get into debt, I believe my financial life will be brilliantly successful. If I can't avoid the temptation to get into debt, there is a high probability that I may never make it. The idea of leverage is different because such debt can be classified as good debt because it generates return. The house we live in does not provide extra income. I have to pay land tax, assessment, and others. I think this is the best thing I can do to increase my odds at financial success. Instead of buying a new car that incurs a debt, I will prefer to buy a second-hand car for the start. I will avoid debt by all means. I share my experiences so that you can become aware of alternatives.

Some Characteristics of Rich People

Please understand that investment alone cannot make you rich. It can also make you poor. It is only one of the many strategies required to become rich. Studies have shown that most rich people do the following things. You are encouraged to form good financial habits as early as possible in your working life. Most rich people know how to balance their need to become wealthy and economically productive with their need to enjoy life. They know that they cannot enjoy life if they are addicted to consumption and the use of credit. They neither borrow nor earn just to consume. They are not credit dependent, and they lead very simple life. They have control over money. This awareness gives encouragement for me to live a life of simplicity and frugality. Such habit has laid the foundation for me to become rich.

Some of the common characteristics of rich people are summarised here. If you choose to ignore the following characteristics of rich people, the chance is that you may not be one of them:

1. They understand and manage their debt. They do not allow debt to manage them.
2. They spend their money wisely, getting maximum value for every dollar.
3. They continuously work to increase both their linear and residual or recurring incomes.
4. They are aggressive savers far outpacing their peers.
5. They are disciplined investors. When they find a good strategy, they stick to it.

I believe I have adhered to the above behaviours to become what I am today. If you aspire to retire comfortably rich, the above qualities can become valuable tools for you to adopt. Remember that Rome is not built in a day. It takes years of perspiration and discipline to become rich. Take care of the penny and the pound will take care of itself.

Chapter Three

HEALTHY LIFESTYLE

I am lucky that I learnt very early some critical changes in my lifestyle to become lean and fit. One day, I hear a self-appointed expert telling me one thing. And the next day, a different talking head claims something that sounds like the exact opposite. Often the advice is contradictory and confusing. Most of the advice lacks scientific evidence. So If I need to start on the path to a healthier life, I need to do my own research. I have friends who are so proud of their cars and houses. I saw some of friends with huge mortgages, spending more than they earn. I did the opposite. I lived way beneath my means. My life is about experiences, not about stuff. I have everything I need. I live lean and healthy. It is true that money can buy a lot of things in life, but it can't buy you fitness. You have to earn it yourself. And ultimately, if you are unhealthy, who cares how much wealth you have? My father had a very good advice for me. He once told me that money is not everything. Good health is most important for all of us. So my first mission is to make my health a top priority. Work and family always seem more important than working on my health, but I have to convince myself that I'm better off for my work and my family if I'm healthy.

I knew very early that the foods I eat each day have the power to renew my body, revitalise my health, and even reverse or delay my ageing process. The cells in our body renew completely in less than a year, and our body is literally brand new every two years or less. So the diet we have with the necessary nutrients will help us build a brand new, healthier, stronger, and even younger body. In addition, eating a balanced diet helps to strengthen our immune system and builds up a strong protective system against diseases including cancer. I am seventy-five years old, but I can still do most of the activities of a fifty-year man. I am disease-free and never get sick. I still have a laser-sharp memory. I also look much younger than my age. I still have inexhaustible supply of energy. I play tennis for two hours without feeling tired and do most of the things I did when I was in my thirties. I have never been hospitalised. I owe all these to the wise philosophy of Hippocrates, the father of medicine, who said,

'Let Food be Thy medicine ... And Let Thy medicine be Food.'

To build a strong body, my approach is to take up a sport seriously and to play like a pro. Enjoy the game, besides getting good exercises for physical development. Sports also cultivate discipline, cooperation, coordination and make ever-lasting friendship. As far as I am concerned, most of my close friends are my sportsmates. Playing together and regular association usually develop lasting bonds of friendship. My active involvement in sports helps to keep me fit and in shape. Besides keeping me healthy, regular exercises and regular competitive sports also help to make life more exciting. My observations of sportsmen reveal many essential qualities such as discipline, determination, team spirit of cooperation, and endurance. These qualities are necessary for success in our working life.

Exercise has been shown to have numerous benefits, even at the level of brain cells. For example, regular, vigorous exercise has been shown to cause special cells in the brain to increase their production of repair chemicals called neurotrophins. This tells us that regular exercise is good even for elderly people. Medical research shows that people with Alzheimer's disease have much lower levels of neurotrophins. It's well known that exercise improves blood flow to the brain and increases protective antioxidant enzymes. People with minimal cognitive impairment, an early stage of dementia, can reverse memory problems with regular exercise combined with a proper diet full of protein, green vegetables, and fruits. Research reveals that exercise causes our body to produce tremendous concentrations and types of free radicals. And the production lasts for hours after exercise is over. It is beneficial because the burst of free radicals stimulates our cells to produce high levels of antioxidant enzymes. Be careful, too much exercise can also be bad. It can also deplete our body's antioxidants, minerals, and other chemicals such as glutathione and others. A little knowledge will help. In this situation, the body needs supplements depending on the intensity and duration of exercise. A doctor or a nutrition expert is essential. For most of us, it's good if we include exercise for all the muscles, including resistance exercises, as these build and prevent muscle loss and prevent loss of bone calcium.

Another aspect of exercise improves blood flow and lymph flow to tissue and organs. A lot of deep breathing takes place during intensive exercises. This specifically increases the flow of lymph, a second circulatory system in the body, in lymphatic vessels, including the heart and lungs. Research indicates that this exercise help to clean the tissues of toxic building. After each exercise, especially intensive exercise, remember to rehydrate. We need about two litres of water or more if we exercise intensively and regularly. I use to add about 500-mg capsule of magnesium to about three litres of water if I exercise intensively. I also drink intermittently to replenish any loss of water in my system.

Irrespective of age, a healthy body requires regular exercise. Taking up a sport like tennis, golf, soccer, or basketball provides a platform for such regular exercise. Healthy body requires eating the correct types of foods. A good knowledge of nutritious foods including protein, carbohydrates, vitamins from vegetables and fruits is essential for good health. Besides providing all the energy and nutrients for growth, many of our natural foods such as broccoli or broccoli sprouts, Brussels sprout, cauliflower, cabbage, and various fruits provide the best medicine. Science has proven time and again that Mother Nature is the best physician. Eating vegetables mentioned above regularly is the best preventive medicine. If possible include blueberries, raspberries, strawberries, or blackberries in your diet. They are packed with antioxidants like vitamin C, beta-carotene, fibre, manganese, flavonoids, and antiocyanins, which give the blueberries its colour. More benefits will follow if these berries are taken with yogurt, helping our body to absorb more of these nutrients.

When I was a student, I did not have such information. My face was full of pimples. In one of my basketball matches, I met our team manager who was a physician. He advised me to take plenty of fruits and vegetables every day. I followed his advice. I spent most of my pocket money buying fruits like banana, pineapple, papaya, various types of berries, and apple from the hawker's store every day. Within a month all my pimples disappeared. I felt very relieved and happy because I looked better without all the pimples. From the time onwards, I started to concentrate on taking foods high in protein and less in fat with special focus on vegetables and fruits. I avoided refined sugar most of the time. It is a white killer. I obtained enough sugar from my fruits. This eating habit served me well in my pursuit to excel in my basketball game and tennis. The eating habits with regular exercises are complementary to my good health. I am now seventy-five, and I could not remember the last time I fell sick. I am always in good shape and active in my new chosen game, tennis now. I am also involved in some form of resistive exercises almost every day to keep every part of my muscles tuned up.

This information regarding the healing power of health-promoting vegetables and fruits is important especially to those in their retiring stage of life. Research is ongoing. Indication is clear that nature's most valuable health-promoting foods such as broccoli, broccoli sprouts, and fruits can help to prevent a number of health issues, including, but not limited to, hypertension, allergies, diabetes, osteoarthritis, and even cancer. Researchers at the University of East Anglia found that eating lots of broccoli may slow down and even prevent osteoarthritis. Further human trials are being carried out. Tests on cells and mice reveal that broccoli contain a compound called sulforaphane that can help to block a key destructive enzyme that damages cartilage. Sulforaphane is a sulphur compound that has an anti-inflammatory and anticancer property. This compound is also found in Brussels sprout, cauliflower, and cabbage. So a healthy diet is a good and safe alternative medicine instead of drugs. Natural foods mentioned above with plenty of fruits can help to keep us healthy like preventing joint pains. Consuming a reasonable amount of these health-promoting foods can help to kill cancer stem cells and slow down tumour growth. These natural foods bring benefits including antidiabetic and antimicrobial activity. Research further reveals that cancer treatment using chemotherapies could not do what these health-promoting foods can. The broccoli compound glucoraphanin, a precursor to sulforaphane, can boost cell enzymes that give protection against molecular damage from cancer causing chemicals. Doctors and researchers believe that four serving of broccoli per week will protect man from prostate cancer. Knowledge is power. Eating healthily is the key towards good health and also serving to prevent unnecessary pains for retiring people.

As we age, our heart and blood vessels are not as flexible as they once were, which may mean it is harder to maintain healthy blood pressure. In 1998, three Nobel Prize-winning scientists, Robert F. Furchgott, Louis J. Ignarro, and Ferid Murad, discovered that nitric oxide, a natural substance in our body, actually signals our endothelial cells to 'relax' and open up our blood vessels. The endothelium is the smooth, supply lining inside every blood vessel in our body. When we are young, the endothelial cells look smooth as silk and just as supple. When we age, our endothelial cells begin to age, too. Over time, our arteries will begin to become less flexible, resulting in harder to maintain healthy blood pressure. So as we age, we need a consistent supply of nutrients to help us protect our body's precious supply of nitric oxide. Thanks to research into extract of green coffee. It has abundant supply of chlorogenic acid content that plays a role of supporting normal nitric oxide level in our body. Researchers in Japan found that the extract from green coffee had significant result in keeping systolic blood pressure healthy (the top number) and diastolic blood pressure normal (the bottom number). It's good news for elderly people to have this information to help them keep their blood pressure under control. Perhaps you need to consult your doctors to have a constant supply of supplement of extract of green coffee to keep your blood pressure normal. Another discovery reveals that an amino acid called L-arginine causes our body to produce nitric oxide. Supplements containing L-arginine can help to improve blood circulation, and they help maintain normal blood pressure. This chemical is converted into nitric oxide that helps to dilate our blood vessels for easy blood circulation. Consequently, the heart does not have to pump too hard, and this helps to maintain normal pressure. As a result, L-arginine becomes a popular ingredient in dietary supplements for helping men to achieve peak performance in the bedroom.

Our environment is important. Life is a choice. I choose to live in an environment full of fresh and clean air. I avoid living in a crowded city. The air we breathe every second plays a significant part in our overall health.

We know that polluted air is filled with various particles so small that they can get into our lung tissue and blood stream. They cause cancer and reduce the effectiveness of our immune system. Having excessive dust, dirt, or smoke in our environment can lead to chronic inflammation, leading to more colds and heart problems. Breathing fresh, clean air is an essential part of having a healthy life. Playing game under the sun especially in the morning can lower the risk of several types of cancer. The vitamin D produced by our body from sunlight may be critical in preventing diseases such as multiple sclerosis and depression. My choice is to get at least twenty minutes or more of sunlight each day instead of taking vitamin D pills. Another choice in life is to have adequate sleep. I need about seven to eight hours of sleep every day. I always discipline myself to sleep early so that I can function efficiently and perform well in the games I love. This disciplined habit becomes my hallmark all throughout my life. I never fall sick for seventy-five years because of this magnificent habit and lifestyle.

Heart Disease and Cancer

The greatest killers of human are heart disease and cancer. Everyone should know that these two causes of suffering and death are preventable. Good and healthy lifestyle including regular exercises and good diet with plenty of health-promoting natural foods mentioned above will go a long way to ensure that you avoid the first killer, heart disease. New researches have revealed that people who consume too much or too little salt are in danger of boosting their blood pressure and cardiovascular risks. So there is a sweet spot for where the optimum sodium intake is. So the message is simple. Moderation of salt intake is a good practice for all of us. In order to avoid the high and low levels of salt intake, people are advised to read food labels to get a good sense of how much salt they consume each day. As a healthy guide, we are encouraged to consume moderately from 1,500 to 2,300 milligrams a day. As a rough guide, the amount of salt is about a spoon full or less. People over fifty-one and those suffering from diabetics should restrict to the lower amount. Some researches indicate that regular intake of potassium, a mineral found in fruits, vegetables, and other leafy greens, can help the body function properly even with an intake of high levels of salt. They found that people with high levels of sodium usually had low level of potassium, suggesting that they did not consume enough fruits and greeny vegetables. This appears to suggest that boosting potassium intake may offer health benefits than focusing on further salt reduction. We need to be careful that these studies are not very conclusive because the urine testing for sodium is not carried twenty-four hours a day. So prevention is better than cure. Keep to the recommended range of salt consumption is still a wise philosophy to avoid high blood pressure and cardiovascular risks.

Misconception of Heart Disease and Cholesterol

When I was growing up, I was advised not to consume more than two eggs a day because eggs have high cholesterol. I was also advised that cholesterol intake should be kept to a bare minimum as doing so would help to decrease cholesterol levels and promote overall heath. At that time it appeared that the theory of lowering dietary cholesterol intake to lower internal cholesterol made sense. But the theory doesn't quite pan out as our bodies are, generally, more complex creatures than our logical minds give them credit for.

The true fact is when dietary intake of cholesterol is decreased, our liver compensates by producing more cholesterol, leaving the total cholesterol levels unchanged. On the other hand, if cholesterol consumption is increased by having more eggs, our liver produces less cholesterol, resulting in the total cholesterol levels relatively unaltered. So our dietary intakes will have little effect on the values of the cholesterol in our blood. The body produces more cholesterol does not imply that cholesterol is bad! The truth is cholesterol actually acts as an antioxidant against dangerous free radicals within the blood. In fact, cholesterol is necessary for the production of certain hormones that help to combat against heart disease. Whenever there are high levels of undesirable free radicals caused by our dietary intakes of damaged fats, processed foods, and large quantity of sugar, our cholesterol levels rise in order to fight these substances. A high indication of cholesterol level in our blood shows that we have dangerous free radicals in our blood causing heart disease.

These undesirable substances in our blood are usually due to our unhealthy dietary intakes high in damaged fats, junk foods, toxic materials, and sugar. So if the body allows cholesterol to fall in the presence of large amount of free radicals, the risk of heart disease will increase rather than decrease. Our bodies do not allow this to happen. On normal condition, our cholesterol levels remain relatively stable. So we need to remember that the answer to decrease or increase cholesterol levels is not in avoiding eating eggs but rather improving our dietary intakes full of protein, vegetables, fruits, and less-processed foods with sugar. In addition, combine that with physical activity, both our body and cholesterol levels will be in better shape. Processed foods, sugar, and excessive carbohydrates will create havoc on our fat-storing hormones, causing not only heart disease but also memory problems, slow brain activity, and increase risk of Alzheimer's.

Cancer as a Killer

The first killer disease of human being is heart disease. The second killer is cancer. This includes the following: pancreatic cancer, liver cancer, brain cancer, oesophageal cancer, and skin cancer. Besides causing diabetics and cardiovascular risks, obesity can increase your chance of suffering from the following types of cancer: kidney, gall bladder, colon, breast, ovarian, liver, and uterine cancer. All of us should put health as our top priority. Start a small immediate goal by getting lean and fit. Adequate knowledge of prevention for each of these fast-moving cancers is essential if you want to enjoy a long and healthy life.

1. Pancreatic cancer can be genetic. We need to know that chronic alcohol consumption and heavy processed red meat can increase the risk of this type of cancer. An effective strategy to prevent pancreatic cancer can easily be done by having five serves of vegetables including broccoli, cabbage, and cauliflower per week. Make it a habit of eating vegetables and fruits every day.
2. Liver cancer has its root in obesity. Maintain good shape or a healthy weight by eating balanced diet including plenty of vegetables and fruits. Take regular exercises by involving in a sport

or regular walking to keep your belly fat to a minimum. This calls for discipline. Try to limit alcohol consumption and sugary foods. It is well known that chronic hepatitis increases the risk.
3. Brain cancer produces the following signs: unusual headaches, nausea, vomiting, vision, or balance problems. Other signs of this cancer include tingling in the arms and legs. The signs of personality changes, seizures, or extreme fatigue provide evidences of brain cancer.
4. Oesophageal cancer is the consequence of refluse, smoking, and excessive alcohol consumption. Checking these habits is the first priority. Avoid foods with high acid content including chocolate, caffeine, mints, and raw tomato. Watch out for signs like chest pains, difficulty in swallowing, hiccups, sudden unexplained weight loss, and chronic pneumonia.
5. Skin cancer can be due to excessive exposure to the sun. As part of the prevention procedure, check for irregular moles, growth, and patches. People with light skin or have blonde or red hair are more prone to skin cancer.

As I grow older, I become interested in problems faced by old people. A little bit of information for people who survive from heart attack. The seventeen-year study showed heart attack survivors had more than double the chance of developing cancer than patients with no history of heart attack. The most common cancers diagnosed were lung and bladder cancers. No direct cause is established. Young heart attack survivors in the age group from thirty to fifty-four years old had the highest occurrence of cancer. Perhaps smoking may be a common factor, but most researchers believe that inflammation is the culprit. Remember heart disease is preventable. We need to take care of our diet with adequate greens, less sugar, and plenty of exercise.

A Simple Peanut Butter Odour Test for Alzheimer's Disease

A common Alzheimer's disease affects my friend's mother. I am interested in practical method of detecting this disease early so that I can help some of my older friends. One simple test is a peanut butter odour test. It interests me because it is simple to carry out. A graduate student Jennifer Stamps, working with her distinguished professors at the UF College of Medicine's department of neurology, came out with this simple test for smell sensitivity. The ability to smell is associated with the first cranial nerve and often that is one of the first things to be affected in cognitive decline. In this simple peanut butter odour test, patients are tested using about a spoonful of peanut butter in a small container. The distance of the container from the nostril is measured by a metre ruler. The patients are asked to close their eyes and mouths. One of the nostrils is blocked. The clinician opens the peanut butter container next to the open nostril while the patient breathes normally. The clinician then moves the peanut butter container one centimetre up the metre ruler at a time during the patient's exhale until the person can detect the odour. The distance is recorded. After about ninety seconds, this procedure is repeated on the other nostril. The scientists found that patients in their early stages of Alzheimer's disease had a dramatic difference in detecting odour between the left and right nostril. The early stage of Alzheimer's patient's left nostril is impaired and does not detect the smell until it is about 10 cm closer to the nose than the right nostril. Patients with other kind of dementia did not exhibit this difference.

This discovery gives us a very practical test to predict or detect Alzheimer's disease among friends without resorting to expensive equipment or full suite of clinical tests for neurological function. Further experimental studies will provide validity and reliability to this test. Since testing for Alzheimer's disease and other dementia is usually tedious, time consuming, and expensive, this simple peanut butter odour test can be an exploratory test for the purpose.

Simple Steps to Improve Your Digestive System and Boost Your Metabolism and Energy Levels

I was lucky that my grandmother taught me this secret when I was a young boy. Every morning she encouraged me to drink a glass of warm lemon juice water. The habit was formed when I was very young, and even today I still drink a glass of warm lemon juice water before I take my breakfast. A fresh organic lemon is cut into four pieces, and the juice is squeezed into a glass of warm water ready for drinking. My grandmother could not explain the benefits of drinking warm lemon juice water because of her lack in scientific knowledge. However I trusted her instinct, and I benefited because the habit improved my digestion and boosted my metabolism and my energy levels. I have formed a good habit, and I continue this good habit until today. I have been always curious to find out the scientific aspects of lemons. Now I know that lemons contain powerful antibacterial, antiviral, and immune-boosting components. Lemons are a great digestive aid and liver cleanser. Lemons contain citric acid, magnesium, bioflavonoids, vitamin C, pectin, calcium, and limonene. These minerals supercharge our immunity so that the body can fight infection. Surprisingly, lemons are considered as one of the most alkalising foods. This may seem untrue as they are acidic on their own. However, in the body, lemons are alkaline; the citric acid does not create acidity once it has been metabolised. The minerals in lemons are actually helping to alkaline the blood. Most of us consume sugar and grains and this habit increases the acidity in our body. Drinking a glass of warm lemon juice water helps to neutralise this acidity, helping to draw uric acid from our joints. This help to reduce pain and inflammation. Besides the habit of drinking a glass of warm lemon juice water every morning encourages bowel movements. This habit is especially helpful for people suffering from constipation.

This simple information will give you three important benefits besides hydrating your body:

1. This habit will improve your digestion and stimulate bile production. It is a good aid for heartburn and indigestion.
2. This habit will boost your energy for the day. Even lemon juice helps to improve your mood and energy levels and reduces anxiety. Plus the detoxifying effect and alkalising effect, this habit can improve your energy levels through the removal of toxins from your body.
3. This habit will help you lose fat. Since the habit of drinking warm lemon juice helps to improve your digestive system, aids

in removal of toxins, and increases your energy levels, this all combines together to help you lose body fats through higher level of metabolism and improving your hormonal balance.

STEPS TAKEN TO PREVENT DIABETES

Diabetes is at epidemic proportions in every country. Diabetes brings a host of complications including heart attack, stroke, kidney failure, nerve damage, poor circulation, hearing loss, erection dysfunction, periodontal disease, and diabetic retinopathy. Recent studies show that it increases the risk of Alzheimer's disease and other dementia. Diabetes is classified as either Type 1 or Type 2. With Type 1, the body fails to produce the insulin necessary to convert sugar and starches to energy, while Type 2 diabetes don't properly use the insulin they produce. A healthy diet is a proven key in the fight against this disease. We need to avoid processed foods high in sugar content and carbohydrates like white bread and others drinks rich in sugar. Include tasty foods rich in protein such as chicken, steak, and other lean meat. Take plenty of vegetables and fruits. Studies have shown that some foods are particularly effective at lowering blood sugar. Knowledge of these foods and intake of them regularly can help in the prevention of this disease. A spice called cinnamon has special effect in balancing sugar level in the blood and cholesterol. Cinnamon helps significantly in the production of insulin. The Diabetes Solution Kit recommends a double C solution: cinnamon and chromium picolinate as super nutrients to help the body cells to control blood sugar level by increasing metabolism. New research is emerging, finding that glucose is manufactured in the liver and kidney even during night-time, and this glucose is added into your blood stream. Chemicals like amino acid, fatty acids, and others are found to be able to control and slow down the process of manufacturing glucose in the kidney and liver. These chemicals are found in certain vegetables, spices, and fruits. Including the following foods in your regular diet will help you fight diabetes or even cure your diabetes:

1. Cinnamon: Taking three or six grams of cinnamon daily lowers sugar level by up to 29 per cent.

2. Vinegar: Drinking two tablespoon apple cider vinegar before meals cut sugar level in pre-diabetics by 50 per cent. Vinegar appears to have effects similar to some of the most popular medications for diabetics.
3. Pomegranates: Drinking six ounces of its juice daily for three months lowers the risk for atherosclerosis, which causes 80 per cent of deaths in diabetics. Other benefits of eating pomegranates regularly include running gamut from arthritis and protection against prostate cancer.
4. Almond: A diet rich in almond improves insulin sensitivity as well as lowering level LDL (bad) cholesterol. Regular intake of 1.4-2 ounces of almond lowers risk of both diabetics and cardiovascular disease.
5. Garlic: It helps to regulate and lower blood sugar. Study shows that the allicin in garlic combines with the B vitamin thiamine can stimulate the pancreas to produce insulin. Other sources of quercetin include onions, tomatoes, berries, and green vegetables.
6. Apples: Study showed that eating two servings of whole fruits a week, particularly apples, blueberries, and grapes, would reduce the risk of Type 2 diabetes by 23 per cent. Another study found that men who ate foods high in quercetin such as apples had reduced the risk of diabetics by 20 per cent.
7. Green Tea: Drink two or three cups of green tea a day can help to prevent or retard diabetics.
8. Chocolate: According to Italian researchers, the flavonoids in dark chocolate help to counteract insulin insensitivity, the condition that prevents Type 2 diabetics from using insulin effectively. Eating 100 grams of dark chocolate a day accelerate the body's metabolism of glucose.
9. Whole-fat dairy product: Study found that the fatty acid in dairy products called trans-palmitoleic acid would reduce the risk of developing Type 2 diabetics. A few servings of whole-fat dairy products daily would probably produce sufficient high levels of fatty acids.
10. Pumpkin: Study found that chemicals in pumpkin had helped successfully to regenerate damaged pancreatic cells in rats. The

compounds boost the pancreatic cells which are the producers of insulin. Regular eating of pumpkin may serve to prevent not only Type 1 but also Type 2 diabetics.

I believe that knowledge is power. Including some of these foods in your daily diet is the first step you should take. Prevention is better than cure. To be effective in preventing all these killer diseases, awareness plus a balanced diet is essential.

PREVENTIVE MEDICAL SERVICES

Recognising Symptoms of Stroke

Stroke is a brain disease in which a blood vessel is blocked and the supply of blood and oxygen to the brain is cut off or greatly reduced. It is similar to heart disease where the blood vessel to the heart is blocked or the supply of blood and oxygen to the heart is greatly reduced. To recognise the signs and symptoms of a stroke, just remember the word FAST.

F stands for Face: ask the person to smile and see whether one side of the face droops.

A stands for Arms: ask the person to raise his or her two arms straight and see whether one of them drifts to one side.

S stands for Speech: is it slurred or strange.

And T stands for Time: don't waste time calling emergency help if a patient shows any of the signs. Time is important not to cause further damage to the brain.

MEDICAL SCREENING

Many medical reports revealed that doctors are overtesting and overtreating patients mainly for commercial purposes. We should be aware of many unnecessary tests for us if we are healthy. But some tests are essential for prevention purposes or for early detection. Expert doctors and researchers recommend the following five screenings:

1. High blood pressure screening
2. Colorectal cancer screening
3. Lipid disorder screening
4. Skin cancer screening
5. Eye disease screening

The first three screenings are given top priority, and the last two screenings are necessary whenever suspicion arises. Other than these, you should consider whether any other tests recommended by the doctors are necessary or not. Knowledge and information are essential for your decision. If you are healthy and full of energy, avoid all the unnecessary medical tests such as X-ray and scanning.

Alzheimer's Disease

A little information concerning the cause of Alzheimer's as we get aged. A possible cause is the formation of toxic chemical called amyloid beta peptide, a nasty molecule that forms protein plagues in your brain. It causes inflammation in the brain tissues and hinders healthy neuron transmission. And this plays a role in nerve degeneration. This problem, if not rectify, eventually destroys your brain function resulting in what we know as Alzheimer's disease. Scientists and researchers have been working on finding natural nutrients to counter this inflammation and rejuvenate the brain neurons. In 1986, Dr Rita Levi-Montalcini and Biochemist Stanley Cohen won the Nobel Prize for their discovery of the nerve growth factor (NGF). This essential protein promotes the growth of the nerve cell processes throughout the body. It helps your nervous system and maintains the brain at top form. They found that NGF prevents neurons from dying, and it also encourages neurite growth. It also helps to organise your nerve cells. So it helps you to think clearly, remember easily, and also learn quickly. This sounds good, but there is a problem. This NGF molecule is too large to pass through the blood-brain barrier, and therefore, it cannot reach the brain. Scientists are working on finding a molecule that can boost NGF production and yet small enough to get through the blood-brain barrier. Researchers in Japan and elsewhere stumble on a species of mushroom taken by Chinese Emperors to keep their mind sharp and alert all the time. This mushroom is known as Lion's mane containing the nutrients for your brain neurons. The special molecules known as hericenones and erinacines found in Lion's mane are small enough to slip through the blood-brain barrier. These nutrients help to stimulate the production of NFG in your brain, thus keeping your brain neurons healthy. In addition to this function, the nutrients also help to fight off toxic brain plague and prevent memory decline. Besides stimulating the production of NGF, these nutrients help to protect the brain from the nasty molecule that forms protein plague. They improve connectivity in your brain, improve your memory, and enhance other mental abilities. Others like phosphatidylserine found in other source can also activate your brain cells and help to rejuvenate your memory. Many natural foods contain nutrients that can serve as rejuvenators for your brain.

Preventive measures for Alzheimer's disease especially for retirees should be noted. Recent research has found that dark chocolate and other host of foods such as green vegetables, broccoli, spinach, fruits like strawberries, and others have the beneficial compound in the form of antioxidant flavonoids that are good for the brain. According to Dr Small, director of the University of California - Los Angeles Longevity Center,

> 'As the brain ages, it undergoes wear and tear in what is called oxidative stress. And these antioxidants in our foods actually protect from that kind of aging wear and tear.'

It is known now that as we age, our levels of NGF decline and that can negatively affect our memory, concentration, and other mental abilities.

Experimental studies carried out in Japan reveal that the nutrients found in Lion's mane help significantly to reverse patients suffering from dementia and other mental disorders. Continuous intake of these nutrients is found necessary to rejuvenate and improve memory for the controlled group. It appears that we need to include nutrients rich in fatty acids, folic, and vitamin B12 including hericenones and erinacines found in Lion's mane. Perhaps nutrients from other sources may equally serve the purpose as revealed later.

Experimental study from Harvard University finds that cocoa consumption boosts thinking and memory performance, as well as something called 'neurovascular coupling' - when blood flow in the brain changes in response to brain activity - which plays a role in Alzheimer's disease and other mental health conditions.

By a study sponsored by the National Institute of Health, researchers have found eating baked or broiled fish at least once a week can keep you mentally sharp as you grow older. Other factors such as reducing physical inactivity, smoking, and obesity can lead to reducing the risk of Alzheimer's and other mental health disorders. For retirees, as a preventative measure, eat moderately some dark chocolate or drink one or two cups of hot cocoa drinks a day and eat enough green vegetables and fruits for the purpose. Regular exercise is essential. Playing a game helps the brain and muscle to co-ordinate. Chances are great that you reduce the probability of developing Alzheimer's early. Knowledge is power, and information is the key to prevention.

Most of us use these products frequently such as plastic water bottles and canned food containers whose linings are made of plastic. The gender bending chemical Bisphenol A (BPA) is part of the equation. Once this chemical gets into our body, it causes a variety of health problems, including heart disease, obesity, infertility, and even cancer. Research finding reveals that once this chemical enters the body, it acts as a synthetic oestrogen that has a devastating effect on human health. Researchers at the University of Kansas Medical Centre found that BPA can worsen symptoms associated with migraines. No remedy cure is readily available. Changing diet to fresh foods and vegetables appears to reduce migraines.

Another source of information may help elderly people who are overweight. As we grow older, we tend to lose muscle and gain fat. Why not try intermittent fasting to reduce weight and help to counter cognitive degeneration. Reports of studies of intermittent fasting in animals for years reveal that older mice and rats and those with Alzheimer-like conditions that practise alternate days of eating and fasting appear to be protected from cognitive impairment or even show sign of reversal of previous impairment. They also appear to maintain more lean mass as they grow older. Those in the control group do not show any sign of improvement. The thinking is that fasting for periods as short as sixteen to twenty-four hours seem to induce a state of stress in the body. The brain releases additional neurotropic proteins that help to stimulate and support the growth of neurons and other cells, heightening their responsiveness and activity. Just as exercise makes the muscles stronger, fasting intermittently makes the brain stronger. It should also be noted that the body chemicals produced by intermittent fasting and exercise also could boost people's mood especially older people. As we age, we are told that our cognitive functioning begins to decline. Our energy level begins to take a dive, and our memory appears to betray us. We become confused and lose our ability to concentrate. The possibility is that we may be suffering from vitamin B12 deficiency. If any of us suffering from the above symptoms, it is good that we take some supplements of vitamin B12 to help recovering our cognitive functioning. For our information, most elderly people are suffering from vitamin B12 deficiency.

Another report from *Journal of Neurology* reveals that the sign of dementia developed four years later for people who are bilingual. It appears that learning a second language increases the cognitive activities of the brain cells or cognitive reserve thus increases the brain's ability to function properly despite damage. So in our old age, we are encouraged to learn a second language through Apple's iTunes which is full of podcasts that allow you to listen to language lessons for free. Pick a language podcast you want to learn. The choice is yours.

There is a strong relationship between Type -2 diabetes and Alzheimer's disease. The latter is also known as Type-3 diabetes. If you suffer from the former, the probability of developing the latter is most likely when you grow old. The prevention from both these diseases is the most critical phase of your life. Both diseases are preventable. Scientific research provides all the necessary clues to prevent them. What do you need to do? Start now, change your day-to-day life style. The first step is to change your diet to a more plant based one with minimum sugar, carbohydrate and processed food. Take up exercise like walking for half an hour daily. Walking is the best medicine you can have. Make sure you drink plenty of water, adequate sleep, reduce stress, avoid toxic food and environment. The science of prevention for Alzheimer's is well documented. Research finding under Epigenetic shows clearly that you can change your genetic expression through life style changes. You can also grow and regenerate brain cells as you age under Neurogenesis. New network for neuron connections can be stimulated and generated under Neuro-plasticity. For detail, consult Google for more information. Investment for your health is the best investment.

Nature's Brain-Protecting Miracle - Curcumin

It's a scientific fact that curcumin, an antioxidant compound found in the root of turmeric plant, a native of India, is one of the most powerful natural brain-protecting substance. This bright yellow spice is usually found in curry powder. Its remarkable healing power is well documented. The people in India used to consume a lot of this spice, and consequently, Indians have the lowest incidence of cognitive decline worldwide.

The hallmark process associated with certain types of cognitive decline is the formation of abnormal protein structures in the brain. Normally, when malformed proteins are formed within the brain, the immune system sends out cells known as macrophages, which engulf and destroy the proteins. If this ordinary function fails, defective proteins accumulate in the brain as beta-amyloid plagues. Soon, cognitive decline follows. Recent research shows that consumption of reasonable amount of curcumin helps to encourage the immune system to send macrophages to the brain to destroy the broken proteins. A landmark clinical trial was carried out involving people with severe cognitive decline that measured the effect of curcumin on their abnormal proteins. Amazingly, the experimental group taking curcumin had significantly higher levels of dissolved abnormal proteins in their blood compared to those in the placebo group. This study indicates strongly that curcumin has the ability to effectively pass into the brain, bind to beta-amyloid plagues, and assist the body in their breakdown. Curcumin is one of the only substances known to have such a profound protective effect in the brain. Other incredible health benefits of curcumin are scientifically recorded here. Besides it protects the brain cells from ageing, it also increases memory retention and clarity thus boosting overall cognitive function. It promotes healthy cardiovascular function and support joint and muscle health. Besides, curcumin supports a healthy inflammatory response; it promotes a healthy digestive system, thus supporting healthy mood balance. It is capable to boost detoxification and liver health. It helps in natural weight loss by increasing metabolism.

Curcumin is used to reduce joint pains especially knee joints and others. First, it reduces inflammation. Unfortunately, curcumin alone is not easily absorbed by our digestive system. Researchers in 1998 discovered that by adding an extract of black pepper called piperine, the absorption of curcumin is significantly enhanced. Piperine helps to prevent curcumin break down in the small intestine and liver, and it increases its bioavailability by almost 2,000 per cent as claimed by researchers.

Turmeric rhizome, grow underground, is similar to that of ginger. It is known as Indian saffron or poor man's saffron because its ability to substitute as a colouring agent for the more expensive spice saffron. Dried and ground into a powder, turmeric is bright yellow, warm, and bitter to taste and is the key ingredient of curry powder. In Chinese medicine, the turmeric rhizome is called Jiang Huang, which means yellow ginger. Chinese use it traditionally to move stagnant blood and Qi to relieve pain including period pain, stomach upsets, abdominal pain, and shoulder pain.

Indian medicine uses turmeric powder for stomach and liver problems as well as skin conditions, wound healing, aches, and pains. Modern medicine investigates its anti-inflammatory effect for osteoarthritis when other inflammatory drugs are not suitable. New findings using curcumin, an active ingredient from turmeric rhizome, as mentioned above are slowly making their appearances.

DANGER OF TURMERIC CONSUMPTION DURING PREGNANCY

Do not be taken in by all the useful effects of curcumin from turmeric rhizome especially for ladies. It is not safe in pregnancy and must be avoided as there is risk of losing a pregnancy. Pregnant mothers must avoid taking turmeric in medical doses. It is known that turmeric may reduce blood clotting. Any person taking anticoagulant medication should seek medical advice before taking doses of turmeric. Any person going for surgery is advised to stop completely taking turmeric at least two weeks before surgery.

Avoid excessive consumption of turmeric either in unprocessed extract or commercial dosage. It is known that 500 mg of unprocessed extract up to four times a day is commonly used and well tolerated. Whenever in doubt, always consult health professional before taking especially commercial turmeric because its dosage varies. Always check the label for the correct dosage. This will avoid abuse and make turmeric a culinary herb with long traditional medical use finding relevance in our modern world.

Natural Treatment for Memory Loss, Dementia, and Alzheimer's Disease

Most doctors will prescribe the drug Aricept for patients suffering from Alzheimer's. This drug does not cure or reverse the disease. In fact, the patients require heavier and heavier doses as the treatment goes on. Many side effects are the consequence of taking this drug. The damage of the liver is one of them. Instead, there is a natural cure for Alzheimer's. Get the book *Awakening from Alzheimer's,* where this natural supplement containing the protein apoaequorin will help to reverse the disease. Other supplements such as coconut oil with MCT oil together can also reverse memory loss, dementia, and Alzheimer's. Another supplement you can consider is known as *cognitine,* which claims to be able to rejuvenate your brain and keep your mind as sharp as ever. Consult your doctor before you try these supplements. Another possibility of declining cognitive functions in elderly people may be due to B12 deficiency. A medical test may be necessary to determine this type of deficiency. Research reveals that a specialist doctor's prescription of vitamin B12 supplement can help you to arrest this type of cognitive decline.

Health Benefits of Omega-3 Fatty Acids from Fish Oil

The omega-3 fatty acid found in fish oil is well known for its health benefits, most commonly associated with dermatological, articular, and cardiovascular health for individuals from all ages. Research reveals that 1.16 grams of docosahexaenoic acid (DHA) supplement per day for any individual can make significant improvement to reaction time of the working memory, although working memory itself does not improve.

Research also reveals that children who have reading difficulty are likely to have low levels of omega-3 fatty acid in their blood. As parents, try to give children more fish or supplement DHA in their diet to avoid many troubles developing in your children.

Conjugated linoleic acid found in dairy products and beef has been proven to have significant effect in burning belly-fat. Many international researches have revealed that this fat burning fat issue conclusively. Pomegranate seed oil has shown to have significant effect to help the body to decrease fat storage especially at the belly. A good combination of conjugated linoleic acid and pomegranate seed oil will significantly increase belly-fat burning via the former and decrease body fat storage by way of the latter. Research reveals that an optimum amount of conjugated linoleic required is about two grams or more per day. This requirement is usually not met in our daily consumption of milk, yogurt, cheese, and beef. I share this information especially for those who lack exercise. To make this alternative strategy to reduce your belly-fat, you may need a doctor's advice for supplement.

Super Antioxidant from Brown Seaweed

People are wondering at the energy level and the physical fitness of elderly women who served as 'mermaids' of Jeju Island off the coast of Korea. These elderly women are from the age range from fifty-eight to over seventy. They wear nothing more than a wetsuit, fins, and goggles when they plunge into the cold sea. They disappear for minutes and return to the surface with octopus, sea urchin, seaweed, and shellfish. They make a living by harvesting the sea floor free diving to a depth of sixty-five feet without oxygen tanks. No doubt daily exercise and a high protein diet help with their remarkable stamina. But they have another secret up their sleeve, too. They eat a nutritional power house, the brown seaweed, in their diet.

This brown seaweed known as ecklonia cava is rich in antioxidants, many times more potent than any land-based antioxidant such as blueberries, green tea, and even resveratrol.

The brown seaweed has an advantage, too. Most land-based antioxidants are water-soluble only. That means they have a hard time crossing the blood-brain barrier to protect our brain cells. On the contrary, ecklonia cava is both water-soluble and fat-soluble. So it is capable of penetrating the membranes of our brain and nerve cells, enhancing its protective benefits for our health especially our brain from degeneration. Studies reveal that ecklonia cava can work wonders for our cholesterol, blood pressure, and circulation. Regular intake of ecklonia cava can sharpen our memory and mental focus. Our brain depends on a neurotransmitter called acetylcholine (Ach) to remember and learn new things. Studies show that ecklonia cava increases Ach significantly within weeks. It also increases alpha waves to our brain. This helps to promote overall sense of calmness and mental sharpness and enhance ability to complete tasks. In a way, it helps elderly people in reducing mental problems. Ecklonia cava is also known to soothe joint pain and inflammation. It does so by its amazing ability to reduce COX and LOX enzymes due to stress, injury, infection, and toxins. These enzymes are responsible for inflammation, joint pain, and other discomfort. Studies reveal that ecklonia cava, unlike other drugs, can soothe joint pain without damaging our stomach or putting our heart at risk. The consequence is that we have less pain, less stiffness, and more mobility. Ecklonia cava also boosts our immune system especially for elderly people. It contains a substance called fucoidans that can protect us from different kinds of flu and cold. Ecklonia cava has an amazing property helping us maintaining our blood sugar level. High blood sugar level can lead to all sorts of health problems. One of them involves an enzyme called aldose reductase. When our blood sugar level gets too high, aldose reductase converts some of the excess glucose into something called sorbitol, which can build up in our eyes and nerve cells and damage them. Great news is that ecklonia cava is a potent inhibitor of aldose reductase. Another benefit is that it boosts our metabolism and fire up fat burning through a pigment called fucoxanthin. Fucoxanthin gives this type of seaweed its distinctive brown colour. Regular consumption of ecklonia cava helps us to maintain a healthy weight. It is know that it stimulates a protein that causes fat to break down, especially abdominal fat. It also helps the liver make more DHA and omega-3 fatty acid that helps reduce LDC cholesterol responsible for weight gain and heart problem. Other minor benefits include younger looking skin and appearance, fight allergies, help detoxify our body, and help to beat fatigue and mystery pains. Remember that success happens when opportunity meets preparation. There is no harm to include brown seaweed or its supplement into our diet. If possible include brown seaweed in our regular diet. An alternative is to take brown seaweed extract in the form of piles.

Form the Habit of Eating One or Two Apples a Day

An apple a day keeps the doctor away. This common saying is repeated for many good reasons. Researches reveal that eating apples frequently improve health in numerous ways. Apples contain high fibre that can help in dieting and weight control because it gives the feeling of being full. People suffering from obesity should take note because the high fibre promotes 'satiety', meaning feeling fuller longer. The ursolic acid, which is a molecule found in apple peels, helps in energy-burning brown fat as well as augmenting muscle mass. Apples contain abundant antioxidant quercetin, which can slow down and prevent cancer cells especially prostate cancer. It is believed that the phytochemicals in apples can also improve lung function and lower risk of respiratory diseases such as emphysema, bronchitis, and asthma. This is partly explained by the presence of the flavonoids, quercetin, hesperetin, and naringenin contained in apples. These chemicals not only help in lowering the risk of diabetes but also can cut the risk of stroke and heart attack, especially a high intake of quercetin. This is partly due to the pectin, a form of soluble fibre found in apples, which lowers blood pressure and levels of bad cholesterol (LDL). Research reveals that eating two apples a day can significantly reduce the artery clogging damage caused by LDL. Another finding is good news for women. Research reveals that eating an apple or two a day can boost a woman's sexual pleasure. High levels of polyphenols and antioxidants found in apples stimulate blood flow to the sexual organs and aid arousal. In addition, apples contain phloridzin, a phytoestrogen that's similar to the female oestradiol.

Weight Control Using Insulin Sensitivity and Carbohydrate Tolerance

People tend to be overweight because of their diet full of processed foods, insulin, and blood sugar spiking carbohydrates. They normally tend to suffer from some level of insulin resistance or leptin resistance, a condition in which insulin is no longer able to efficiently remove blood sugar from the blood stream. In simple term, the rate of metabolism is greatly reduced. This results in reducing fat burning, increases blood sugar level, and increases sugar storage. This condition can lead to Type two diabetes and risk of Alzheimer's and other cognitive disorders. Heart disease and stroke can follow.

By promoting insulin sensitivity and carbohydrate tolerance, we are helping the following processes to work efficiently in our system. First, with minimum insulin release when our body is highly sensitive to insulin, this small amount is sufficient to effectively clear sugar from our blood system to its storage sites: muscles and liver. Our body has incredibly difficult time burning fat in the presence of insulin. So the less insulin and sugar in our blood, the better for fat burning. Second, when our body is sensitive to insulin, it serves to quickly and efficiently clear sugar from our blood. Third, it facilitates maximum glycogen uptake. Glycogen is the term used for stored carbohydrates in muscle tissues and the liver. When these tissues are highly sensitive to insulin, the vast majority of blood sugar will be stored within them as energy reserve in muscle tissues, instead of being converted to fat at the belly. Finally, the increase of insulin sensitivity will lead to minimum fat storage. Consequently, our body chooses to store carbohydrates intake as energy in lean muscle tissues and the liver, avoiding forming body fat. The chance of being overweight with fat at the belly will be slim. So to have a lean body we need to improve our body's insulin sensitivity to provide carbohydrate tolerance. The following strategies to enhance insulin sensitivity are recommended.

Strategy for a Slim Body and Flat Belly

First, consistent exercises in the form of games or repeated resistive weight training for each part of the body for about an hour per day will definitely improve insulin sensitivity. This appears difficult for most people because it requires discipline and spare time. Taking up a game like tennis or any other sport will help.

Second, a diet of fresh fruits, vegetables, and less carbohydrates will also help. Take mostly one ingredient food, that is, food containing itself without additive or sugar. Avoid sweetened processed drinks and can foods with preservatives. You may have reduced your leptin or insulin hormone level resistance and promote fat burning process, that is, increase your metabolism.

Third, take enough of cinnamon herb compound to increase leptin level and promote insulin or leptin sensitivity.

Finally, take proven supplements such as IC-STM or other clinically proven herbal powders like LeptiBurn or BioTRUST to enhance insulin or leptin sensitivity.

Natural Cure for Many Types of Cancer

Thanks to the advancement of herbal medicine and the spread of herbal healing knowledge; it is now possible for us to find an alternative cure for many types of cancer. I am duty-bound to share the knowledge of this cancer-blasting miracle tree, the soursop tree, found in tropical climate. Its fruit is known as graviola in the Caribbean and the Tropics. This particular tree is one of the many herbal plants whose extracts have healing power over many types of cancer cells. Extracts from the leaves, seeds, fruits, and stems of the soursop tree are capable of killing about twelve different kinds of cancer cells because of the plant's nutrients called annonacerous acetogenins. These compounds are reported to have the power to pull the plug on the energy source cancer cells to survive. It is reported that the acetogenins in the extract are effective against lung carcinoma cells, human breast tumour lines, prostate adenocarcinoma, pancreatic carcinoma cells, colon cancer, hepatocarcinoma cells, human lymphoma cells, and multidrug resistant human breast cancer cells. Researchers in Taiwan, Japan, and elsewhere report that acetogenins have a devastating impact on ovarian, cervical, breast, bladder, and skin cancer cell lines. Acetogenins from the leaves and seeds of the soursop tree are found to be toxic to liver cancer cells. They are also poisonous to colon cancer cells and killed them 10,000 times the potency of the anticancer drug Adriamycin. Even leukaemia and lymphoma cells can't stand the power of acetogenins. In Japan, researchers find that it destroys cancer cells in leukaemia and lymphoma with great efficiency. The soursop fruit, known as graviola, is delicious. It contains easily absorbed proteins, healthy fats, vitamins B and C, and minerals especially potassium and phosphorous.

The knowledge of this alternative cure for cancer such as certain type of mushroom and seaweeds should be made available to everyone.

Other Alternative Cures for Cancer

There are many alternative cures for cancer available today. These methods are usually covered up by the main stream medical world. The drug industries are too powerful and too commercial in the main stream approaches to cure cancer. The use of surgery, chemotherapy, and radiation do not help. For a hundred years, the rate of death of cancer patients remains the same. Other than natural foods mentioned above, there are many other natural alternative cures known today. A natural way to enhance a patient's immune system is the use of newly born mother's milk or cow's milk (available in health stores) which contains special ingredients to boost the patient's protective system of destroying cancer cells and getting rid of toxins. This natural alternative therapy is one of the easiest ways to treat cancer, and it's very effective. Another approach is using the same therapy used by astronauts using oxygenation to boost their energy of the cells and to enhance the patient's immune system. This approach supplies plenty of oxygen to the body cells which helps to kill cancer cells. Oxygenation therapy approach for a period boosts a patient's immune system but also provide extra energy to the patient to fight cancer. Another approach is making use of artificial-induced fever-like temperature or heat therapy known as hyperthermia to kill cancer cells leaving the normal cells unharmed. There are many other alternative approaches available. For full information, you should try to contact 'The Alternative Cancer Research Institute' for details. The publication *The Complete Guide to Alternative Cancer Treatments* is available.

Iodine: the Anticancer Agent

Iodine contains many cancer-fighting and cancer-preventing properties. It is known that iodine has been shown to cause 'apotosis' or cell death in breast and thyroid cells. Cancer cells are usually deformed cells which do not die according to the specification of their DNA. An accumulation of these deformed cells constitutes cancer in the breast or thyroid. In addition, iodine functions as both antioxidant as well as oxidant in the body. This duel effect makes it a strong antioxidant agent. A healthy body has a balance between antioxidant and oxidant, and iodine compound helps to maintain that balance. Thus, iodine becomes the most powerful anticancer agent known.

It is important to get a simple iodine test to measure your iodine levels in your body. And while good iodine levels help fight back against cancer, lowered levels provide fertile ground for cancer to begin in your many different hormonally tissues such as thyroid, breast, uterus, and ovaries. It's critical that you take care of your iodine levels to help promote your optimal thyroid, endocrine, and immune system functioning. Ocean fish or sea vegetables like seaweed contain adequate iodine if eaten regularly. Avoid bakery products where bromide is added, since bromine will interfere with iodine utilisation in the thyroid and other areas iodine concentrates in your body. Plus it's known as carcinogen. If you are tested with low iodine levels, consult your doctor for iodine supplements.

Key to Living Longer and Healthier Life

Before we look into studies regarding living longer and healthier, we need to be aware that there is a link between positive thinking and health.

Our immune system functions well when we have positive attitudes. Positive thoughts about our ageing offer us additional survival advantage. Being an optimist brings feeling of content with one's life and such self satisfaction has been associated with better health outcomes. It is easy to conclude that if we anticipate healthy and satisfying golden years, that expectation is more likely to come true.

A longitudinal study conducted by researchers at Cardiff University involving a big sample finds five simple rules which are vital for reducing chronic diseases to enable people to live a long and healthy life. These simple rules include regular exercise, healthy weight, healthy diet, little alcohol, and not smoking. I believe that I have almost fulfilled all the requirements. I think I am still enjoying my life at the age of seventy-five and am able to play tennis regularly because of the lifestyle adopted in all stages of my life.

All of us are aware that the cells in our body die and renew themselves within a year and our whole body reshape itself every two years. So it is important that we include nutrients that will help us rebuild our body. At the same time, we need to include food that will help us to fight cancer and cardiovascular diseases. A well-known scientist from the National Cancer Institute, Rachael Stolzenberg-Solomon, said,

> 'The easiest, least expensive way to reduce your risk of cancer is just by eating a healthy diet.'

Most of the experts agree that a diet rich in cancer-fighting substances should be predominantly plant-based. Deficiency in minerals such as potassium, magnesium, iodine, and others can affect our health, immune system, and overall well-being. As we grow older, we may need nutrients especially plant-based food rich in amino acid, vitamins, and minerals including potassium, iron, magnesium, copper, zinc, chromium, manganese, selenium, calcium, essential fatty acids, nucleic acids, gamma linolenic acid, phytonutrients, and other antioxidants. These nutrients are found in big quantities in these super foods: chlorella, moringa, maca, spirulina, cacao, wheatgrass, camu camu, and acai. It is not possible for most of us to get these super-rich foods. If our diet is not rich in vegetables and a variety of fruits, we may need to take this supplement extracted from these eight super foods mentioned here. This mega-nutrient organic super food is available from the Quantum Wellness Botanical Institute. It may be worth trying to help your body replenish and rejuvenate to enjoy a healthy and energetic life. I am lucky to be aware that our body tomorrow is equal to what we put in it today. Our entire body has the miraculous ability of rebuilding itself in less than a year. To enhance your body in the process of regenerating ability, you need to supply your body with nutrient-rich foods.

People in Europe around the Mediterranean Sea enjoy long life because of their diet rich in fish, fruits, vegetables, whole grains, and olive oil. This diet is believed to help improve digestion, decrease strokes and heart attack risks, and lower risk of diabetes. Another factor is that this diet helps to encourage longer telomeres responsible for longer life. Further discussion regarding telomeres will be dealt with later. It appears that olive oil has a significant role to play. Olive oil contains significant amount of antioxidants and monounsaturated fats that helps to lower the levels of low density lipoprotein or bad cholesterol. Olive oil also helps to keep insulin levels in check, helping to control diabetes. Its chemical structure and function also helps to protect cholesterols in the body from oxidation. Thus, it discourages diseases of inflammation, heart disease, and high blood pressure.

Besides our diet, there are certain things we should observe if we want to live longer and healthier. My own experiences seem to agree with the intensive research carried out by the University of California involving a big sample of participants. The following factors regarding your lifestyle and diet are helpful to help achieve a longer and healthier life:

1. Keep yourself lean as possible without becoming underweight.
2. Keep yourself physically active as part of everyday life. Take up a game and play regularly.
3. Avoid sugary drinks and limit the consumption of high calorie foods.
4. Try to eat mostly food of plant origin.
5. Try to limit intake of red meat to less than 500 g per week and try to avoid processed meat.
6. Try to limit consumption of alcoholic drinks. For men less than two glasses a day and women less than a glass a day.

7. Try to limit consumption of salt, specially processed foods with added salt or sodium.
8. Try your best to meet nutritional needs through diet alone. Dietary supplements unless from natural sources are not recommended because of their side effects.

For our body to function smoothly as we age, we need to control the build-up of free radicals especially singlet oxygen which stay inside our body. They cost oxidation stress, and these free radicals pound away at the healthy cells causing damage and depleting cellular energy. In fact, they damage our very DNA, accelerating the ageing process and raising the risk of serious health problems. Many of us, as we age, experience wrinkled skin, blurred vision, clogged and hardened arteries, loss of memory, and diminished energy level. For your information, you do not have to suffer this way. Researchers have found a 'magic bullet' to counter all these suffering. An extract from natural algae species known as 'astaxanthin' is now available. Study reveals that astaxanthin can scavenge free radicals and singlet oxygen in your brain, eyes, joints, and central nervous system in ways ordinary antioxidants simply can't. The uniqueness of astaxanthin is that it has powerful ability to neutralise free radicals including a particular unstable and destructive type called singlet oxygen. Singlet oxygen is linked to deadly cholesterol oxidation in the arteries, DNA damage, damaging skin, eyes, and other tissues of the body. In fact, its destructive effects have been tied to a wide gamut of age-related health concern. The good news is that astaxanthin molecule composition allows it to cross the blood brain and blood-retina barriers that other antioxidants can't cross. Astaxanthin is many many times more powerful than antioxidants like beta carotene, vitamin E, CoQlO, and vitamin Cl. Taking astaxanthin regularly can help us in cholesterol management and ensure our joints stay flexible and comfortable. It has the ability to lower the production of inflammation and pain-causing enzymes. Study shows that astaxanthin lowers LDL (bad cholesterol), raises food HDL cholesterol, and reduces triglycerides. It supports artery health as we age. In addition, it helps to ensure our vision stays clear and focused. It protects our skin and helps us to keep our lifelong memory. It keeps us energetic by helping our mobility and stamina. For extra information, try to pick a natural supplement in astaxanthin such as PurZanthin. Consult your doctor for a better supplement.

Include Walking into the Good Life Style for Older People

People who are over sixty need a practical lifestyle to reduce stroke and other disabilities. Besides acquiring skills of keeping us happy, good financial management, good hobbies, and purpose to live on, older people need information to prevent diseases like diabetes, heart disease, high blood pressure, and stroke. Research reveals that stroke is a major cause of death and disability for older people over sixty. Regular exercise will help to suppress the harmful proteins that are associated with depression. Regular exercise will enable you to acquire the ability to express the class of enzymes that have the ability to detoxify the chemicals formed during stress and others.

Dr Ralph Sacco, chairman of neurology at the University Miami Miller School of Medicine, advocates that any form of exercise is beneficial to older people regarding physical and mental health. Many studies suggest that getting into the habit of walking every day for at least an hour can protect against stroke. Walking can come in many forms like running errands, going to the shops, walking around indoors, as well as walking for leisure such as walking in the parks. Study suggests that just walk does the trick regardless of pace. Besides stroke prevention, exercises bring other benefits. Studies suggest that older people should aim for 150 minutes per week of moderate physical activity, which includes walking at a brisk pace or light gardening or 75 minutes per week of vigorous activities such as jogging or tennis … It will protect against heart disease and diabetes, as well as protect against stroke. We need to be aware that heart disease is preventable. I would suggest that we follow a healthy diet with plenty of greens and avoid sugar, the white killer.

A major study was carried out by Jefferis in Briton. It involved 3,500 healthy men aged sixty to eighty in twenty-four British towns for ten years. This big sample was divided into five groups. The first group of men had 0 to three hours of walking per week. The second group had four to seven hours of walking per week. The third group had eight to fourteen hours of walking per week. The fourth group had fifteen to twenty-one hours of walking per week, and the last group had more than twenty-two hours of walking per week.

After ten years of research, Jefferis found that men who had more than fourteen hours of walking per week reduced their risk of stroke by one-third compared with men who walked less than three hours per week. The result was more dramatic for men who walked more than twenty-two hours per week. The risk for stroke dropped by about two-third. Although the study does not establish a cause-and-effect relationship for walking and stroke, but the revelation is enough for older people to take special note for healthy lifestyle. No special tool is required for walking. What we need is to establish the habit of walking and be active whenever possible. Remember walking is just as good as running. It prevents dementia, improves our immune system, and lessens our symptoms of depression.

I am aware that once I hit middle age, my muscles start to vaporise, and it gets worse as I get even older. The name of this muscle loss is called sarcopenia. Many a time after sixty years old, I woke up and felt old because of my vanishing muscle. Studies reveal that we will be losing at an average rate of 1 or 2 per cent of our muscles per year. From fifty to seventy years of age, we will be losing about 30 per cent of our muscles if we do not take preventive steps to slow down the vanishing muscles. The awareness of such phenomenon drives me to take drastic action to reverse the process. After my fiftieth birthday, besides my regular tennis and walking daily, I included exercises with muscle resistance to replenish lean muscle and to negate the effect of age-related muscle loss. I also include stretching to improve my flexibility and build lean muscle. I share this information so that anyone who is above fifty years old can retain partly his or her lean muscle by stretching or practising resistive exercises.

Knee Joint Pain and Osteoarthritis

I played basketball for many years, and I had knee injury. My left knee was twisted, and one of the ligaments was torn. Although I have recovered from the injury, my knee is never the same as before. During that time, surgery was not a common practice. In modern surgery, I should have the ligament mended and repaired. I have been taking glucosamine and chondroitin to help reduce joint pain and swelling associated with arthritis. In my retirement, I have been playing tennis three times a week, and this supplement seems to help relieving my knee joint pain. Most athletes, as they age, usually suffer from joint pain, a condition known as osteoarthritis. This is a condition in which the cartilage that cushions the joint wears down and leaves bone rubbing on bone. For advance cases, surgical joint replacement is available. But it is rarely the first line of defence. Rather, treatment typically starts with pain relievers in the form of injection of substance into the joint which acts as a cushion between the bones. The substance is usually a gel-like thing called hyaluronic acid found in human body. This chemical is made from non-animal source. It is injected directly into the knee over a three-week period, essentially lubricating the joint and acting as a cushion between the bones, to relieve chronic knee pain and improve movement. If you need this injection, you are advised to consult your doctor for further advice.

The Length of Telomeres and Overall Health

The DNA tips called telomeres are associated with the ability of our body cells to replicate. Does the length of each telomere matter? Today, the science is crystal clear that shorter telomeres are associated with dead and dying cells. Shorter telomeres also suggest that a person is susceptible to age-related diseases and even early mortality. Telomeres protect the useful programmed parts of our DNA. This protection is important when our cells divide or make new cells. There is a limit to the size of each cell, and once its limit is reached, the cell divides and create more cells. This replication allows our body to grow and develop and replace dead cells. The process goes on in every part of our body including our stomach wall - cells killed by acidic chemical are replaced. The most important function is the protection of the programmed coding DNA. An enzyme called telomerase helps to replicate and replace the caps of DNA. Cell division is a natural cause of telomere shortening that we cannot control. However, we can manage some of our stressors that shorten our telomeres faster than normal. You need to understand some of these stressors like inflammation, stress, and lack of sleep. Avoiding these stressors will not only protect the length of the telomeres but also protect our overall health.

To provide adequate protection for our telomeres, we have the responsibility to practise regular exercise and get enough vitamin D and adequate antioxidants. Regular exercise reduces stress, releases endorphins, improves brain function, and improves cardiovascular health. Try to get enough sunshine vitamin D which is associated to telomere length. Vitamin C is one type of antioxidant. Others like vitamin E, beta-carotene, and selenium are also antioxidants. Eating adequate amount of chocolate, popcorn, red wine, blueberries, green vegetables, and broccoli will ensure enough supply of antioxidants. All these will certainly help to ensure lengthy, healthy telomeres and good health.

Never too Old to Learn New Things

I was interested in meditation as early as I started my secondary schooling in Penang. I did not go through any formal training. I was searching for a good instructor to help me enhance my creative visualisation power during meditation. I accidently knocked into Burt Goldman's discovery of Quantum Jumping. Being curious I wanted to know more about this mysterious man's background, his philosophy, and his discovery. The title appears to suit me. Quantum mechanics was my optional subject during my honours year study. I never really understand the subject. Anyhow, Burt Goldman's proposal of the existence of infinite number of parallel universes attracts my attention. His remarkable concept of my alternate selves or doppelgangers in theses infinite parallel universes is really something new, mind-boggling, and yet inspiring. According to him, he had waited three decades gathering evidences form great minds like Professor Stephen Hawking, Professor Alan Guth, Professor Albert Einstein, and Dr Michio Kaku regarding the possible existence of infinite number of parallel universes before he formally introduced the concept of Quantum Jumping in 2009. No physical contact between any two parallel universes is possible because of the vast distance apart. Quantum Jumping provides an imaginary technique for each of us to come into visionary contact with our alternate selves residing in alternate parallel universes. The conduit is meditation and creative visualisation. This is the beginning of a new thinking revolution about our physical universe and its alternate parallel universes. The discoveries of new physics in the digital age including relativity and quantum mechanics appear to reach well beyond our perceived vision based on the concept of concrete and solid reality. Hundreds of thousands of radio, TV, and cell phone waves are being transmitted throughout the world. Having the right equipment like our cell phone or radio and by tuning to the right frequency, we are able to receive and transmit messages in various languages in our own room. Similarly, there is a possibility of an infinite number of alternate universes and infinite number of our alternate selves whose frequency or vibrating energy similar to ours in our own room. The concept of Quantum Jumping enables us to contact and interact with our alternate selves whose expertise we are seeking. Imagine that you could examine their ways and learn their methods, draw upon their skills, experience, and wisdom, and find out how they become so happy, talented, and successful. This process is made simple in our own room through the process of creative visualisation in meditation. This meditation technique is available to all of us. What a wonderful idea. Say now I aspire to be a writer. Believing in this remarkable concept of Quantum Jumping, I could jump into a parallel universe to meet a doppelganger who is already a well-known writer. I can hold discussion with my doppelganger to learn his skills in writing, his experiences, his attitudes, his knowledge, and other essential qualities involving writing. I have enrolled as a student to learn this new technique. I have just received my first few creative visualisation lessons and have experienced a few Quantum Jumps. I am now a basic jumper. Slowly, I will move up the four levels: from a basic jumper to a novice jumper, then to a master jumper, and finally a quantum jumper. As soon as master this technique, I will be sharing my new experience at the end of this book. I was attracted to learn and master Quantum Jumping technique for a very good reason. The concept of Quantum Jumping, which involves our subconscious mind, has vast applications: professional development, business, investing, well-being (healing and health), hobbies, relationships, and an infinite ways to improve our lives. The details of this remarkable technique will be explored in Chapter Seven.

As I listen to Burt Goldman, an eighty-seven-year ex-soldier, who discovered this remarkable concept, I am inspired. He claimed that he had been practising Quantum Jumping for almost three decades. His achievements speak for itself. His creative advance visualisation in meditation enables a believer to jump through a door in your room into another parallel universe to meet a successful version of your alternate self. This remarkable idea enables each one of us to travel into an infinite number of parallel universes to meet the successful doppelgangers you intend to meet. This power of the mind is infinite. Imagine that you could jump into any universe and learn to be the dream person you wanted to be.

I believe in the power of the mind. Age, according to Burt Goldman, is just a number. He is eighty-seven, and I am seventy-five. The number does not matter. What I intent to live the next fifteen or twenty years of my life is important. My intention to be a better grandfather, a better husband, a better lover, a better sportsman, a better writer, and a better investor can be my next dream through the process of Quantum Jumping.

In retrospective, I can compare my life with the act of mixing a cocktail drink. I have spent my entire life sipping on a cocktail of hope and action. I must have mixed it right because my cocktail tastes right. My life journey had been smooth because I knew that mixing my cocktail well would ensure my happiness and success. They depend entirely on how I balance these two elements. Perhaps my processes of mixing my cocktail can serve as example to you so that you too can mix the elements right and experience happiness and success. Now I will take you on my bullet train to experience the journey I have made. Hopefully, you would be able to reproduce another successful journey of life to share with the future generations.

Success in life brings happiness and abundance if our cocktail recipe is right and balance. According to the well-known writer Wallace D. Wattles, the author of *The Science of Getting Rich:* 'There is a Science of getting rich, and it is an exact science, like algebra, and once these laws are learned and obeyed by anyone, that person will get rich with mathematical certainty.' I believe that in my working stage of life, I had followed these laws unconsciously. I worked hard and planned mathematically to unleash my inner abundance. I must have explored the logic why I should get rich. I agree absolutely with Wattles that without money I can't live at my highest potential and my entire purpose in life is to give myself most fully; therefore, I must be rich to fulfil my moral obligation to my creator. That has given me the freedom to give back to society in many forms: publications, curriculum materials, helping others, and charity. The various approaches I adopted can usher some light for anyone to emulate.

The Values of Meditation and Mental Training

When I started my student days in Penang, I was terribly affected by my past memories. I always felt that life was unfair. The situation at home and all the negative headlines in the media left me feeling helpless. Everything was out of control. All the negative energy seemed to work in bringing me down. I was facing all the external roadblocks the seemed to be getting in the way of my goals. My practice of meditation each day before I started learning and playing my favourite game basketball allowed me to go back in time and encourage me to change direction. My visualisation sessions triggered my senses that there was no reason to hold on to those poor memories that did not serve my situation then. I no longer had to work in the morning, study in the afternoon, and work again in the night. I had chosen to abandon this negative energy that had worked to bring me down. This practice of meditation is a good way of getting emotion out of the way. Personally, I experience many health benefits because of my regular meditation. In my lesson preparation, meditation brought about sharper focus. Through meditation, I derive a stress-free mind, a deeper contentment, and an emotional balance. I am free from high blood pressure partly because of my regular meditation. Once after each meditation, I am ready to embark on a new venture like studying a new topic or working on a new project.

There are many methods people use for meditation. From my own experience, I had adopted a simple method of meditation which initially I thought it was daydreaming. My approach is different from the new concept introduced by Burt Goldman in Quantum Jumping. During my school days, this simple meditation had really complemented my study and sporting strategies. Especially important is mental training riding all types of emotion through deep meditation. I knew of some players who were very skilful and outstanding during practice sessions. But when they were put in a competitive environment, they could not replicate their skills and performances due to lacking in mental strength. Perhaps my usual involvement in meditation and active visualisation of playing situation before each important match had enhanced my performance. Most sportsmen require mental training and repeated drilling plus physical development to perform at their peak. Meditation provides a mental rehearsal, creating mental images of the exact movements I wanted to emulate in my sport. Active visualisation in deep meditation provided me the necessary ingredients such as inner calmness, patience for the right moment to execute, and contemplation to create chances for teammates. All these elements had helped me to perform optimally during a match.

Whenever I practise meditation, I learn how to put myself into a deep level within minutes. This ability came after months and years of practice. I do not allow anything to border me. Sounds don't disturb me. This helps me to manage stress that seems to melt away. Perhaps, we need a simple notion regarding meditation, according to Osho:

> 'Meditation is a state of no-mind. Meditation is a state of pure consciousness with no content. Meditation is the awareness that "I am not the mind". When the awareness goes deeper and deeper in you, slowly, slowly, a few arrive-moments of silence, moments of pure space, moments of transparency, moments often nothing stirs in you and everything is still. In those still moments you will know who you are. This is meditation. When mind knows, we call knowledge. When heart knows, we call it love. And when being knows, we call it meditation.'

During my form two to form five time, meditation plus my sound self study strategy of pre-preparation before lessons, my learning productivity soared. Ambitions and goals stayed clearly in my focus without distraction. Worries of performance did not suffocate me in both sports and study. My mental strength was boosted to complement my dribbling and shooting skills in important matches. This practice seemed to have an important impact on my style of playing by creating chances for my teammates to shoot whenever the opponent team used two players to stop me. Visualisation helped in creativity of play and helped my team's performances.

There are other benefits that I enjoy because of my regular practice in meditation and exercise. It leads me to develop positive thought pattern, helping me to become more discipline in adhering to my self-study strategy, playing strategy, positive attitude towards my family members, and better social image. I became less critical of myself, family members, and friends, thus boosted my ego strength. I began to see the world and my future differently. My self-assurance and warm-heartedness made their appearance. It prevented shyness, and I became more outgoing. To me, meditation is a proven method for stress reduction, and it improves my quality of life. Meditation always slows down my mind to a deep state of relaxation. It enables me to focus on the 'now' rather than dwell on what happened in the past or having fear for the future. It had tremendous health benefits to me. I always felt good during and after each meditation. It provided me the clarity of thought before I studied and helped in my self confidence. I seem to have acquired a sense of peace and a direction of life. In brief, my regular meditation and exercise seem to have created what science has discovered, a happy hormone like serotonin which helps me feeling great. It sharpens everything including my concentration and study, and it enhances my appreciation of my surrounding. It keeps my new life fresh. These combinations create dramatic improvement in my health, boost my energy level, and help me in manifesting creative ideas and problem solving related to my studies. It enhances my success in both study and game. People seem to associate meditation to Buddhism. Now I am aware that I can use other psychologies of religion like prayer, yoga, or mindfulness to develop my spiritual life without believing in relative truths. Stories of any religion are relative truths because some people believe them but others do not. I am spiritual but not religious. I use a tool of religion to raise my state of awareness and experience a sense of oneness with the universe without necessarily following the relative truth. I am seeking the absolute truth which everyone who practises it and believes in it. I know I am in the minority. Most people believe in relative truths.

Since schooldays until now, I could not remember the last time I became sick. My regular meditation and my regular exercise have ensured me a life of good health. Looking back, I had used meditation to help me getting optimal performance each day. That is because meditation does more than make me feel good. It heightens my sense, explodes my creativity, boosts my productivity, and develops a scary accurate sense of intuition. It helps to increase my focus, solve problems faster, and enjoy deep relaxation. It reduces anxiety, lowers stress, and quietens my mind. I believe I have learnt to naturally accelerate my body's rate of healing. Perhaps the mind is the driving force behind all healing. Imagine that you could have a system designed to accelerate your mind's and body's natural capacity for physical and emotional healing. I adopted such a system through meditation. Listen to what Buddha says,

> 'The secret of health for both mind and body is not to mourn for the past, not to worry about the future, or not to anticipate troubles, but to live in the present moment wisely and earnestly.'

I believe that I have used deep meditation to help me boosting my creativity in both study and game. Deep meditation complemented my creative mind to think of solutions to my mathematical and research problems. It enhanced creativity of new ideas and allowed inspiration to flow. In my game, creativity came in the form of opening up space for teammates to score. Superior skills in dribbling and shooting had brought in other psychological advantage to my team. The opponents became uncertain and this usually led to poor teamwork. Confidence soon disappeared and the game was lost.

Daily meditation helps me to think big and attain powerful goals. Without such regular practice, I would not have left my comfortable job as an industrial arts teacher to take up a new challenge in science at the age of twenty-six. My colleagues staying with me while I was teaching in a small town, Sungei Petani, in Kedah, Malaysia, once told me that it was not easy for me to do science subjects when I was preparing for HSC. To them, many of the sixth-form school students, with teachers' guidance, could not do well in such subjects like physics, chemistry, pure mathematics, and applied mathematics. Only a few students in upper six in a regular government school dared to take such option. I was not discouraged. I knew my own mind. My meditation taught me to think big and set my goal. I became permanently more self-assured and positive. I set forth to accomplish and to achieve things that can contribute to humanity. I had proven them wrong. I went on not only passing my HSC but also obtaining my bachelor of science degree with honours. I didn't stop there, and eventually I went on to get my Ph.D. As my contribution to sixth form education, I had written three textbooks: applied mathematics, pure mathematics, and statistics. I had also written modern mathematics textbooks for form one to form five plus the additional mathematics textbook for forms four and five. In addition to these textbooks, I had written revision guides for students from form one to form six. The intention of writing these educational materials is to help make learning of mathematics easier. This is also my contribution to the educational needs of the community. I was lucky to be rewarded richly for all these contributions. I believe I took the challenge well. I followed what Dr John Eliot wrote in his book *Overachievement:*

> 'Overachievement is aimed at people who want to maximize their potential. And to do that, I insist you throw caution at the wind, ignore the pleas of parents, coaches, spouses to be "realistic". Realistic people do not accomplish extraordinary things because the odds of success stymie them. The best performers ignore the odds.'

Daily practice in meditation gives me the power to control my creative mind. I enjoy sleeping well and learn to practise creative dreaming. I have learnt the power to 'command' my mind to let me fall asleep when I choose to. I do not need an alarm clock. It also shows me how to set my internal clock to be able to wake up anytime I want. All these good night sleeps have contributed to my productivity in studying, working, and writing. I have all the energy to endure every hard fought game I played. This has given me the ability to remember my dreams and even able to ask my dreams to find solution to a problem. Some of my new ideas came from my dreams. Once I dreamt of my father who passed away many years ago. In my dream, I was driving towards my old home. My brothers and sisters were asking my father for financial help by predicting four digit numbers at the next draw. Seeing me coming in my car, my father told them that he would not entertain them. But he wanted me to come and told them that he would not help them but he would rather help me financially. I was not interested because I could earn myself. I told the story to my mother-in-law who used to buy four-digit lottery. She bought a few dollars on the number plate of my car for me. After the weekend, I was richer by a few thousand dollars. It might be a coincidence. Anyhow, one of my dreams brought me financial benefit.

Another aspect of the power of the mind comes in the form of intuition, which can be a valuable asset. Everyone is born with intuitive abilities. Through meditation, I was able to learn to manifest these abilities and let it function at a higher intuitive level. Imagine that you are able to use your psychic abilities in everyday life and use your 'gut feeling' for a happier, more successful, and more enlightened you. I was able to accomplish that. By mediating and researching in my mind, I discovered that I was much stronger than I thought. I avoided wasting time dragging myself under. I did not allow negative thoughts to emerge in my mind. I only made important decision after my deep meditation. The power to get what I want, be it personal or financial, professional or sports, lies 'inside' me. It does not matter what the external situation is like. When I was a college trained teacher, I fell in love with girl who had just completed form five. She was about to join Regional Training Centre to be trained as a teacher. I remember the incident when I accompanied her to her uncle's place in Penang. We were happy talking about many things. Then suddenly she told me that she had a boyfriend studying medicine in Australia. I did not utter any word after that. I was disappointed. We were supposed to go for a night show after dropping her bag at her uncle's place. Graciously, I excused myself and left the place. That night I had my meditation before I slept. My intention was to make a decision whether I should continue my relationship with her. My 'gut feeling' told me not to lengthen such relationship. I made the right decision. When I was in the university doing my final year, she wrote to me, telling me that she was still a bachelor girl. She wanted to see me. I remembered vividly what Helen Keller once said,

> 'When one door of happiness closes, another opens: but often we look so long at the closed door that we do not see the one which has been opened for us.'

The next day I joined a picnic organised by my house mate teaching in Sungei Petani. He rented a house at the seaside in Penang for his form three students after their LCE exam. They stayed there for a couple of days. They had picnic and fun there. This was the place I met my soulmate. She had just completed her form three study. I was a young college trained teacher teaching in another school. We were attracted to each other. I did not pursue the relationship at the time because it might not be appropriate. A few years elapsed without much contact except a few letters we wrote to each other when I was in the university. When I was returning to the university for my honours year, she was in the same train with me. She was joining the University Hospital to be trained as a nurse. The nursing hostel was behind my First Residential College. Our relationship began, and eventually we got married. I really found my true love.

The subsequent three chapters will describe those experiences and discoveries I have made during the four seasons or the three stages of my life. I have experienced those series of insignificant events and simple discoveries along the path towards where I am now. It's fascinating how even these insignificant events and simple discoveries can create a massive ripple across time and change the lives of people in unsuspecting ways. What brings success, happiness, and enlightenment to me can also do likewise if you have an open mind, discipline, and good intent. Many happenings occur through strange encounters. I know of a friend who met his soulmate because he missed the bus by a fraction of a second and bumped into the girl while walking to work. Another basketball friend of mine got his dream job after a chance encounter with a perfect stranger at the taxi stop. The stranger whom he gave a lift happened to be the chairman of the company. So it might happen to you because you accidently pick up this book, read it, and decide to follow the steps towards a successful and enlightened life.

CHAPTER FOUR

THE WONDERS OF THE FOUR SEASONS OF MY LIFE

The three stages of my life can easily be classified into the four seasons. The period of childhood from the time I was born during Japanese occupation until I left for my secondary education in Penang matches with the cold winter season. The three periods from secondary school to college and then university are classified as the spring season of my life. My formal working life as a teacher is the summer season, and the retirement phase is considered as my autumn season of life. The reasons for the comparison will be discussed in the subsequent headings.

EARLY CHILDHOOD AS THE ECONOMIC WINTER SEASON

I was rather unfortunate to be born into a large family which did not focus on education and intellectual development. Time was tough, and all the kids had to work to help our parents made ends meet. My family was fighting for survival and only focused on putting food on the table. I was caught in a situation where my physical contribution mattered. This period of my life is comparable to the winter season. Everything is cold and tough. I do not remember much about my early childhood. I was born during the Japanese occupation in a small town in the state of Kedah, Malaya at the time. My father had eight brothers and two sisters, making a total of ten. His father also came from a large family of eight brothers. According to my father's story, my great-grandfather had almost eighty acres of farmland in China, and my grandfather was allotted about eight acres. When my grandfather passed away, my father was allotted an acre. At that time, my father was seventeen years old and he was fifth in the family of eight boys. He did not want an acre of land. In his mind he was thinking that if he had eight boys, each would only get one-eighth of an acre. How are they going to earn a living by working on that small piece of farmland? His imagination or visualisation came true. He had eight boys and six girls after two marriages. He decided to migrate to Thailand where his elder brothers had started business in Bangkok. He landed in Bangkok helping his elder brothers making soya bean curd and selling soya bean water. He wanted an independent life very strongly, and he moved to a small town in a bordering state to Thailand. I was born in this small town, Serdang, in Kedah, a northern state of Malaya. He started as a worker in the farm and then started his own sundry shop, a small business. He did not have much education. He made enough money and went back to China to marry his first wife. She gave him two sons and two daughters. The four of them were still very young when his wife passed away. I do not know the cause of her death. My father then married my mother, his second wife. On top of taking care of the four children of my father's first wife, my mother was very productive. She gave him six sons and four daughters. Imagine my father's heavy responsibility. He had to feed sixteen mouths. I remember once my father told me that even 'the mountain' would be eaten by all of us. Life was tough and time passed. All of us survived. I am fifth among the boys in the family. My father was a very thrifty man. None of my elder brothers and sisters had received secondary education. They had to start working very early in their life to help supporting the big family. This period of my life is cold and difficult, and I call it the winter economic season of my life. When I was two years old, my grandmother came from China to help looking after the many children. My mother helped to manage our sundry shop. She had no time to take care of all of us. I was under the care of my grandmother. She told me later that I shared the same bed with her until I was fifteen years old when I left for Penang to continue my secondary education. Though I did not remember much regarding my childhood, my grandmother's story was the only source I had. She lived to very old age. She passed away when I was doing my second-year course at the University of Malaya. I was already a twenty-seven-year-old bachelor boy. I came home and attended her funeral. She was like a mother to me for almost fifteen years. She always reminded me to bring home my girlfriend for her to see. I failed her because for the first twenty-eight years of my life, I did not have a special girlfriend. I was too busy pursuing my basketball career and education. She died disappointed that she never saw my girlfriend or wife. I did fall in love a few times but never had the courage to propose to any of them. I think that cowardice had helped me in my game and academic pursuit. Otherwise, I would have been tied down to family life instead of my academic pursuit. I may not be what I am today.

I am never proud of any of my elder brothers, but I appreciate all my sisters. I have four elder brothers. None of my elder brothers had become good role model to me. I started my primary school when I was seven. All my elder brothers and a sister from my mother were in the same Chinese Primary School. I remember the first day in school. I was squatting beside the school basketball court watching a practice game. My third elder brother was one of the players playing before the school bell rang. My interest in the game was kindled. I started playing the game when I was in the second year at the school. When I was in year four, I represented the school team. I began to form a vision or dream that one day I would represent my town, state, and country in the game. This visualisation enabled me to see myself training under strict discipline routine like dribbling, shooting, and practicing almost every evening in the basketball court. All these hard works produced fruits of success. When I reached standard six in primary school, I was included into the only team representing the town. Life was full of excitements whenever there were friendly matches played at the school basket court by the town team. I became the match creator and shooter because of my extra skills in dribbling and shooting. This achievement had given me confidence, and I began to trust myself for further achievement in the game.

My childhood life especially at primary school was tough and hard work. I attended school in the morning. In the afternoon, all my brothers were given specific tasks to take care off. In a big family like ours, my father had to make full use of his human resources to survive. We had a two bulls used to pull cart for the purpose of transportation. These animals worked during the daytime pulling bullock cart, and they needed to be fed during the night. My immediate elder brother and me were given the responsibility to gather grass from the fields to feed these two animals. From my primary three to primary six, I had to gather two bags of grass every day. It became a routine, and I accepted my responsibility without questioning my father. I accidently cut my own palm twice during these years. The evidences are still prominently shown on my left hand. I also remember when the rubber trees had passed their prime, they were replanted with grafted young trees in our small holding. My father started to grow sweet potatoes and banana trees in between the young rubber trees while they were growing. I was asked to help in clearing the land for growing our crops. I had to gather rubber woods for home-cooking purposes. I enjoyed the harvesting season. I used to sell sweet potatoes to the village folks cheaply. In modern day's term, this can easily be classified as child labour. Anyhow, I enjoyed selling the product and got some extra cash to buy my basketball shoes. In addition to this responsibility, my mother was involved in rearing about a dozen of pigs to bring extra income for the family. These domestic animals were kept in cages behind my house, and they had to be fed twice a day and needed to bath them each day to keep them cool so that they would grow faster to be sold for slaughtering. I was given extra responsibility to gather yam plants from the wild so that these plants could be cooked with others ingredients to feed the animals. All these responsibilities going out to the rice fields, river banks, and jungles brought some risks to my life. I was brave and fearless. Imagine you asking your eight- or nine-year-old boy to go to these places to cut grass and gather wild plants. I was chased by wild animals like wild boars before. I also encountered snakes like python and cobra. I did not know the danger at that young age. It was rather fun for me trying to outrun these snakes. Cobra was especially dangerous when their nests were around with the eggs or young ones. Even some species of birds would attack if you disturb their nests with eggs or young ones. All these experiences stood well for me in later life when I needed to survive. Perhaps it is nature's way of preparing me for a tough and challenging life. I should be thankful for such a tough preparation for my life.

Primary Education

I was just an average student in Chinese Primary School. I don't think any of my teachers had a high opinion about my academic ability. Other than my basketball skills, I had not achieved much to shout about. I could only remember the occasion when I was in standard five. I was chosen to represent my class in oratory contest both in Chinese and English. In both events I emerged as runner-up. Six years of primary education soon ended. I remember my last day in school after my graduation ceremony. My graduating class had only sixteen students, and only six of them were receiving graduating certificates with distinction. I was lucky to be one of the six. The rest just managed to pass. Being a senior student in the school, we were allowed to lock our books in our desk drawers. While I was removing my books, tears flowed down from my eyes. I felt so sad that my schooling had ended. There was no secondary school in my hometown. I had to start working the next day to help my parents supporting his big family. Some of my lucky classmates were admitted to Chung Ling High School and Penang Girls High School in Penang. I really envied them. Penang is a city about forty kilometres from my hometown.

My father was a very thrifty man. He did not pay much attention to a sound education because he was not educated himself. He had a big family and a heavy responsibility. In spite of that, he was able to save enough money to buy a small rubber holding planted with rubber trees. The next day after my graduation, I was asked to help my elder brother, who is two years my senior, to tap rubber in his small holding. It was hard work for me. I was only a twelve-year-old boy. We had to get up five o'clock in the morning to have our breakfast made up of biscuits and a cup of coffee. We had to cycle about six kilometres to reach our rubber small holding. Rubber tapping is a tedious job. Each tree is tapped every day once using a sharp tapping knife. Latex will flow from the grove cut by a sharp tapping knife into a small container. Each person can normally tap about 300 trees a day. After about four or five hours, the latex in each container is ready to be collected into a big tin container. A day's work began at 6 a.m. and ended about 12 p.m. The latex was poured into a bigger container placed behind our bicycle to be carried to a factory to be processed into rubber sheets. The coagulated latex formed in each cutting groove of each tree and that remained in each of the container were also collected to dry and for sale to provide extra income. This period is part of the history of my life. The only memory left is the scar of a big cut on my left hand when I fell from my ladder and the tapping knife cut my left wrist. These three years of hard work served well as reminder of where I came from.

Imagine you live in a small town fenced up by wire fencing. That was the situation we were in during the communist insurgency period in early '50s. We were not allowed to bring food and other essential items with us while we left the town to work. Checking at the exit of the town was very tight. The British colonial masters used this technique to cut off supply of foods to the communists loaming in the nearby jungles. Many of the essential foods sold in our sundry shop were controlled items. We had to keep a record of every customer who purchased them. Regular checking was done by government agents to control these essential daily foods from reaching the communists. Since I received six years of education I was given the responsibility to keep the records. Every night after the shop closed, I had to start counting the numbers of each item left so that they tallied with the sale recorded and the number we purchased from wholesalers. This extra responsibility required further knowledge of accounting and English language proficiency. I was allowed to attend an English Missionary School in another town, Parit Buntar, about fifteen kilometres away. Because of my low command of English language, I was allowed to attend standard five. I spent about three years from standard five to form one in this afternoon school which catered for averaged students.

During these three years, I had a heavy responsibility. In the morning I had to help my brother to tap rubber. I usually left earlier leaving my brother to collect the rubber latex and process the rubber sheets. After a quick lunch, I headed for the bus station to catch a bus leaving for Bandar Bahru at about 12 p.m. Bandar Bahru is a town next to Parit Buntar separated by the river. There was no bridge at the time. I took a small boat called 'sampan' to cross the river from Bandar Bahru into Parit Buntar. From there I had to walk about three kilometres to reach the school. The afternoon session school began at about 1.30 p.m. and ended at 6.15 p.m. I followed this routine for three years while I tried to improve my English and kept my educational pursuit alive. Each day when I reached home, it was almost 7.30 p.m. I had to eat my dinner alone from Monday to Friday. After my dinner, I had my responsibility to keep the emergency sundry records for the government. Imagine working in this condition without electricity in the home. We had kerosene lamps to help us accomplish these tasks. There was not much time to study. I do not remember I did any study other than what I learnt from my schoolteachers. I tried to do most of my works in the school. Being an afternoon school, the weather was hot; with most of the teachers just completed form five with a minimum Senior Cambridge Certificate, not much learning actually took place. That was the situation then. But I am still grateful for the opportunity to attend the school. From Monday to Friday, my time was fully occupied. There was not much time for me to develop my basketball skills. Only Saturday and Sunday left for me to train and play my passionate game. By then I was already a prominent player for the town team. The team depended much on my dribbling and shooting skills. We were already an outstanding team in the state.

The Wonders of the Spring Season of My Life

A sudden change of environment allowed me to welcome the spring season of my life. After three years of part-time working and schooling in the afternoon, luck began to smile at me. A friend, who later became a relative through marriage, had good news for me. He studied in Penang and happened to stay in the same street as my eldest sister who was married to a Penang businessman. Without asking for permission from my brother-in law, I enrolled into a high school in Penang to begin my form-two study. Life began to change. I had more time to do the things I like such as training my basketball skills and indulging in reading to improve my English. My father was not happy that I played basketball seriously. He commented that playing the game did not bring food on the table. My brother-in-law, though not educated, seemed to like me and encouraged me to study. My own father failed this test. He did not believe in education. He would rather have us helping his small business and worked in his small rubber holding.

I was an averaged student. When I was studying in form two, I was already sixteen years old. Because of my regular training to improve my basketball skills and regular competitions, I was rather physically well-built for the age. Immediately, I was noticed and was included into the school basketball team. The next year when I was in form three, I was drafted into the Penang Champion Team (Penang Fisheries Association Club Team). At first, I was a reserved player because I was new to the team and was only seventeen years old. In one of the matches, one of the older players was not performing well, and I was directed to replace him in the middle of the game. My dribbling and shooting ability mesmerised the couch. From that replacement onwards, I was a regular starting five. This achievement and experience gave me a critical lesson in sport. Any skill whether in sports or industrial skill, requires repetition or drill to achieve perfection or near perfection. The standard of play of the school basketball team was gathering momentum as an outstanding school basketball team. By the time I reached form four, the team emerged as the champion team in the inter school competition. The school boasted in having two state players: Sunny Leong and me. In 1959, Sunny Leong was an outstanding Penang State player, and he represented Malaysia. After form five he left for Australia for further studies. He was never seen again in the basketball court. This is the first time in the history of basketball inter-school competition in Penang state that an English Afternoon School became a champion team. The prominent schools were usually Chung Ling High School and Han Chang High School. They played in the Penang senior basketball League. This is an extra feather to my basketball achievement. During these few years while I was studying in Penang, I helped my hometown team to become the champion team in South Kedah basket inter-team annual competition held in Kulim, Kedah. I represented South Kedah in the annual inter-district tournament: South, Central, and North Kedah districts. I was the outstanding player helping South Kedah to capture the inter-district tournament many times. I was also the most promising player from Kedah. In 1959, at the age of nineteen, I was drafted into the national team for training. The following year, I was selected to represent Penang State. My club team in Penang continued to dominate the Penang Senior League until I left for college in 1961. While on holidays, I still wore the basket jersey for Penang State team and Kedah

State team. While in TTTC, I was the star player from 1962 to 1963. Most of the players in college were only school players, and there is no much to crow about the team. We played many friendly matches and toured Singapore. In one of the matches against Day Teachers Training College in Seremban, I fell and twisted my left knee. I worked too hard in the game because the team was too dependent on me. This signalled the end of my basketball career as a state and national player. Most of the results of friendly matches during my college days were not outstanding. During college days, I also took up soccer and represented the college in the game. I was not very good at the game because I took it up too late. But I enjoyed the two years playing basketball and soccer for the college. I tried many games while I was in school and college. When I was in the university, I was also the star basketball player. I played in the inter university games. Other than basketball, I also played badminton and table tennis. I played these games reasonably well. I think I was very competitive. This factor must have motivated me to excel in any game I was involved. Tennis and golf were not within my reach during my school and college days. I was not financially ready for these two games as facilities were not available. I picked up tennis and golf when I was teaching in Petaling Jaya.

Playing Basketball during Secondary School Days

I believe I am one of the few lucky people in this world. While I was in Penang when I was about sixteen years old, I became interested in meditation. I thought I was involved in daydreaming. I was attending an afternoon school in Penang staying with my eldest sister. Every morning after my breakfast, I sat down to prepare my lessons for the day. I had a chair and a study table at a corner of the hall. I had an ideal place to meditate before I started my study. Meditation is just like a game, the greatest game, the game of human consciousness. I practise this game every day, and it becomes a routine. I began to find peace, and the silence gave me plenty of time to think and feel. After many practices I began to shift from thinking to feeling. I soon realised that it is living from the heart, not the mind, that is most fulfilling. I live each day from my heart centre. I find life more gratifying, more harmonious, and more joyous. My mind has filters and judgements, but my heart does not have such things. I practise conscious breathing from the heart and find peace and harmony. My name Sin Mong meant 'new dream' in Chinese reflects this dream given by my father. I did not learn formal meditation, but I was indulged in daydreaming by closing my eyes when I had nothing to do. I used to count number slowly from ten to one and repeat as many times as possible with my eyes closed until I began to visualise that I would be playing basketball in front of a big crowd in the future. This dream became reality in my later life. I also visualised that I would be playing in different towns, cities, and countries. This dream to excel in the game became entranced in my subconscious mind. It helped me to solve problems, changed habits, and practised creative visualisations. I did not only dream of this feat. I took action to realise my dream. I began to read about American NBA players and studied their training schemes. I made cutting of outstanding players and pasted them on my exercise books. Most of the cuttings came from old newspapers used by my father for wrapping goods. At that time, I did not have the money to buy newspapers. I had set my bold goals. When I started my schooling in Penang, I started to work towards these goals. There was a basketball court belonging to Penang Port Commission Club behind my sister's house. Every morning I woke up at 6.30 a.m. From 6.30 a.m. to 7.30 a.m. I began my basketball training in dribbling and shooting all alone. Students cycling to schools used to wave at me, and they provided me the inspiration to develop my skills in ball handling and shooting. Little did I know that these extra training in various skills came in useful when I started playing competitive games. I became one of the top players in my team in Penang, my hometown team and the state team. For a few years while I was a student, I was a star player, and my photos in shooting and dribbling appeared in local newspapers. I was well known to basketball enthusiasts in the states Kedah and Penang where I played very often in many tournaments. I remember once an enthusiast who was a taxi driver refused to accept taxi fare from me. He provided me free transport to play in Kulim, Kedah. I was so touched by his gesture. All the attentions and competitions in various basketball tournaments spanned over four to five years during my student days in Penang had made my life very exciting and memorable. I looked back with satisfaction that my goals in sports had fulfilled.

This little discovery in drilling and repeated practices in shooting can further be developed and perfected with modern facilities. With modern gymnasium with its training facilities, an athlete can reach optimum power not only in dribbling and shooting but also in enhancing his airtime by strengthening his leg and hand muscles. Consistent and regular fine-tuning can bring out the best possible performances and powers of any sportsman.

Any sportsman who aspires to excel can adopt this simple strategy of drilling and regular practice. Repeat a skill as many times as possible regularly to gain perfection. The digital age can help. Go into Google or other websites from your Internet to get further information regarding how to execute particular skills. Get DVD videos of expert players using that particular skills you try to develop. Put into practice your newly acquired skills by playing and competing with others regularly. To add to this advantage, try to develop your leg muscles to improve your airtime. Repetitive practice in particular skill development trains discipline and perfection. It helps to cultivate good discipline and habits. Practice makes perfect applies.

In reflection, my experiences in mastering my passionate game basketball can provide some evidences on how to improve and master any game you choose.

1. Try to study the history of the game. Choose the game that suits your physical endowment. Once you have chosen the game, try to develop your passion with skills development.
2. Study a few current experts on the game. You can get it through books, magazines, or videos. Videos are the best because you can replay particular skill where you can emulate in the same way. Without practice, all theories do not help. Try to play the game as often as possible. Join a club team and involve in competition. Besides competition, practise different skills through drill to cultivate conditional reflex or automatic action.
3. Take lessons from someone who has already mastered the game. This can help you to avoid bad habits. Allow senior players or coaches to criticise your current skills and try to improve them through repeated drill. It takes great discipline to master a game.

Mastering a game brings great benefits too. It builds discipline and let you socialise with people of all ages and backgrounds. It develops bonding among people with the same passions. Mastering a game helps to develop your instinct of a killer without having to kill anyone. Finally, mastering a game keeps you in good shape, an element essential for good health. Remember, mastering a game doesn't happen from inspiration. It happens from perspiration, discipline, and passion. It's the system of body muscles you need to build. Why not build it while your brain is still creating new neurons at breathtaking rate than learning it when you are older. To many people, it may be too late. To change your life and to develop your passion for any game, you have to start immediately when you are young. There is no exception. The simple idea is consistent practicing and persistent doing the same skill until it is automated.

Secondary Schooling in Penang

In the field of education I had a wonderful journey. This is really the spring season for my education. My season began the moment I started my formal schooling in Penang. I was enrolled in Methodist Afternoon School in Penang. I was free from the care and control of my father. Ther was no more working from morning to evening. I had all the time to explore a new dimension of my life. I was looking for ways to motivate myself to do well in education. I began to ask myself what I wanted to be and how to get there seemed to resonate. I was involved in daydreaming and later meditation. This is the technique for me to communicate with by subconscious. Every morning after my exercises in dribbling, shooting, and developing other basketball skills through drilling, I had a good morning bath. After a simple breakfast and drinking a glass of warm lemon water, I sat down on my desk to begin the day. Drinking a glass of warm lemon water was a habit encouraged by my grandmother when I was a young boy under her care. I enjoyed the benefits of healthy digestion, being alert, and good energy levels. I was excited by my new life, and I looked forward to each day instead of spending my time longing and hoping for better days. I woke up each morning with a bounce in my steps, a smile in my face, and a sense of purpose in my heart. I was ready to begin a new day by engaging in meditation first. I used to close both my eyes and start counting from 10, 9, ... until 1 and then repeat until I was cool and calm. Silence is one of the greatest answers to visualisation. Meditation requires silence. This provides me an opportunity to experience peace and calm for ideas to flower in my life. My Chinese basic education allowed me to know a little philosophy of Lao Tze, who said, 'Silence is a great source of strength.' I have found my personal routines that not only work for me but also enhance my focus in my study. All these activities helped me to set goals, to understand the importance of taking action, to visualise my dreams, and not to be afraid of rejection. I just never forget to discipline, to follow my dream and joy.

While I was a small boy, I seemed to have developed subconscious self limiting beliefs without realising it. These subconscious self-limiting beliefs, according to Natalie Ledwell, may fall into three broad categories:

> 'If I try, I may fail; No one will want me; and I am not worthy.'

In my short meditation, I wanted to access the core of these limitations and tried to eliminate them in my life especially in education. In each of my meditation stage, I visualised two pictures: one small one showing the failure I encountered and another one showing the success I could achieve. I began to visualise replacing the small picture of failure by a bigger picture of success. I kept on repeating the process of replacement by visualising a process to help me achieving this goal. My visualisation began to explore and dream of all possibilities: from being an excellent sportsman to a professional educationist. I could sense and visualise where I was heading. This ten to fifteen minutes mental training seemed to give me the necessary concentration and focus in my self-studying strategy. Bill Harris wrote in his book, *Threshold of the Mind*:

> 'The human brain has the quality of plasticity or malleability throughout life if it receives the kind of stimulation that allows it to grow and adapt.'

Each meditation appeared to be able to slow down my brain waves, bringing it down from high level to a very calm level, and enabled me to focus and learn my lessons subsequently without much effort. Distractions and interferences seemed to disappear. Each meditation session lasted only a few minutes, and it helped to awaken my inner potential. I usually had a good intention whenever I closed my eyes for each session and my creative visualisation began. The first few sessions of my meditation I focused on finding study strategy to help me achieving my academic pursuit. My short-term goal was to improve my English so that I could master all the subjects I was doing. I must have awakened my subconscious mind telling me to prepare lessons first every day before attending class. So each school day, after my short meditation, I started to prepare lessons according to my school timetable. I used my dictionary to help me understand each new word I encountered. Usually, it involved three or four lessons involving mathematics, geography, history, and general science. I was fully committed to this routine each morning before I had my lunch. This habit became my daily routine. I was eager to learn before I reached the school. This predetermined state gave me full concentration for each lesson. I felt happy and motivated because I was always in the state of preparedness and was able to follow each lesson closely and attentively. This important habit of awareness and pre-prepared lessons became my corner stone to academic success. I had started a mini-habit routine which I eventually built into a major habit in my later life. I was lucky by thinking small enough to get the strategy started. This habit soon became my self-study strategy which I repeated so often that it moved on autopilot during my school days. I spent almost an hour on each school subject to prepare myself for the day. All these routines and preparations gave me an advantage when I listened to my teachers explaining the contents of each lesson. All lessons in school were merely talks and chalk method used widely by most teachers. I believe that this method of teaching is still widely practised in most schools. I was able to follow every lesson closely because I had already gone through the content earlier. I even wrote down questions asking my teachers to clarify ideas or concepts I did not grasp through self-study. I think most my teachers knew that I was their exceptional student. When I was attended form two, I remember my English teacher who was at the time undergoing Normal Teaching Training and under supervision singled me out to answer questions when his lecturer observed his teaching method. I was obliged to help him by giving my best answers possible. I was an outstanding student in mathematics and general science. Being well prepared for each lesson, I was able to spot the calculation errors of my mathematics teacher. I knew very well that my mathematics teacher was not gifted in mathematics. He learnt first before coming to class. He had just finished his form five and passed the Senior Cambridge Certificate. He was not a trained teacher and struggled to make his teaching effective. I believe I had shattered a little bit of his confidence. But we got on well together. I used to help him checking his errors. Most of my teachers when I was in form two were just having form five qualifications with the exception of one or two retired teachers. I felt very happy in my new school environment because my personal routines seemed to work well for me.

I chose the following tips to keep me motivated and inspired. Whenever people asked me, 'How are you?', before I came to Penang for my secondary school, I usually told them, 'I am okay!' But after coming to Penang, I changed my tune. My response was, 'I am great!' The more I repeated these words, the more I believed it and started to feel great in every area of my life. I realised that I needed to change my routine once in a while. I could not keep practicing my basketball skills and keep studying. Once a week, I used to take a break and cancel my usual plans. I did something unexpected just to avoid routine fatigue. Once in a while I needed to spice up my life and tried something new like seeing a cheap matinee film on Saturday morning. I said 'yes' whenever friends invited me for picnic at the seaside. After the break, I usually felt rejuvenated and ready to start my routine again. I also learnt to release any negative energy I had accumulated throughout my childhood. When I started schooling in Penang, I was holding on a lot of negative energies such as fear, anxiety, sadness, and anger. Before I started meditation after closing my eyes, I usually took a deep breath. As I inhaled, I focused on my breathing in uplifting feelings of peace and happiness, and with each exhale, I released any tension or stress. After a few exercises, I was ready for my morning meditation and visualisation. Now I realised that the happy feeling I had increased my productivity, and it must have a huge effect on my success as a student. Soon thinking big just became natural to me. I had developed a positive mental attitude. I began to entertain thoughts of someday becoming a teacher myself. This soon became my immediate goal in my life.

I must admit that I was conditioned by my parents, teachers, friends, and the media with a set of beliefs that were silently influenced my reality then. Some of these beliefs were good, but many of the negative beliefs and paradigms were embedded in my subconscious mind. Initially, they were sabotaging my educational progress and my reality. My routine meditation each morning seemed to have awakened my inner potential and helped me to overcome these limiting beliefs. With my new environment, my daily optimised routine, the network of relatives, and friends' support, my confidence and progress took a great leap. My new endowment in creative visualisation gave me the direction for my future. I was an averaged student and more mature than others. I was ahead of the class because of my self-study strategy. Most lessons were imparting facts, beliefs, and theories. There was lacking in other aspects of education. Teachers were not trained to prepare students for real-life situations. We were not trained to think critically and creatively for ourselves. No lesson was given to teach relationship skills, thinking skills, and other living skills necessary to succeed in life. At this early age of my schooling, I could see clearly the educational gaps between school curriculum and the real-world situations. It would be good for the country if kindness, gratitude, love, and other values were included in the curriculum. At that point of time, it might be true that our educationists were not familiar with the benefits of these human variables could help students attain happiness, positive attitude towards life, better self-esteem, assertiveness, higher energy level, more willing to be creative, better well-being, and more willing to come forward to learn new things. The failure of our educational curriculum was glaring. I was lucky to stumble upon creative visualisation every morning during my short meditation before studying. The imagination I had in each of my creative visualisation helped to prepare me for 'out-of-the-box' thinking and helped me to make my dream a reality. According to Dr Bruce Lipton at Stanford University Medical Centre,

> 'It is your subconscious mind that "ultimately casts the deciding vote" on how much success, abundance,

happiness, health and freedom you experience in your life.'

He explains, 'Most people don't even acknowledge that their subconscious mind is at play, when the fact is it is a million times more powerful than the conscious mind and that we operate 95 to 99 per cent of our lives from subconscious programs.'

Before I came to study in Penang, I used to wonder why so many 'bad things' were happening to me. I thought I was a good boy. I was thinking that life was simply unfair. And I was not alone. I knew that the response to this question would have huge impact to my life. If I was not careful, this issue could lead me into a spiral of negativity and victimisation. On the other hand, if I could overcome it by believing in myself, it could put me on a path of self-improvement and transcendence. I began to believe that there should be some good reasons for the unfavourable things that happened to me when I was young. Many of the so-called bad things happened in my childhood must not be a permanent feature in my life. What could I do about them? I was in an environment where everything happening affected me. I was pulled in the thoughts, feelings, beliefs, ideals, and rationalisation of those around me. Everything I had accumulated became my reality, and I began to attract more things I grew up believing. These beliefs included relationship, finance, and others. Now I had a new environment. How was I going to change all that so that they no longer had any power on me any more? Change I must so that these events could become part of someone else's story. My perception of the world must change so that such events would not be a problem in my later life. I began to believe in myself, and I began to view that such 'bad things' were really gifts to me telling me to work on something. Many bad things included: people did not like me, my health was not very fantastic, my happiness level was sucking, my dreams were not manifesting, and others. I must not allow such things to repeat in my life. These were signs the universe telling me my realities and I was now responsible to clean them up. These were vital information the universe was telling me and I had to do everything to overcome them. I should be happy that something bad was happening. Yes, happy that I knew what was wrong with me! These events were pointing out the gunk in my life and giving me the opportunity to get rid of them forever. I knew I did not have a choice. I could not pretend I was an ostrich and put my head in the sand. I had to believe that the universe loved me and would keep showing me the patterns I needed to work on so that I could clear the bad events. Once I achieved that I would emerge and embrace the happy version of my life. I now believed that these so-called bad things were really gifts telling me to take action by fixing whatever came up. The success of the journey of my life would depend partly how I kept working on these issues and overcome them.

I was lucky to realise this important intuition that if my subconscious mind was not set for success, nothing that I learnt, nothing that I knew, and nothing that I did will make much of a difference. I was determined to change my subconscious limiting beliefs I inherited from my family background. By changing my subconscious programming, I had taken the first essential step to change my results. Armed with my new imagination, I ventured to 'rewrite' my subconscious blueprint to help me to become more confident, more creative, healthier life, and better goal in life. This was powerful, and it helped me to live the life I wanted. I began to experience a life filled with increasing success, happiness, excitement, and unforced motivation that I jumped out of my bed every morning, thrilled to be alive. I was revitalised by the inspiration of achieving my dream in basketball and in my academic pursuit. Constant practice of visualising what I wanted to experience in life seemed to produce fantastic results. Regarding visualisation, there was nothing new, strange, or unusual. I was using it every day because it was our natural power of imagination. We were busy most of the time, and we were not aware of it happening. The advantage of meditation seemed to bring out this phenomenon vividly, and I used it as my basic creative energy constantly. I realised that my nervous system had difficulty differentiating real memories and creative visualisations. This offered me the chance to 'trick' my subconscious mind to intentionally, effortlessly, and effectively improve the two areas of my life: sport and academic, by visualising about what I want to experience. I disciplined myself to constantly and persistently practise what I visualised in relation with my self-study strategy and my skills development in the game I loved.

I was actually involved in habit-stacking to create simple and repeatable routines both in sport and in academic. I had unconsciously created a checklist for my daily routine. I had been following my routine by doing the same set of things in the same order and same way each day. Linking these habits together, I was able to get more important things done in less time, resulting in positive change in my life. This awareness of spending my time effectively gave me the advantage in both fields of my interest. After my breakfast, I usually had a big glass of warm lemon water to keep me hydrated for the whole morning to follow my daily routine. My basketball couch instructed me to drink plenty of water especially after vigorous exercise in training. I had great respect for him, and I followed his instruction closely. According to him, even a mild dehydration can cause headaches and fatigue, affecting your concentration, impairing short-term memory, and impede mental function. I always made sure that I was hydrated sufficiently before I start my basketball skill training and studying. I had formed the habit of scheduling my day and prioritising my tasks. I realised very early that if I did not have a basic schedule, it might frighteningly easy to get to the end of the day and I achieved nothing of importance. Each day I had my checklist of tasks I wanted to accomplish. My priorities usually lied on the following: first meditate to calm down and refocus for the day. Thanks to the awareness that I could tame my random thoughts and change my emotion by relaxing my breath. My breath does indicate the state of my mind. I notice that when my emotions are high and my mind is not at rest, my breathing becomes unsteady and shallow. When I am relaxed and at peace, my breathing is usually slow, rhythmic, and deep. I practise this natural way of breathing whenever I begin my morning meditation. Next, all homeworks had to be done first before I applied my habit of self-study strategy following the timetable of the day. I would focus on the first three most important tasks so that I did not waste the day on tasks of low importance. I would touch on other tasks if there were time available to me. This habit seemed to have enhanced my productivity in study. When mathematics was involved, I would break each task into small steps and accomplished each step separately like solving a problem involving a concept just learnt. This reinforcement seemed to make learning different concepts effectively. I usually took a break after every thirty minutes by walking around for ideas. I usually kept my table with only books relevant to my study and kept other distractions away. Just before my lunch, all books were kept in my bag and in my bookself. The table was left clean for others to use.

I started with a wish that I could cope with my study, crystallise it, and do well. My attitude was essential to see my wish became true. After the first semester, my report card showed that I was one of the top students in my class. I had overcome the first subconscious self-limiting belief that if I tried, I would fail. I really tried and I achieved. My first obstacle was overcome. With the achievement I got after one year of applying my self study strategy, I managed to overcome my second subconscious self limiting belief that no one would want me. People were looking up at me now. The third subconscious self-belief, 'I am not worthy' had no ground to stand on. I started to form a long-term goal. I dreamt of a university education. But how do you go from dreaming to doing? How do I turn my dream into reality? I took action daily, consistently, and persistently. You need to follow my story closely. There were two other students in my class who were equally outstanding. Later on, one went on to join a Malayan Teachers Training College to become a trained teacher. The other joined me at the University of Malaya and went on to become a doctor. I finally obtained a bachelor of science degree with honours. Two of my classmates in form two were rather weak in their studies. One of them came from Perlis. He came from a reasonably rich family. They approached me to give them personal tuition in science and mathematics. They had faith in me. I agreed partly because by repeating the lessons to them, it would help me to remember the facts and enhance my understanding of the two subjects. In addition, I got some extra pocket money. I did not have to depend on my father any more. This arrangement went on until we finished form three, and all of us passed the Lower Certificate of Education with flying colours. Little do I realised that I had actually discovered an effective self-study strategy together with group discussion by circumstances. Not only I repeated the same lessons in science and mathematics to my classmates during tuition sessions, I also ventured to prepare them lessons in advance so that they too could follow school lessons closely like me. This arrangement provided me a platform to be assertive and assumed leadership role. Practising self-study strategy and leading a small study group changed my attitude and made me a more confident student. Knowing self-study strategy helped to change their attitude towards science and mathematics, and their confidence in the two subjects slowly gathered momentum. This shows that when you can control your mind, you shape your reality. Every student has the same ability to learn but just do not know how to get started. If you get the right teacher and the right strategy, you can get a jump-start with your own learning abilities. We were doing very well in form three. All of us passed the Lower Certificate Examination with flying colours. Three of us made an attempt to sit for Senior Cambridge Qualifying Test in English while we were in form three. This test was normally taken by private candidates in form four before they could sit for Senior Cambridge Certificate Examination. I was the only one managed to pass the qualifying test. I was allowed to sit for Cambridge Certificate Examination while I was in form four. I did not do so. I was patient enough to wait until I completed form five. Now I realise that patience is a virtue. I made a good decision partly because of my regular meditation helping my decision-making. I did not want to belong to the group of people who had problem with patience. All good things came to me because I could wait. I knew I was facing the right direction, and all I had to do was keep walking. I realised that I had a busy schedule in my basketball game. I was already a star player for my school team, my club team, my hometown team and represented the states both Kedah and Penang. I learnt to manage my time and stress. I learnt to trust myself in both study and game. I realised very early that the most important person in my future was me. Education was the key to my future, and I did not want to be the victim. Not only I excelled in my game, but also I completed form five with a string of distinctions in most subjects in the Senior Cambridge Certificate Examination. All these experiences of practices either in self-study strategy or in game skills leading to mastery needed consistency, persistency, diligence, and playfulness. Learning the lessons of mastery gave me a purpose to my life at the time. Practice consistently, diligently, persistently, and playfully provided extra ingredients for growth both physically and mentally. All these seemed to contribute to my well-being and happiness. Now I realise that happiness is essential for success in both my game and my study.

A change of environment and freedom from works enabled me to discover an effective self-study strategy during my early education. This general study strategy of pre-preparation can be modified and explored further to help students in secondary school to learn effectively. A little of training and practice will do the job. Instead of tuition, another alternative approach will be small group discussion. A little bit of leadership is required for group discussion to succeed. I feel strongly that school authority should initiate this move to develop this self-study strategy and group discussion technique. An effective system can nurture leadership quality, cultivate the team spirit, and develop cooperation and good training in communication.

While helping my classmates to master a simple self-study strategy to learn effectively and giving tuition to a few of my neighbour's kids, my interest in teaching was ignited. I wanted to be a qualified teacher and at the same time pursued my basketball career. I started looking for government advertisement asking students with Senior Cambridge Certificate to apply for teacher training colleges. While waiting, I attended FEC held in the evening. I completed lower six and sat for Higher Certificate of Education (HSC) in two principal subjects. I got through the two subjects: principal level in physics with chemistry, mathematics, and a pass in general paper. I didn't know that at that time with two principal passes, I could apply for a science degree course in the University of Malaya. Instead, I applied for teacher training because I wanted to be a qualified teacher.

Teacher Training at the Technical Teachers Training College

I was overjoyed when I was accepted as a candidate to follow a two-year course at the TTTC in Kuala Lumpur. The minimum qualification for entry to the college required a credit in English and three credits in other subjects. Now I think back, I was overqualified. I had a string of distinctions in Senior Cambridge Certificate. I passed my general paper and two principal passes in HSC. I should be in the university. Anyhow, I took up the training and was quite happy to pick up some new industrial art skills like woodworking, metalworking, electrical installation, drafting, bricklaying, welding, metal art working, and physical education. Two years of training passed, and I became a qualified teacher specialising in industrial arts. During the two years training and staying in hostel together, I made a few close friends with common interest. I was active in the student union activities. I served as treasurer for a year. A few of us formed a discussion group to pursue our interest in mathematics. This was the strategy I advocated because I found it to be effective self-study strategy. Each of us was required to prepare a topic in mathematics and made presentation for others to discuss and learn. I strongly believe that teaching a topic after preparation is the most effective way of remembering and mastering the topic. We managed to cover many topics because of our collective efforts. When I joined the University of Malaya later on, some of this group of friends were also there, working for their first degree. My good friend Leong Fook was one of them. He went on to win a Full Bright Scholarship in mathematics. He obtained his Ph.D. in mathematics from the United States. I was told that he became a mathematics lecturer in University Science Penang. Another friend I met and stayed together during university days was Yu Cheng Sun, a Chinese scholar from Taiping. He studied pure mathematics and Chinese studies. Another friend from the same college was Teh Pick Ching. We were together for three years in the university. Yu went back to teaching in Kuala Kangsar, Perak, and later became principal of the school. He studied pure mathematics and Chinese studies. Teh worked in the Curriculum Development Centre. He was given a scholarship to study his master's degree in the United States. When he retired, he lectured at the University of Brunei. I was the exceptional one. The others joined the arts faculty and studied economics, Chinese studies, and Malay studies. I joined the science faculty and graduated with a bachelor of science with honours in mathematics specialising in mathematical physics. Although I did not teach industrial arts after that, I did not consider my two years spent at TTTC a waste of time. In fact, the experiences gathered really enriched my journey of life. Many aspects of life like friendships and relationships do not come from academic studies. Interacting, caring, cooperation, and sharing have much to offer us to live a more satisfying life. I learnt to practise kindness and showed gratitude to those who had helped me.

Two years of hostel life at TTTC had a special impact on my life. I learnt how to manage human conflicts and how to manage human relationship. I remember the struggle for union power in student politics had an impact on my later life as a school administrator. I had made some enemies but also made some good friends. Most importantly, the struggle for union power provided me a platform for training in communication, critical thinking, and planning. When I became an administrator as principal, I was able to provide clear and direct communication to those under my care. Leadership, integrity, trust, firm, and understanding became my mission. I set my goals clearly for them to follow.

The two years spent in TTTC is rich with memory. It enriches my learning journey. It adds colours and human favours to my early stage of learning life. It is part of the history of my learning journey. Most of my lecturers in industrial arts at the college were from Canada, under the Colombo Plan. The principal of the college was Mr S. P. Didote. He had a bachelor of science degree in industrial education from Bradley University, Peoria, USA. He lectured us electricity, electrical installation, and pedagogy. Being a science student, I took special interest in the subject. I was rewarded with high distinction in the subject. Another lecturer Mr J.M. Stokotelny lectured us pedagogy and technical drawing. Mr R. J. Toutant lectured us in art metal and pedagogy. Both of them had a bachelor of science degree in industrial education from Bradley, Peoria, USA. Mr R. J. Sutton lectured us woodwork and pedagogy. He held a bachelor of science and a master of science in industrial education from Stout University, Minominie, USA. The rest of the lecturers were from local universities and colleges. I did not have much aptitude towards these subjects. I passed all of them with credits with an exception of distinction in electricity.

According to Mr S. P. Didote, skill training was not a new thing and was practised in the West under different names. In the United States and Canada, they called such training as industrial arts. This type of practical training commenced at grade 7 or form one and might be carried on until grade 12 or form six. Industrial arts is a broad-base programme, and it does not offer any depth in training. Not all schools offer such programme in their curriculum. The inclusion of industrial arts programme in some school curriculum enables students to experience several skill subjects.

The exposure to these skill trainings provided me a better and a wider choice in my career. Industrial arts education became part of my general education. All these exposures enabled me to decide my career according to what I like and according to my ability. The objectives of learning industrial arts are to experience practical skills to enable students to make vocation selection wisely; to acquire skills that are useful in everyday life; to encourage creativeness and design; to bring about an appreciation of materials, machines, tools, and processes of industries; and to develop self reliance, self-discipline, and resourcefulness, safe working habits, cleanliness, and orderliness. I believe I had acquired a more rounded education. All these extra information and skill training served me well when I started a family. Many of the skills are useful in my house maintenance and upkeep.

Developing Ways to Increase My Will Power

When I was in the secondary school in Penang, I was lucky to stumble into various ways I could increase my will power to succeed. Most people I know are lack of self-control. Most people like to claim that they have will power but my observation tells me that they are the people more likely to give in to temptation. I had many schoolmates who were smokers. They told me that they could easily give up smoking because they had will power. But the truth is that they are the people who suffered from relapse when tempted. Many of my fat friends who were overoptimistic dieters, but they were the ones least likely to lose weight. I am lucky to discover earlier some secrets that help me to succeed in my education and basketball game.

First, I accidently came to realise that good habits were critical to help succeed in my life. A few minutes of meditation every morning before I started preparation my lessons for the day gave me a clear and calm mind regarding my mission for the day. The discovery of my self-learning strategy was actually a keystone habit which became my magic bullet to succeed in my education. The habits of practicing my dribbling, shooting, and other skills eventually became my weapons in competition. I always had an advantage or 'one-up' when these skills became automatic weapons. These habits did not only give me more discipline but also help me become more productive and patient in my study and games. They spilt over, and they made it easier for me to form other good habits in life. All these habits formation provides the ground for my self-discipline in my later life.

Second, I learnt to do important things first early in the morning. Soon I discovered that I too had limited will power. It was highest early in the day, but as I made decisions, it emptied like a gas tank. Until today, I try my best to do the most important things first. As the day goes on, it will only get harder to face big challenges.

Third, I discovered that I did not use will power when something was a habit and my behaviours were automatic. My drill involving practice in dribbling and shooting in basketball were clear habits that did not require will power. It takes a lot of hard work and time to build new habits. You can manipulate your environment so as to make what you should do easy and what you shouldn't do hard. In study, always open up the page you need to master ready and put your comic book away. Always try to make it easier for you to jump-start a positive change by lowering the activation energy for good habits you want to adopt and raise it for habits you want to avoid. Do not overdependent on your will power.

Fourth, exercise your will power muscle regularly. If you compare your will power with your muscle, you must not use it too much as you will get tired and give up. But by exercising it, over time, it gets stronger. A good method is to make use of your habits to build will power. Research has shown that students who practise good posture by sitting up straight seem to strengthen their will power and perform better in their tasks. Those who have the habit of slouching without being reminded to sit up straight do worst in their tasks. These tasks have actually nothing to do with posture but will power.

Others such as fundamentals like eat and sleep can influence will power. Improving will power is as easy as eating and getting enough sleep. An easy way to boost self-control is just eat something. If you want to wake up full of will power, then you should make sure you have enough sleep at night. If you have not enough sleep, it will result in less self-control. By putting things off that you enjoy is another way of enhancing your self control. The art of postponing instead of say no can help too. Test yourself by adopting 'not now, buy later' is better than 'no, you can't have it'. I believe that anything other than just giving up helps to strengthen your will power. So delay, distraction, or even caving in in a defined way can strengthen your will power muscle.

Finally, if you give in to your temptation, it's okay. That does not make you a defeatist. What matters is what you do after. Adopt an attitude not to blame yourself for giving in. Instead, show self-compassion will increase your self-control. Study after study reveals that self-criticism is consistently associated with less motivation and worst self-control. It is also one of the simple biggest predictors of depression, which drains both 'I will' power and 'I want' power. In contrast, self-compassion - being supportive and kind to oneself, especially in the face of stress and failure - is associated with more motivation and better self-control. It is well known that people who cut themselves slack go on to keep trying and end up succeeding.

Two Years of Teaching Industrial Arts after College

After two years of intensive industrial arts training and pedagogy, I became a qualified teacher in the eye of the Ministry of Education. I had got a license to teach in government schools. I was posted to a secondary school in Sungei Petani, Kedah. I started my teaching career as an industrial arts teacher for two years in a secondary school. It was a new school, and it took me a few weeks to get a room for technical drawing and a workshop for woodworking. Most of the tools and equipment were given by the Canadian Government. As soon as I started teaching, I was preparing to sit for my full HSC Examination. I was thinking big. My goal was to pursue a degree in science in University of Malaya, the only university in Malaya then. I started attending practical lessons in physics and chemistry at FEC in Penang, a city about thirty kilometres from the town I was teaching. I was busy studying, teaching, and travelling for almost two years. Finally, I passed my HSC examination in the following subjects: physics, chemistry, pure mathematics, applied mathematics, and general paper. I was given a place in University of Malaya. I was twenty-six years then. With a little bit of saving after teaching for two years, I left for the university to pursue a degree in science. At that time, a college-trained teacher was paid a basic salary of RM310 per month and general degree graduate got RM430. An honours degree only got RM600 as basic salary. The difference is not that big. My fellow teachers appeared not very supportive for me to take up the course. Most science students will end up with a general degree because the course is generally tough, competing with young and good students from schools. Anyhow, I had already made up my mind to give myself a chance to fulfil my dream. In May 1966, I left Sungei Petani for Kuala Lumpur to continue my further studies.

I must admit that I love teaching. My ability to influence learning was shown during my secondary school days. When I graduated from a teachers training college, I had the security of knowing where I was headed. My future was secure. My dream at the point of time was to gain more knowledge. I knew that if I wanted to realise my goal as an educationist, I had to gain admission to University of Malaya, the only university in Malaya at that time. When I was teaching after graduating from TTTC, I was staying with five other teachers in a single-storey terrace house in Sungei Petani, Kedah. Some of them did not encourage me to pursue a science course because, according to them, it would be too tough. Even young school students in schools with teachers' guidance failed to make the grade at HSC level. Here I had to teach, mark papers, and not much time to study. In spite of the handicap, I managed to pass my HSC with good results to qualify for a science course. This may serve like an enviable position. Yet what I didn't count on was the uncertainty of life and what uncertainty of life could do to a person. I am aware that I do not have to know exactly what I am doing or where I am heading. I just have to be willing to take the next step. My goals are sometimes clear and powerful, yet sometimes with blind unwavering faith. I have a conviction, and I know I may have to bleed a little, cry a little, and sweat a little. I am ready to make the commitment. Not only there would be no income for three or four years, I was not financially sound after teaching for two years. With the small income as a college-trained teacher, I did not have much saving. If I did not make it, I would have lost valuable time and income. All the doubts and uncertainty kept circulating in my brain. In particular, I thought security was my friend and uncertainty my enemy. If only I knew then, as I know now, that that there is wisdom in uncertainty. It opens a door to the unknown and only from the unknown can life renew constantly. Deep in my heart, I wanted to be a more knowledgeable teacher. I wanted to explore my potential and to fulfil my dream of being a curriculum maker and an educationist. I embrace the principle of the wisdom of uncertainty, that is, everything happens has a reason. I was uncertain of my future. I used to imagine that I had an invisible thread in my hand. And I would be holding it all my life. It led where I needed to go for my greatest fulfilment, not where my mind, my fear, my expectations, and my insecurity told me to go. This invisible thread, though fragile as it appeared to me at the time, was my guiding force, leading me in the best direction I had. The risk was there. But being invisible, it guided me in unexpected ways - out of seeming uncertainty, there was hidden wisdom.

So the best way to strive and live, which I didn't know when I was twenty-six years old, was to embrace the wisdom of uncertainty. I believed that I managed to accomplish the feat by attuning myself to the following values: the feeling in my heart to follow my dream, a worldview larger than myself, a sense of empathy with others, a desire to be of service, an understanding that I was unique in this world, and an understanding that I deserved to be productive, happy, healthy, and fulfilled. I had to take my chance or the opportunity would never surface again in my lifetime.

University Education

Three years of science courses ended before I realised anything. I was doing physics, chemistry, pure and applied mathematics. After three years, I was awarded a bachelor of science degree. Without knowing whether I qualify for honours year, I was posted to teach in a big Malay Secondary School near Alor Star, Kedah. I taught applied mathematics to the first batch of form six students there for about four months before I joined the university as an honours year student majoring in applied mathematics. With the saving from the four months' salary as a general degree graduate and working as a tutor during my honours year provided the financial strength to see me through my last year in the university.

When I was in my first two years in the university, I spent each of the three months long vacations, helping my mother managing her sundry shop. I gave her new ideas how to make trading more efficient. I rearranged the setting making the display more prominent. My mother was quite impressed and wanted me to take over the shop instead of studying. At the time I was almost twenty-seven years, old enough to get married.

During school holidays, I gathered my younger brother, sister, and nephews for special tuition in a room next to my shop. They benefited learning a new study strategy using interaction and discussion. I also taught them my self-study strategy and encouraged them to use it when they were back in schools. My nephew's report card was transformed from red to black after one term holidays spent with me. My younger brother did well and went on to get his engineering degree from the University of Singapore. My sister came to stay with me later on and went on to get her bachelor of economics degree with honours.

After my first year at the university, I was running out of money. I applied for a bursary from the Kedah State Government. I was awarded a $2,000 bursary per year for two years to complete my second and third years. The state insisted that I should provide a guarantor for the agreement to serve the state for Five Years. My nephew's father, my second brother in-law, was asked to be my guarantor. He asked me why I wanted to be tied down to work in Kedah. He gave me $4,000 and asked me not to accept the bursary. I was delighted because I was free to work anywhere I like after my graduation. I am very grateful to him. I remember that after teaching for about one and a half years, I returned the $4,000 to him. He appreciated my effort because I turned his son from a weak student into a promising scholar. My nephew went on to get his degree in statistical economics from University of Malaya.

I was doing well in the university. Initially, I was doubtful of my ability, but after one semester, I was full of confidence. Most subjects I did from first to third years were rewarded with distinctions and credits. I worked hard, and I was rewarded. I was very focused and determined to make it. I was selected to do my honours year and finally awarded a bachelor of science degree with honours. I dare to dream big, and my dream had become a reality.

Playing Basketball at the University

When I joined the university, I had already passed my peak as a basketball player. I had knee injury, and my performance was below my best. The first day in the university, I met a Penang player who knew me as a state player. He asked me to come for selection for the university team the next day. Without much ado, I was included in the university team. Again I became a star player for the team. My shooting and dribbling skills still dominated most of the matches I played for the university. I played in the inter-college tournament every year. The university team was too good for the other colleges. We also played in the senior basket league in Selangor State. The university team made its annual tour of neighbouring countries every year. I really enjoyed each of the tours. In 1968, we played in the inter-university games held in Hong Kong. Facing strong opponents from Singapore and Hong Kong, we still managed to win the championship. I was one of the outstanding players chosen to represent the Combined Universities' team to play against the Hong Kong city team. I was chosen to captain the team and directed to control the pace of the play. We did well to give them a good fight and finally won the match. My contribution was valued by the couch from Hong Kong. How do I regain my confidence in my game? Confidence is a funny thing in sport like basketball or tennis. Before the inter-university games, I actually worked on my confidence. One of the ways I used was to work on basic skills like dribbling, shooting, and passing. I improved my mobility by doing regular skipping and shadow-boxing. All these improvements required technical inputs as well as the right mindset in order to make the changes that allowed me to regain my confidence.

Playing for the university team for more than three years seemed to enrich my university life. I made some very good friends until today. Many of them went on to become doctors, engineers, and businessmen. When I was principal of La Salle High School later on, one of my team players who was a successful developer gave my school a badminton hall because of our relationship. When I started teaching in Kuantan Pahang, some of my basketball teammates rented a house and stayed together in Petaling Jaya, a city next to Kuala Lumpur. Most of my weekends, I came down to stay and play basketball with them. This offered me a chance to see my girlfriend regularly. This arrangement only ended when most of them got married.

Meeting My Soulmate at the University

For the first three years at the university, I concentrated on my study. There was practically no social life for me. My sole goal was to get my degree. Because of financial constraint, I chose to stay outside the campus. Three of my friends and me shared two motorbikes. We lived together for three years. I remember during my first year, four of us shared a room to reduce cost of living. Only from second and third years onwards, two of us shared a room. We managed to stretch our money to reduce cost. For my first three years at the university, my life was restricted to study and basketball. The latter kept me fit and healthy. Most of my time was spent in the library because of the hot weather. I played basketball three times a week in the evening. Most matches in tournament were played during night-time.

My romance started during my honours year. After teaching four months in Alor Star, I had some saving. So I chose to stay at First Residential College. My girlfriend stayed at the nurses' hostel behind the First Residential College. I had a small Honda motorbike. It was convenient for me to attend lectures. Most evening I used to carry my girlfriend out to the garden or shopping centres. This was the best year of my life. I was in love and preparing to settle down. I was almost twenty-nine years old. I had fallen in love a couple of times, but I did not have the courage to propose to the girls I admired. My girlfriend was doing her first year nursing course. Our relationship soon grew into love. I was ready to experience love in every moment of my life. This was the opportunity of my lifetime. I was ready to propose to her, but I did not have much confidence. I was ready to get any setback if the answer was no, and I was ready to move on in my life. I realised that I should instead concentrate on my honours year's study. My past experiences served as good lesson for me. I learnt early that relationship meant something complete, finished, and closed. We had a good relationship. We could talk about everything. So let it be a relationship, and I should not pursuit further. I played my basketball game as usual, and I went to the library very often to concentrate on my study.

Everything changed when I received a phone call at my residential hostel. I was wondering who made the call. She talked to me happily and wanted to see me. I was thinking she might need transport from me to do some shopping. I was not sure of her motive. Anyhow, I obliged and visited her again at her hostel, which was behind my residential hostel. We went out in my Honda motorbike. We were both very happy going out together. Most of the time I was very careful because I knew my time in the university was limited; I had only a few months before I graduate. I really wanted to know whether she really loved me or just using me as a convenient transport minister. I asked about her boyfriend who was a medical student. She explained to me that he was a classmate of her sister in form six in Alor Star, Kedah. He was not her boyfriend. I told her that I did not come to see her for many days because I did not want to interfere in her relationship with the medical student. I began to trust her because of her simplicity, sincerity, and great friendship. I grew to like her and eventually fell deeply in love with her for being very trustworthy. Finally, I proposed to her, and she accepted my love. This was the happiest moment of my life. I discovered early that love is never a relationship; love is relating. I imagine that love is always a river, flowing unending. I also realise that love knows no full stop; the honeymoon begins but never ends. I started to prepare for my new beginning, welcoming love in my life. I was determined to see that love is not like a novel that starts at a certain point and ends at another point. We agreed that love is an ongoing phenomenon. We made that commitment to let love continue wherever we go. We had been seeing each other very often, and we enjoyed every moment of our outings. Time marched on.

All good things soon came to an end. I graduated and was posted as an applied mathematics teacher in Kuantan, a town about 160 kilometres from Petaling Jaya. I still had my teaching contract with the government because of my two-year teachers training course at the TTTC. I had served only two and a half years as an industrial arts teacher and about five months as general degree teacher. I still had another two years teaching contract with the Ministry of Education.

CHAPTER FIVE

THE WONDERS OF THE SUMMER SEASON OF MY LIFE

Two Years of Teaching at Kuantan, Pahang

I enjoyed my spring season in my life as I journeyed from secondary school, teachers training college, and then university life. The season offered me opportunity to equip myself with enough skills, experiences, and knowledge to start my professional working life. I also learnt how to avoid people's bad ideas. With such a long period of preparation, I was ready for my working life. This new stage of my life was full of challenges and pressure. This was the summer season of my life. I could feel the heat and the responsibility coming. I said myself that I had always been on the right track. Everything I had done till this day, I had to do it. Every decision I had made whether I liked it or whether it gave me a great experience or great lesson, I needed to make that decision. I had to make the decision to get me right here. Just before my graduation, I received a letter from the Ministry of Education directing me to report for duty at Technical Institute in Kuantan, Pahang. I arrived at Kuantan in January 1970. I did not know anybody there. I put up at a local hotel for a night, and the next morning, I reported for duty at the institute. In the institute, I met Mr Chin Shin Peng, who taught pure mathematics for form six, and I was supposed to teach applied mathematics. He helped to get accommodation in a friend's home. I rented a room from his friend. My formal working life began.

Mr Chin had a bachelor's degree in pure mathematics from the University of Adelaide, Australia, where he studied under the Colombo Plan, sponsored by the Australian Government. He was an excellent teacher in pure mathematics. I adopted his teaching strategy focusing on immediate assessment after every chapter. His strategy appeared effective. Students were put under stress all the time, and they had to learn to manage their stress. Perhaps they also learnt to manage their time and learnt to trust themselves. In addition, I introduced my own self-study strategy to my students hoping that they, too, like my student's days, could learn effectively. Occasionally, I picked a few students to make presentation to ensure they pre-studied the lesson before coming to class. This emphasis had made learning more effective for my students. The two years I taught there, the results were beyond expectation. Many of my students went on to become engineers, science, and mathematics graduates.

Besides teaching, I was given the responsibility to prepare the institute basketball team for the state league. I was the couch-cum-player. I was still a good player at state level. While I was there for two years, the school team took part in the state inter-team tournament. I played along with the school players. I was actually better basketball player than the students because of my experience and exposure. The team did not do well because most of the players were inexperienced. Anyhow, the spirit of participation was there. The students were given exposure to such adult tournament of higher standard. Because of the exposure, the school team did well in the state inter-school basketball tournament.

A few teachers including Mr Chin were keen badminton player. I picked up the game during my two years there and became an average player. We played three times a week from Monday to Thursday in the school hall. Occasionally, the principal of the institute joined us in the game. All these activities kept me in shape.

I spent most of my weekends in Petaling Jaya, where my girlfriend had her nursing training at the University Hospital. Every Friday, when the school bell rang at 1.30 p.m., I was ready to travel to Petaling Jaya.

A few of the teachers there were in the same boat as me. So we used to make arrangement to travel together. For two years, I lived under such arrangement. Most school holidays I spent my time in Petaling Jaya together with some of my university teammates who rented a bachelor mess in Petaling Garden. This arrangement made it possible for me to be near my girlfriend. I really seized the moments of happiness, love, and be loved! At that point of time, that was the only reality in my world, and all else was folly. My world rotated around the girl I was interested in and the girl I loved.

My habit of meditation was still with me. The two years I spent in technical institute ignited my interest in education. My first year teaching applied mathematics to lower and upper sixth students was a success. I began my second year with great confidence. I had a great applied mathematics teacher who taught me at the FEC in Penang. I do not remember his full name. We called him Dr Cheah, a Ph.D. graduate in mathematics from Cambridge University. He played tennis and enjoyed his life in Penang. I learnt that he was the son of a very rich man in Penang. He did not take up any appointment in the university because he had everything he wanted. In one of my deep meditation before I took my afternoon nap, I visualised myself as the new author for sixth-form mathematics textbooks especially applied mathematics. The power of the mind fascinated me. I believed that I would succeed and actually I did. In my second year teaching applied mathematics, I emulated the teaching style of Dr Cheah. I used to come to class without anything. I did not follow the textbook which was very inadequate. I was able to humanise the teaching of applied mathematics relevant to everyday experiences. For example, when I taught Newton's First Law, I brought in daily examples to illustrate the law. Let us examine Newton's First Law, which states that everybody continues to be in its state of rest or uniform motion in a straight line unless it is compelled by external impressed forces to change that state. I asked my students why a passenger fell backward when the bus made a sudden move forward? I wanted my students to experience mathematics in everyday life. Students' fear for applied mathematics was evident! I encouraged them to think creatively. I also encouraged them to dream creatively. Most of the time I tried to impress on them that they were what they think. This aspect of education encouraging thinking was neglected in the school curriculum. It takes a creative teacher and a curriculum maker to complement the examination-oriented curriculum.

Let us examine Newton's First Law again. Why is a passenger in danger of falling backwards? The upper portion of the body continues to be at rest while his feet in contact with the floor are carried forward by the moving bus. So he falls backwards. Most students experienced that while standing in a bus. This only accounts for the first aspect of the law. What about the second aspect regarding uniform motion? Say when a bus is travelling at a constant speed and it suddenly applies brake when facing danger, what happen to you? Why you are thrown forward? The reason is that your body is moving with the speed of the bus before the brake. Discussion and speculation by students helped them to experience mathematics. This surely enhances learning through the process of humanising the teaching of mathematics. I taught my students not only mathematics but also imagination. I told them to imagine that they were sitting in another planet and were looking at the planet Earth, what they would see? They knew that the Earth orbits around the sun. So the Earth is moving with certain constant speed. People on the earth do not realise that, thinking that the earth is at rest. Therefore, more specifically, when I place a marble on the table, the object will be at rest only relative to the earth. The concept of relative motion and relative velocity emerges as an important experience in life. If Newton's observation is right, why, when I roll a marble on the floor, the object eventually comes to rest again? It is supposed to continue moving with a constant speed. Why? Their experiences in speculating enhance their learning. Here there are opposing forces such as frictional force, air resistance, and energy required for rotation and others which act on the marble, bring it to rest relative to the floor. These external and internal forces cause the marble to come to stop. Imagine that if you can find a perfect place on the earth where the floor is perfectly smooth and there is no air resistance and other forces, then the law asserts that the marble will continue in motion uniformly. But such conditions do not prevail on the earth, and therefore, such uniform motion does not exist on the earth. Because of such situation, most of us do not conceive such a concept. It takes a great and creative mind like Newton to realise that and refine it as a law of physics. I used to pose them another question. What happens to a rider on a fast-moving motorcycle if the front wheel strikes an obstacle and stops moving? According to Newton's First Law, the rider continues in his motion even the motorcycle has stopped and there is practically little force to stop him from moving. The head of the rider moves with the velocity of the motorcycle at the instant of the accident, but his feet and hands are in contact with the machine, resulting in lessening the velocity of the lower part of the body at the instant of collision. Hence, the rider's head goes forward and hits the road first. Now you know why you need to wear a crash helmet to protect your head.

I will show you another example illustrating how I humanised the feeling of frictional force. When I placed a block of wood on the table, I told my students to imagine that they were the block of wood. The explanation goes on like this: first, when I place you on the table, what is your first feeling? Yes, you feel that somebody is supporting you otherwise you fall because of the force of gravity. I will draw the cross-section of the block of wood resting on the table. The weight of the wood is represented by mg, where m is its mass and g is the gravitational force per unit. This force is acting vertically downwards. The feeling that the table is supporting you is indicated by the reactional force R acting vertically upwards. So you are balanced and at rest. Therefore, R =mg.Now if I tie a string at the centre of one of the surfaces of the block and start to pull the block forward, what do you feel? You have to imagine that you are the block! Yes, there is force resisting your movement forward. You can feel it. What is that force tries to prevent you from sliding forward? That force is the force of friction acting horizontally. I will indicate that invisible force by the symbol F. So F is the frictional force. I will slowly increase the pulling force in the string that is the force tension in the string is increasing. What is your feeling? Yes, the frictional force appears to be increasing! As I gradually increase the pulling force, there will come a time when the block begins to move. What does this phenomenon tells you? Yes, the frictional force between the block and the table has a limiting value. The value is known as the limiting frictional force. So the general conclusion is that when two surfaces in contact, there is always a limiting frictional force preventing the block from sliding. This limiting frictional varies from surface to surface. The horizontal tension of the string at the moment of sliding will represent this limiting frictional force. Why? This limiting frictional force divides by R is always a constant for two given surfaces. This characteristic constant is recognised as the coefficient of friction. Different surfaces of materials will have different coefficients of friction. To help students feel and realise this difference, concrete experiences will help. In physics laboratory, this type of experiment can easily be carried out. Throughout my teaching experiences, the humanising effect does play a role in feeling and understanding applied mathematics.

Another aspect of teaching embraced by me is to promote inquiry and imagination. For example, when I introduced relative motion, I usually brought in Einstein Theory of Relativity in very simple form. Imagine that there are infinite numbers of universes, each with its own stars, inhabitants, and system of beliefs. This imagination is found in the 'Puranas', a collection of ancient Hindu texts, which believed that there are infinite number of universes, each with its own stars, planets, inhabitants, and gods. Imagine that we can travel faster than the speed of light and we can indulge in travelling from one universe to another. A man in his thirty has a son who is five years old. He goes on into space travel. Relative to him at the new universes he visited, he has spent twenty years in his life travelling. As he travels, he gains time. He comes back to the earth and now he is in his fifty. But relative to his son on the earth in our universe, the duration is more than fifty years. When he returns to our planet, his son is already fifty-five years and he is only fifty. Now his son is older than him. Can you think of such imagination? This is the beginning in the exploration of time, space, and relativity. Promoting imagination and thinking not only makes the subject interesting but also inculcates the thirst for more knowledge and skills. I am not an expert of motivation. In 1959, Dr David J. Schwartz wrote his famous book *The Magic of Thinking Big*. He had given me useful methods of getting the most out of my job as a teacher. I learnt how to think positively, knowing that I am what I think I am. I started to dream creatively and think like a leader in the educational field. I dreamt of taking the lead in curriculum reforms and strategies for mathematics curriculum renewal. I dreamt of producing curriculum materials to make learning simple and interesting. This was the beginning of my awareness that ideas were linked to wealth. Can I use ideas to help students learn and in the process of making me wealthy? I also dreamt of helping students getting rid of the fear of applied mathematics. I learnt to create new ideas so that I can sell them at the highest value possible. I wanted to be an idea machine to help me become rich. All these seemed to manifest themselves in my deep meditations subsequently. All these dreams became my ultimate goals in life. Even at my initial teaching career, I believed I could succeed and eventually I did.

My thinking appears to reinforce what Marianne Williamson said in her best quote:

> 'Your playing small does not serve the world. There is nothing enlightened about shrinking so that other people won't feel insecure around you. We are all meant to shine, as children do. We were born to make manifest the glory of God that is within us. It's not just in some of us; it's in everyone. And as we let our own light shine, we unconsciously give other people to do the same.'

These basic beliefs were passed to all my students in my first two years of my teaching. Too many of us underestimate our own potential and shrink away our own dreams and what we are truly capable of. We have to learn to trust ourselves and believe in our abilities. Let the infinite power of the mind bloom. The two batches of students taught by me went on to do well in their HSC examination. I met some of them who were engineers when I was teaching in Petaling Jaya. There are many other examples which I will illustrate as you follow the journey of my life.

Teaching Life in Petaling Jaya, Selangor

After two years of teaching in Kuantan, I applied to the Ministry of Defence for a post as a captain in the army. My application was successful, and I was supposed to report for physical and weapon training at Port Dickson for three months before taking up the post as an education officer with the rank of captain. Luckily, my girlfriend and my deep meditation helped me to make a good decision. I rejected the offer. Instead, I took up a teaching post at a La Salle High School, in Petaling Jaya. Brother Lawrence was the brother director there. He welcomed me and made me in charge of sixth forms there. The year was 1972.

I rented a room from a family in Section 17, Happy Garden in Petaling Jaya. I had two years of teaching experience in mathematics especially applied mathematics. My experience was my asset when I started teaching in La Salle High School. The first batch of form six students was at upper six, and they did not have a qualified mathematics teacher guiding then when they were in lower six. They were overjoyed when I started teaching them with such confidence. I had to teach not only applied mathematics and pure mathematics but also physics. I did physics in my first and second years in the university. My honours year optional subject was mathematical physics. I was able to handle physics at sixth-form level. Imagine a class had to face me most of the time, five days a week. I took it as a challenge. The students were happy because they had an excellent teacher who made learning easy and fun.

I always thought that I could make a difference in the educational field. I did not have a diploma in education but a certificate of education from TTTC. Since I was teaching in Petaling Jaya next to University of Malaya, I enrolled as a candidate for a master's degree in education, specialising in mathematics education. I had to attend lectures every weekend for a year, and I had to produce a dissertation in my special field in relation to instructional strategies. After two and a half years of research and studies, I was awarded a master's degree in education. It was a joyful occasion. I remembered my mother, together with my father-in-law, attended my graduating ceremony. At the same time, my son was born. My first kid is a girl. We had a big celebration in my new home we had just bought. Looking back, such celebration is critical. We have to make it a point to celebrate our partner's successes. Such gesture can enhance relationship.

Life for me at that time was full of responsibility. The university had fifth residential college, and my house was the sixth residential hostel. Both of us were working. My wife was a theatre nurse at the University Hospital. We had a maid to take care of my two kids. My sister was studying for her HSC before joining the university. She stayed with us. My wife's two younger brothers and a sister were also staying with us. We had nine mouths to feed and to accommodate. I had a younger brother doing his engineering degree at the University of Singapore. He also needed my financial assistance. Our salaries were meagre, just enough to provide the basics. Luckily, I was at the right place at the right time. My reputation as a sixth-form mathematics teacher became known to most sixth formers in Kuala Lumpur and Petaling Jaya. I started a tuition class to help them achieve better results during my second year of teaching in Petaling Jaya. The class became popular and attracted a big number of students from various schools. Most of my weekends were used for that purpose. This brought me extra income. I was able to put aside some for rainy purposes and for investment.

I had a passion for writing! When I was a secondary student, I dreamt that one day I would become a writer. That remained unfulfilled until then. If happiness is an expectation met, then a dream fulfilled is even better. I knew I had a good dream. I even knew that I had to dream because most people bothered to pursue their dreams with actions, achieve them. Usually, the mistake of most people is that they only dream but do not take action. Then it becomes daydreaming because they don't dream hard enough.

My dreams of becoming a curriculum developer began to materialise during my third year of teaching in Petaling Jaya. To me it seemed natural. I needed to explore. I was curious. I had to adapt to a new situation and use part of my brain that evolved specifically so that I could create new works. My first production emerged. My first textbook for addition mathematics for forms four and five was accepted by the Ministry of Education of Singapore and also the Ministry of Education of Malaysia. It became a standard textbook for both countries. Soon, royalty began to flow in, providing me extra money to start my investment ventures. I did not rest on one achievement alone. I began writing another textbook for applied mathematics for form-six students to fulfil another dream. Within two years, the book was adopted by the Malaysian Ministry of Education to replace the outdated mechanics textbook used for years in schools. My concept of humanising the teaching of mathematics especially applied mathematics was in display in my second textbook. Now I realise that wealth is the side effect of my idea machine. I dream to become such a machine and let my idea muscles develop fully. One good thing is that I enjoy every moment in my writing.

I had adopted a new concept of mathematics curriculum in a way which highlighted the role of the teacher in the making of curriculum. This new type of empowerment requiring the teacher as a curriculum maker might be totally new at that point of time. I was ahead of time. The modern concept of mathematics curriculum was well explained in my Ph.D. dissertation. In brief, mathematics curriculum involved students, teachers, actions and interactions in classrooms, schools, educational system, textbooks, instructional methodologies, and intentions. An account of curriculum materials including syllabus, together with students' lives over time and the teachers as 'curriculum makers', constitute the mathematics curriculum.

I was well rewarded for my first two textbooks. My idea machine did not stop. Production continued. Soon other textbooks like *Principal Level Pure Mathematics* and *Basic Statistics* for sixth form made their appearances. They were also adopted as form-six textbooks. Even some of the universities used my basic statistics book as an introduction to statistics. When the medium of instruction was changed into the national Language, all my textbooks were translated into Malay language. The challenges remained. My dreams continued to drive me in writing. I also competed with other writers in writing modern mathematics for secondary schools in the national language. I got my series of textbooks from form one to form five accepted. Even my new additional mathematics for forms four and five written in the national Language was accepted. I was not allowed to use my name in that textbook. So I made use of my sister-in-law's name. She was an additional mathematics teacher at St. John Institute at the time. The policy of the Ministry of Education was clear. They wanted the cake to be shared by many writers. Since I had form four modern mathematics textbook, I should not be seen as monopolising the textbook market by having my name in additional mathematics textbook used by science students in forms four and five. Anyhow, I did not bother. I was still entitled to my 10 per cent royalties. My publisher knew the procedure, and I was rewarded.

I was well rewarded with annual royalties, year after year, for many years. I did not stop. My dreams of producing other curriculum materials to make learning interesting and simple drove me on. Learning aids like revision courses for Lower Certificate of Education, SC of Education, and HSC of Education were published by various publishers. I even started a publishing company known as Hexagon Publishing to produce learning aids and marketing them. I was a very busy man trying to balance my job as a mathematics teacher together with my extra responsibilities in writing and conducting tuition classes during the weekends. I look back with great satisfaction because my efforts are well rewarded.

Investment Life during Working

After a few years of very busy life in my new environments, balancing family life with my teaching job plus extra responsibilities, my financial situation began to strengthen. The extra income from my tuition classes and my annual royalties gave us the initial money to invest for our children's education and our retirements. My purpose was clear. I dreamt of early retirement to further my education, to improve my writing skills, and to embark on another mission in life. I needed to adapt constantly to my new environment and used part of my brain that evolved specifically so I could create new wealth through various available investments. With this goal in mind, I started investing into properties using the leverage system. My royalties and extra income provided the initial down payments for two shop lots. Loans from the government and banks provided the rest. I did my investment mathematics well. The rentals were more than enough to cover the monthly instalments. After fifteen years, the two properties were paid up before I took my optional retirement. During these working years, my extra annual royalties and other side incomes provided me the initial sum for me to invest in equities. I was amateur then. The first few years, I lost some money and was discouraged. I did not give up. I started to do some research and began to formulate my own strategies to profit from my equities investments. My aim of investing in properties and stock market is not about becoming rich. It's about wealth. And wealth is never measured by my bank account. It's measured by how I worked, how I fulfilled it, and how is my life. It is about how I laugh, love, and enjoy this world. That's how I perceive wealth. The stock market provides everyone an opportunity to fulfil one's dreams and builds one's wealth. Anyone who wants to build wealth should embark on this mission. It's a challenge for anyone to accomplish something, earn something, and grow something. Another idea I used to increase my wealth is compounding. It is making money off the money I make. What is compounding? Suppose you own an asset that pays rental or a stock that pays dividend, you use the income to buy more of the asset. If you own more of the asset, you earn even more income. This process keeps repeating itself during my working days. It's a snowball effect. Reinvesting your dividends or rentals increases your income exponentially. Over a long term, it can turn even a small investment into a fortune. I am a living example. In any country, there is always a group of stocks that you should use to start compounding your wealth right away while you are working. That was exactly what I did when I was working for twenty-three years. Luck seems to smile at us after many years of investing; we manage to build our wealth and retire with financial security. My successful strategies were well documented in Chapter Two and earlier.

A Successful Career as a Teacher

I had a passion for teaching. I believed in myself. I started my teaching career well. The first two years as an applied mathematics and additional mathematics teacher brought me confidence and success. I started my teaching career in a high school on a right footing. When I was doing well as a teacher, I was approached by a Singapore commercial company to start a new career as an analyst. I could not make up my mind. I was told the potential was great in terms of financial rewards. I meditated and explored all possible aspects of my life. The uncertainties remained strong. I had the happiness of my family to think off. I was very committed to my teaching profession. I was doing well in school. I had started writing well, and my reputation as an innovative applied mathematics teacher was well recognised. My weekend tuition classes attracted big crowds. I was financially rewarded. On tops of all these, I was very happy with my profession. My annual royalties kept on increasing. So the final answer I gave was a big no.

Initially, I was the only qualified graduate teacher at the high school. A few years later, other qualified teachers joined the staff. Soon, we had the most formidable team of sixth-form teachers. The La Salle High School was recognised and considered the most successful sixth-form science school in Malaysia. We topped the national science results in the Higher

School Examination results. My service to the school was recognised, and I was promoted to deputy principal. Soon, I was promoted and made principal of another big secondary school in Selangor. The new school was about sixty kilometres from my house. I had to drive an hour to reach the school. I accepted the responsibility as a new challenge in my teaching career. Being a sportsman, I started to improve the school field and other facilities to attract more students to get involved in sports. In the afternoon, I encouraged teachers to play games like basketball and netball. I practised basketball with the students and teachers. We formed a teacher basketball team and played friendly matches with the neighbouring schools. The new school was famous for gymnastic. They were the national champion. My service to the new school was very short. I managed to bring some changes to the school. I started a Resort Centre equipped with English books to encourage students to read and improve their English. The fund came from a Canteen Day organised by the school initiated by me. Canteen Day was an annual affair at the La Salle High School in Petaling Jaya. The purpose of the food fair was to allow parents and ex-students to participate in school activities. Every one put in some efforts either financially or otherwise. The fund raised was used for the improvement of facilities and students' welfare. In the high school in PJ, a school Canteen Day could bring in $40,000 to$50,000 of fund. Surprisingly in a smaller town like Sekinchan, we managed to raise over $30,000 for the purpose. It was the first time in the new school history that such a full-scale food fair was organised. I had started the ball rolling. Hopefully, future principals would follow the footstep to raise fund for students' welfare and other critical projects for the school.

During the short period of two years in this new secondary school, I was selected to be the chairman of the fund-raising committee for Selangor and also Malaysian Schools Sports Councils. I was involved in a lot of travelling because the new school was far away from Kuala Lumpur. It was inconvenient. During the period when I was there, Selangor State was given the responsibility of organising the Malaysian National Sports Festival in Kuala Lumpur. The fund-raising committee was given the task of raising enough money to organise the national events. As chairman, I had to be in Kuala Lumpur many times a week to contact commercial firms for sponsorships and chair the committee meeting. The director of education for Selangor saw the difficulty I faced. I was then directed to take over as the principal of my former high school. The fund-raising committee chaired by me was given a year to raise enough fund to organise the Malaysian Interstate School Athletic Meet the following year. Back in Petaling Jaya, I was able to call for regular meetings. The committee was made up of school principals and a few department officials. I suggested three immediate projects: a singing concert at Stadium Negara, a 'Thousand Persons Dinner', and an appeal letter for denotations from companies and well-wishers. Without much opposition from the members, the three projects were given the green light. We were lucky that a big corporation Nestle agreed to sponsor the singing concert known as 'Malam Mesra **MSSM'**, that is, 'Fun Night for Majlis Sukan Sekolah Malaysia'. All the professional fees for the singers were sponsored by Nestle. To our surprise, the response was fantastic from all the school children around Petaling Jaya and Kuala Lumpur and the public. The concert was a great success, and the Selangor Education Department headed by Datuk Hussein was very pleased. The harvest was great, and we were ready to launch an appeal letter to all the companies and well-wishers for the Interstate School Sports festival. A thousand-person dinner was included in the appeal letter to companies and the public. To our surprise, Malaysian public including parents and companies took up all the hundred tables for the dinner held at the Shangri La Hotel, Kuala Lumpur. The appeal also gave us a handsome sum of donation for the sports festival. The committee had done a good job, and the State Department was ready to organise the sports festival the following year. I was given a pad on the shoulder by the CEO of the state for the job well done. During the sports festival, I was rewarded a sport coat to commemorate the occasion. In my school La Salle, we had fund-raising dinner almost annually at the Hilton Hotel or Shangri La Hotel in Kuala Lumpur. The 'Thousand Persons Dinner' with entertainment, mostly singing, was popular. Parents seemed to like it and they supported us strongly. Many of my school parents supported me for organising the **MSSM** dinner as well as my school dinner. There was a big La Salle crowd at the dinner. I wished to thank all of them from the bottom of my heart.

The students and teachers were happy, and they rejoiced when I returned after two long years. A friend told me quietly that the school was full of activities again when I returned. I had a plan for the school both in academic and in sports. My first big plan for the school was to improve the academic standard within three to four years. My second goal was to get most of the students to be involved in sports. Every student was encouraged to master a sport. It was important to be able to communicate in a crystal clear way the vision and purpose of the school I was heading. My focus was on the students and teachers including facilities to help their potential growth. I wanted to have the right and well-prepared teachers on the bus. This is the single most important factor for leadership success and for institutional success.

To improve academic standard, I started a staff development programme aiming to encourage every teacher to become 'curriculum maker'. Some teachers did not appreciate the programme because they had to attend in service courses during the weekends or in the afternoon if they taught in the morning and vice versa. This staff development programme aimed at helping teachers to be familiar with recent research findings encouraging them to promote inquiry and critical thinking in class room instructions. Lecturers from local universities and Ministry of Education were invited to provide input for the purpose. I believed strongly that the role of the classroom teacher is critical. The teacher is, after all, the point of contact between the curriculum and the students. The impact of any new programme or innovation on the students operates through the students' teachers. Therefore, maximising the teacher effectiveness is the most critical goal of education. Regular supervisions and discussions with teachers became my daily routine. The aim was clear. We wanted to raise teachers' effectiveness and made thinking part of the students' learning process.

My passion for sports compelled me to set goals for each sport. I knew that mastery of a sports required perspiration, consistency, persistence, discipline, and passion. In addition, it took time and training to master a sport. I tried earnestly to place the right teachers to take charge of each sport according to their interest. A goal-oriented programme was put in place. Training was mainly focussed on form-one students in any sport. The goal was to allow each student to master his chosen sport in two to three years. The programme's goal was to produce a formidable team for each sport or game within three to four years. This process would be allowed to replicate so that the school would have plentiful supply of good athletes or players with mastery skills year after year. This system was effective, and within a few years, the school won most of the inter-school team games including athletic meets. This seemed to boost the school moral and brought unity among students. They were proud of the school. This gesture was clearly revealed when big student crowd cheered the school team in each game to victory.

We also realised that to improve academic and sports standards, we needed good facilities. When I took over the responsibility of administrating the school, my first goal was to update and renovate the science laboratories. Five spacious and modern laboratories were in my plan. A new sixth-form block with six new spacious classrooms was in the blueprint. For two years, we were busy raising fund for the purpose. We had all types of fund-raising mechanisms put in place like Job-A-Long, Walkathons, Singing Concerts, Thousand Persons Dinners, Canteen Days, and other fund-raising projects. Being a missionary school and the property of the school belongs to the missionary, we got limited government's grant. The school also appealed for help from the public and other school associates to help building our dream. I began to explore my network of friends from the university. Luck was on my side. One of my ex-university basketball players agreed to donate partly a badminton hall for the school. He was a developer and a businessman. The school had to come out with 100k first, and he would pay the rest of the building cost. In honours of the main contributor, the hall was named after Datuk Chan Ah Chye. I was lucky because one of the companies initiated by my wife's partner came out with the money first to help me. The money was wired from Australia into my personal account, and I wrote a cheque, 100k, to the school development account. Payment was then made to the company building the badminton hall to start the project. I promised the Australian company that the school would pay back the money in stages through the renting of the courts to the public. Everything went as planned; within four years of my administration, these projects became reality. The canteen was also renovated and enlarged to cater for the students.

The students were motivated. All the noises of construction appeared to boost the students' enthusiasm in their studies and their sports. On the fifth year of my administration, the high school was the best boys school in Petaling District in terms of both academic and sports. Since my mission was accomplished, I was ready to take my optional retirement at the age of fifty-one. I was already a wealthy man with by rentals, annual royalties, and dividends from my long-term value stocks. Thus, I ended my twenty-three year teaching career with good memories.

To me, teaching is a calling, and this is my guiding principle in my twenty-three years of service. My only hope is that my legacy lives on not only in the students who now lead fulfilling lives but also in my colleagues who have become better teachers and principals because of their association with me. We used sports mixed with academic achievements as a means of raising the school's dignity, the status, and the spirit of the school. We were all very proud of the school spirit. We tried to make the students proud of the school. I believe that when students are proud of the school, they will do their best to maintain the name and standard of the school. This is a big step to cultivate discipline. Indiscipline occurs when students don't have a sense of ownership or loyalty to their school. Since we cannot insist on it, we need to build this quality in them - that the school belongs to them. My rallying point is that the students should be proud of their school. The best way forward is by sports and games with good facilities. Good academic achievement is a successful initiative in promoting good school attendance. Students' interest and support for the school becomes clear when they give their support to their school activities. Another big challenge for me as principal of the school was to motivate and mobilise the teachers in the school. I did it by setting a good example. Punctuality and discipline were given great emphasis. I had to do myself what I asked of others. Good relationship was essential for the success of most of the school projects. I knew I had to be firm and strict, but they must also know they could come to me for anything. I might have made some mistakes along the line. I remembered a teacher came to me late to ask permission to sit for her law examination. I told her to fill in the normal form though it was already late. I told her I would keep the form in case of trouble. She could sit for the exam as scheduled. Nothing happened, and she passed her exam, and now she is a famous lawyer. My duty as school principal was to work on the students. I needed to create a situation and an environment in which students' progress was possible. Good students and good sportsmen were encouraged to become role models in the school. To me, every child is special, and he or she is entitled to academic and physical progress. I am proud because I still cherish these memories that I succeeded in most of my educational missions. After accomplishing all these dreams, I realised that it's time to move on. Time to release and detach from every person, every circumstance, every condition, and every situation that no longer serves a divine purpose of my life. I believe that all things have a season, and all seasons must come to an end. I need to make a choice. So I chose a new season, filled with purposeful thoughts and activities. I planned to embark on a bigger mission to do research, hoping to bring about a wider curriculum renewal especially for mathematics and education. I was on my way to join University of Queensland in Australia. My next dream was to look into strategies to bring about mathematics curriculum renewal especially in Malaysia and Asia. I always treasure and feel good to have an end to journey towards, but it is the journey that matters in the end.

Office Politics Affecting Your Career

As I moved up the ladder of success in my chosen career in education, my observations and experiences revealed that one of life's greatest ambitions was to remain authentic. I realised early that I must not underestimate the many circumstances that would challenge my ability to be myself, particularly in my earlier career. I was lucky that I learnt early how to navigate office politics as a challenge. It became a big test of my character and my belief. Looking from the perspective of a principal plus experiences of a teacher gave me a predictable and vivid view about office politics. Especially for beginners in a career, it is much easier to see personal agendas, competition, false relationship, and even 'backstabbing' which can be costly and demoralising distraction. I had experienced most of these destructive forces at work when I started serving as a teacher, later as a deputy principal, and then as a principal. I remained authentic and believed in myself. The following are the tips I would like to share with you so that you can overcome these obstacles when you confront them in your career. Politics is everywhere and is present in your place of work. Be aware of it can help you from falling into the trap.

First, learn how to influence. Instead of being influenced by others, I was lucky that I learnt the power of self-control earlier in life. My journey of secondary education in Penang gave me a good start in influencing others especially my peers. My consistent and persistent habits in meditation, self-study strategy plus leadership in group discussion, and game skill training shape my will-power. I knew that influencing is an invaluable asset of leadership, but it is also complex to attain and wield. I stumble upon the secret which is the core of effective influencing. It is the art of building authentic relationships in your work or play environment. My interest in people was developed earlier when I helped my fellow classmates and my neighbours' children to study effectively. I was curious about others regarding their interest, motivation, and ambitions before helping them. In later life, I was able to extend beyond just those that might directly work with. This curiosity helped to shape my effectiveness as an influencer. I was able to build a broad and honest relationship across my environment as a school administrator. I always adopted an attitude that it was not necessary to agree on issues but I would remain respectful of others' views. The simple principle of getting to know people will more often than not smoke out disingenuous agendas.

Second, I learn not to resent others' success. This attitude was rooted in my life very early when I helped others to succeed not only in academic but also in sports. This sleeping giant called envy was slain very earlier in my life. I had no problem seeing people succeed in life. I always offered my congratulation. I had the generosity spirit planted in me early. I learnt this important habit early, and I enjoyed playing my long game. In my teaching career and, I believe, in almost every work environment, the least gracious people are the most unsuccessful. It can be tough to acknowledge others' success when you are highly competitive. I learn early that people recognise those who are generous. There is nothing more appealing than the genuine support of colleagues who are promoted. These moments can shape the nature of relationship for the better. It also sends a signal that you are above any petty jealousies. People who are bully and mean are usually insecure. They deny that but it's the truth. Be brave, confront them, and tell them so. You can change the whole situation but show kindness.

Third, I learnt to ignore the pack. My observations in most schoolyards, the challenges are easily be influenced by the working or playing environment. The temptation of jumping into the bandwagon of popular opinion or pack mentality exits. Each of us is shaped partly by our experiences with people. The perception of ourselves can easily be influenced. But most successful people are able to manage and build relationship with many and varied individuals, without being pressured, coerced, or influenced to join a destructive pack. I learnt early to remain a collaborative individual rather than a compliant groupie. I strongly upheld the simple principle of rendering help when help is needed. Experience tells that this gesture is always reciprocated.

Finally, I learnt to play the long game keeping in mind my goal in life. I learnt early to have a positive attitude towards my job and my responsibility. So I did not allow office politics to distract me from my long game. I learnt to ignore unnecessary and nasty comments regarding my responsibility. I knew my mission was to help others to learn and to succeed in life. So my attitude was to take every opportunity to build and maintain relationship across the working environments both within and outside my place of work. My exposure to competitive games and voluntary works provided me the capacity to work alongside people who faced different issue and challenges in their respective roles. I used to make it my business to initiate projects which were beneficial to the students and teachers alike. So I focused on my long-game objectives which helped to shape my judgement and helped to insulate myself from the petty politicians in my working place. If you need support, be gracious to provide it to others. Any gesture of kindness and helpfulness will be repaid many times. Hopefully, the above issues raised will serve to sensitise career builders regarding the handling of office politics initially.

If you believe in practicing generosity of spirit, at heart you believe in the power of an individual to make a difference and at heart you treat individuals with deep respect and want to see others flourish. Unfortunately, not all people do that. Many of us do not practise generosity of spirit are usually selfish. We are usually mean and very quick to make judgement. We are intolerant and sometimes big bullies. Partly we are insecure ourselves when we exhibit such behaviours. We want to claim credit for being superior and take credit for work that others do. Be aware of such situation and do not allow office politics to affect your career or profession.

What Predict Success in a Career?

It is well documented that academic abilities do not predict how well you do in life. But we know that academic achievements are necessary for you to land on a good job. So it appears necessary for us as educationists to explore the other social skills to be included into the school curriculum to help students succeed in their careers and become star performers.

Many big organisations used to hire high achievers from well established universities. They were puzzled regarding the performance of their employees. Not all of them are equally good at their work. A bell shape curve of performance is usually exhibited: a few outstanding, most in the middle, and a few poor. This puzzle persists regarding high achievers in the middle and poor sections of their performance. They do not turn out to be leaders in their work. What are the reasons for their failing to become star performers? One possible reason is proposed. The relative poor performances of students who score average grades at highly competitive schools suffer from a low self-confidence or low self-esteem from being small fish in a big pond. My experience tells me that the reverse can be encouraging. I was an average student in a low achievement school. I came out top, and that gave me confidence subsequently. Research reveals that even students who do not have high IQ in their class but obtain high grades share an attitude called 'grit'. They keep plugging away despite setbacks or failures.

Research involving a thirty-year longitudinal study uncovers relationship between behavioural variables and financial achievement. It is found that students with the best cognitive control had the greatest financial success in their thirties. It seemed that cognitive success predicted financial success better than IQ and better than the wealth of the family they grew up in. Cognitive control refers to the abilities to delay gratification in pursuit of your goals, maintaining impulse control, managing upsetting emotions well, holding focus, forming good habits, and possessing a readiness to learn. Grit requires good cognitive control. These variables explain partly their financial and personal success. Further researches into attributes that predict success pinpoint a constellation of abilities include grit and cognitive control, but go beyond. The abilities that set apart star workers from the average at work cover emotional intelligences spectrum: self awareness, self-management, empathy, good habits, and social effectiveness. Both grit and cognitive control exemplify self-management, a key of emotional intelligence. IQ and technical skills matter, of course; they are crucial threshold abilities. It's the distinguishing competencies that are the crucial factors in workplace success. The variables displace by a star performer is largely due to emotional intelligence. These human skills include confidence, striving for goals despite setbacks, staying cool under pressure, harmony and collaboration, persuasion, and influence. Those are the competencies require for success at workplace. I stumble upon this requirement that the higher you go up the ladder, the more emotional intelligence matters. So I was well prepared when I became principal of my school. I listed these competencies and tried my best to follow them in words and actions. In my school assembly each morning, I attempted to impart these life skills to my students. I told them stories regarding the importance of attitude and life skill competencies that would help them to succeed in life. Initially, it is your academic achievement and intelligence that get you the job, but your emotional intelligence, good habits, attitude, and competencies that make you a successful person. I gave an example of the important of attitude in order to succeed. I told this story to my students on many occasions.

A shoe salesman was sent to an African country to promote a certain brand of shoes. He arrived there, and he gave up when he saw the people without wearing shoes. So the company sent another salesman to do the same job. The new salesman had a different attitude. He saw the people without shoes as an opportunity to promote his brand of shoes to protect their feet. He persisted and promoted his brand of shoes, and finally, he succeeded to convince the people the need to protect their feet from the elements of nature. This approach was part of my contribution to breach the gap between academic achievements and emotional intelligence for success in life.

Another story I related during my short assembly speech regarding students not knowing their own potential. A few young eagers were brought up with a pack of chicken. For days, they were happy enjoying their food together. One day, a young eager looked up the sky; he saw an adult eager flying in a circle looking down at the pack of chicken. The young eager was thinking that he was a chicken. He told the others that it would be great if he could fly like the eager above. I told the students that many of them were just like the young eager not knowing their own potential.

Student Exchange Programme with Junshing College, Japan

I remember that when I was principal of La Salle High School, we had a student exchange programme with Junshing College of Japan. Every year, we received students from the college and placed them in foster homes for a few weeks. This valuable programme is once in a lifetime for the students. They stayed with Malaysian students and learnt their culture and their ways of life. The programme also encouraged relationship, and this might grow into everlasting relationship between two families. Some of the families would keep their relationship for life. In 1989, I led a group of about forty students to Kagoshima, a city on the southern tip of Japan. The group included my wife, my two children, a few teachers, and the principal of St. John Institute, Kuala Lumpur, Brother Michael Wong. We flew from Kuala Lumpur to Tokyo and took a connecting flight to Kagoshima. The vice chancellor of the missionary college is a nun, and she offered my family a bungalow staffed with plenty of provisions for our comfort. We were very thankful for such hospitality. The students including my two kids were distributed to various homes for their two-week stay. They had a magnificent experiences staying with Japanese families. The college also arranged various programmes for the students during the days. The teachers, my wife, and me were invited to many functions to make our visit exciting and memorable. I remember one of the old La Salle Japanese ex student who is a surgeon gave us a fabulous dinner in his apartment. The ex-La Salle students in Japan also arranged a round of golf for me and Brother Michael in one of the famous courses in Kagoshima. We wanted to visit other cities in Japan. We bought a two-week bullet train tickets so that we could travel freely in Japan for the period. My wife and me made Koyto our centre. Each morning, we took a bullet train from Koyto to the nearby cities like Nagasaki, Hiroshima, and others and came back to our youth hostel in Koyto in the evening. It was really a good experience for us. We also visited Tokyo famous Disney Land while staying in the youth hostel, which is the old Olympic village. Two weeks of adventure were soon over, and it was time for us to say goodbye to all the friends of the college. This trip is once in my lifetime experience. I always remember and value this memory. May be some time later, I will visit Japan again as a tourist.

Life in my school was not only studying. Sports were encouraged. We had many activities including visiting other countries. I remember our school badminton team which won the Malaysian badminton tournament was given a trip to tour Australia. The trip was sponsored by Datuk Chan Ah Chye. We were very grateful to him for such a gesture. They were many other trips for other winning teams within the country. They are too many to mention.

CHAPTER SIX

THE AUTUMN SEASON OF MY LIFE

Retirement Life

The month was March 1992. I began my optional retirement. The summer season of working life was over, and the autumn season of my life began. The pressures and responsibilities of my working life became part of my history. I was given a rousing send-off. All the facilities built by the school under my care were ready and used a few months ago. I waited for almost a month for the official opening by the Minister of Education. Four sets of ribbons were prepared for the following: the science laboratories, the new canteen, the sixth-form block, and the badminton hall with four badminton courts. I left with pride because I had accomplished my mission of providing better facilities for the students, and the school was the top boys school in the state. Immediately after the official opening, I left for my next mission: new experiences, growth, and contributions. My wife waited for me, and we left for Australia at the end of April 1992. The children were already studying in Australia.

We had bought a piece of land at Chapel Hill, and we built a nice home for ourselves. We are still staying at the same house now. The new home is in a very good suburb at the foot of the mountain named Mt Coot-Tha, the highest point in Brisbane city. The house is surrounded by hills covered by green trees everywhere. The air is invigorating, and the atmosphere is quiet. This is an ideal place for meditation, reading, and research. I have a new environment, a new beautiful property, where birds sing at dawn in extensive woodlands, and a garden just not big enough to build a tennis court. The edge of the garden is lined with palm trees and bisected by various types of fruit trees including guava trees, mango trees, and other fruit trees. The house is bathed by the rising sun. It offers tranquil shade provided by the trees. The weather is excellent. The summer is not that hot and the winter is just cool and it's nice.

My children were attending a high school nearby. I just got enrolled at the University of Queensland to finish my doctoral study. My daughter finished her form five in Petaling Jaya, Malaysia. She joined year 12 in a nearby high school in Brisbane. My son finished his form three in 1991 and sat for his LCE. Immediately after his examination at the end of September, my wife packed him to Brisbane. He passed his LCE with distinction in all the eight subjects including Malay language. He joined year 10 for three months until December. He sat for the year 10 final examination and he got through. When I arrived at Brisbane in April 1992, my son was already in year 11. My study began. Every morning I reported for my doctoral study. I used to meet my personal supervisor Prof. Peter Galbreth once in a while to consult him regarding my project. Most of my times were spent at the library. As usual, my morning ritual began with a fifteen minutes of meditation. Each meditation was brought to an alpha level with a visualisation of the immediate objective of the day. These meditations were especially useful in the earlier stages of my preparations in designing my research methodology. The first year was mainly spent in the review of relevant literatures and in designing instruments to measure various variables affecting the study. As a curriculum developer, I was interested in mathematics curriculum renewal especially in Malaysia. At that time, Google and other websites were not well established yet. I depended much of publication materials on research and books relevant to the field of interest. A computer search of the relevant materials and books was necessary to gather information. I was not very familiar with computer at that point of time. My daughter was already in the university doing an applied science degree. She used to show me how to take advantage of the computer to search for the materials I needed.

Searching just for materials relevant for my research might sometimes be monotonous. Satisfying just my five senses: sight, smell, hear, taste, and feel seemed not enough. I began to explore into my sixth sense involving psychic and the soul. When I was in the secondary school, I was exposed to the Bible. I took Bible study based on Saint Luke for my SC examination. I did not take spiritual growth seriously until now. My son used to mix around with many Christian friends when he joined the university to do his double degree in engineering and computer science. He became a six sensory psychic and soulful person after his baptism. He appeared to be getting better and better each day. He went out to help other students. One day, his pastor visited me. He happened to be one of my ex-students. At that time, he had just completed his Ph.D. in civil engineering from a University of Monash and had started working at the CSIRO as a research scientist. At the same time, he also founded a church called 'Hope of God'. So Dr Wilson was a research scientist from Monday to Friday, and on Sunday, he was a pastor, spreading the gospel to the undergraduates. My son happened to be attending the church at the University of Queensland. They had no building of their own. So they made use of lecture theatre for their Sunday services. I was invited to attend Sunday service in the morning. For the sake of my son, I agreed. For a few years while I was doing my research, I attended the church regularly. I also attended some of their courses conducted during the holidays.

A Born-Again Christian

My son wanted me to be a Christian and encouraged me to make the commitment. My belief in Christ slowly gathered momentum. I sense it very early that a happy family is but an earlier heaven. My philosophy for any venture or undertaking has always been straightforward. I am always ready to take up a new adventure by doing the following three steps. First step is to participate to get rid of any fear. Second step is to learn the new undertaking or new way. Third step is to decide whether I like it or not. If I like it, I will continue. Otherwise, I will just ignore it. Believing in Christ is a relative truth because many people do not have the same belief. So I have to be aware that I need to respect others' beliefs. During most of my meditations whenever I reached alpha level, I began to tap into my sixth sense involving intuition, visualisation, and emotion. The idea of living with an extra sensory ability had always intrigued me. I longed to become a six-sensory psychic and soulful person. I began my exploratory reading into this phenomenon and hoped to learn the 'secret tools for six-sensory living'. Sonia Choquette, the writer of *Trust Your Vibes,* said it eloquently:

> 'Trusting your vibes is a way of life that creates a partnership with God and moves through each day as though it were a dance with the Divine. What you will discover when practicing these six-sensory secrets is that for every step you take toward Divine Spirit by trusting your vibes, it will take a step toward you - and together, you'll create a life of grace, harmony, simplicity, and abundance. This may seem far-fetched and unlikely to the five-sensory person, this is only the beginning. It keeps getting better and better.'

After attending many cell group family meetings and learning the Gospel, I became convinced of the existence of God. This is a new wonder I experience. In my imagination of the possible existence of an infinite number of universes each with its own stars, inhabitants, and may be their own creator or God. The possibility is always there. The general philosophy is that by embracing God I hope to become a better father, a better husband, and a better person. I must have made many mistakes and committed some sinful things during my lifetime. I was desperately asking God for forgiveness. Even Moses who had committed murder was forgiven and chosen to lead his people out of Egypt. Finally, I was baptised by my own student and became a born-again Christian. Besides my life insurance, I had just accepted a free insurance for my soul. This insurance is freely given to anyone who believes in Jesus and follows him. I also believe that I have nothing to lose. Remember God only helps those who help themselves. Believe without action and effort will not bring any success to our life. It began to dawn on me that a life of abundance and spirituality can coexist. I discovered the false belief I inherited that money is the root of all evils. Money is only a tool for exchange and a means for us to live a comfortable and purposeful life. The Apostle Paul points out that it is the love of money that is the root of all evils. The love of money refers to greed and abuse. You can compare money we have to any tool or hammer of a worker. A tool can be used to build a house or it can be used to destroy a house. Similarly, money is also a tool that can be used to abuse or to help others as well as our own family. I begin to enjoy my simple way to be kind, loving, peaceful, balanced, spiritual, and rich person. I think I have managed to become a spiritual millionaire. With this mental block relating wealth and spirituality that cannot coexist, removed, I begin to experience an acceleration of abundance in every aspect of my life. I have found the secret to matching my purpose with the profits of investments. I continue to pursue knowledge with the intention of helping others and follow my passion. I am also aware that spirituality can come from other sources like meditation, yoga, prayer, and other forms, not necessarily through embracing religion. More and more people relate to the term 'spiritual but not religion'. According to the philosopher Ken Wilder, there are two 'types of truth'. Most ideas, myths, and stories in religions are relative truth because many people find them to be true but others do not. Another type is the absolute truth, which everyone who experiences it shares the same view. Examples of personal realisation are awakening by psychological technologies like yoga, meditation, and prayer. They experience immaterial and invisible sensations like feeling peaceful and encouraged. Most people seem to engage in relative truth and only a small number of people are engaged in absolute truth. In relative truth, difference of opinions can lead to conflict. On the other hand, absolute truth can alleviate conflict and suffering. I think I am blessed with both types of truth.

A Memorable Trip to Watch Tiger Woods at the Master Golf Tournament at Augustus, USA

When I was serving as the principal at La Salle High School, I was entitled to a world trip with other principals from Petaling District. But unfortunately, the year was 1992 when I put in my paper for optional retirement at the age of fifty-one. The director general of education cancelled my name from the group because I was retiring soon. But God is always kind to me. He has a greater plan to reward me. In 1997, I enjoyed a trip to watch the Master Golf tournament, and I played a few rounds of golf in some well-known courses in the United States. The trip was sponsored by Mitsubishi, a Japanese company. My brother-in-law and his wife were invited to join the trip because of his business deal with the company. The group included the Japanese company CEO, many managers of other companies, and the well-known golfer Peter Leonard. My brother-in-law did not play golf. He asked me to go on his behalf. At first, I invited my university basketball friend Mr Lee Guan Seng to come along. He is also a keen golfer. But he was too busy in his business to make the trip. So I invited my golf mate Mr Tan Teng Hee to come along. The group of about ten players flew business class from Sydney to Los Angeles (LA). I wanted to thank the sponsor who made the trip such a memorable one. We stayed one night at a prestigious hotel in Los Angeles and had a lovely dinner, a courtesy of Mitsubishi. The next morning, we flew to Augustus to watch the Master Golf tournament featuring Tiger Woods who had just turned pro at the age of twenty. I was told that tickets to the Master were sold out a few years before each tournament. The Japanese company managed to buy the passes of some of the old members of the Augustus Golf Club for us to watch the Master. On the first day of the tournament, I was approached by a golf enthusiast who wanted to buy my pass. He was ready to part with $7,000 for a chance to watch Tiger Woods in action. I did not sell my pass because I knew this was once only in my lifetime to watch the Master. For four days, I made an effort to follow Tiger Woods to watch every stroke he made. His skill and accuracy simply intrigued me. He was such a fine athlete and so polite. On the last day, he seemed to recognise me following him so closely. He wished me, 'How are you?' I was shocked beyond words. This is the memory I will cherish throughout my life. He was too good for the rest of the golfers. He won the Master by twelve strokes. The year was 1997.

    The group started playing in various well-known golf courses in other cities including Pebble Beach in California. We were given VIP treatment everywhere we went. This is the most memorable trip in golf for me. I played along with Peter Leonard, who later won the Australian Master and the Australian Open. I was told that Peter and the CEO of Mitsubishi were members of a Sydney Club, where Peter was the residential couch.

After two weeks of golf in various cities around the United States, the group left for Sydney. Mr Tan and me left for Vancouver, Canada, instead. He wanted to visit his eldest brother in Vancouver. We stayed in a good hotel downtown in Vancouver. He caught up with his brother, and we had some good time with his brother's family. I checked through the telephone directory and found the name of my former schoolteacher who had migrated to Canada. I gave her a call, and she was excited to see me. The next morning, she and her husband came to see us at the hotel. They had prepared all the necessary provisions for a picnic in one of the parks in Vancouver. Vancouver is such a beautiful city in April, and the weather was very good for outdoor activities. We spent the whole day at the park having such a wonderful picnic. We talked about the days in school and also our new environments. She and her husband love Vancouver. We love Brisbane, all the same. We talked of our children and enjoying our retirement. I expressed my thanks for their special efforts that made my trip to Vancouver so memorable.

I invited them to visit us in Brisbane. After a few days in Vancouver, we really enjoyed the food in China Town. The roasted duck is famous there, and the 'Tim Sum' or 'Yam Cha' is comparable with that of Sydney and Hong Kong. We had a wonderful time walking around Vancouver. Every good thing has an end. We flew back to Los Angeles and got a connecting flight to Sydney and then back to Brisbane.

A Few Memorable Visits to the United States

After graduating with his double degrees from the University of Technology in Brisbane, my son took up a job with IBM at the Silicon Valley. During the second year working there, we paid him a visit. At the same time, my daughter was working at Stamford in Connecticut, near New York. We flew from Sydney to San Francisco, and my son picked us up there. We spent a few days in Saint Jose, where my son worked at that time. There was not much things to see there. So my son arranged for us to visit Disney Land in Orlando.

We flew there and had a wonderful time. The trip was paid by my son, and we expressed our gratitude for such a memorable time together.

From Orlando, we left for New York, and we were greeted by my daughter there. We stayed in an apartment rented by the company for my daughter working there. She was there for exposure for almost a year. While we were there, we visited some of the historical places on the east coast of the United States. Some of the mansions built for the very rich at the time were fabulous. A few of them had over twenty or thirty rooms to cater for entertainment and parties. As usual, the economic cycles took their turns, and soon, many of the mansions were abandoned and the government took over. Now many of them are museum pieces for visitors. We drove up to Boston and had their famous lobsters there. It cost us a fortune.

Anyhow, we had a good time spent with our daughter. After almost two weeks there, we left for Los Angeles and back to Sydney.

After working a few years in the Silicon Valley, my son got a job as a manager in Freddie Mac in Reston, near Washington, D.C. His responsibility was on computer security and the system there. Initially, he was happy there, and he bought a bungalow with half an acre of land. I visited him a few times and helped to maintain his garden. We enjoyed a good relationship for a long period while he was there. During the weekends, we drove to most of the nearby towns for short visit and did some marketing. We visited Washington, D.C. many times and visited most of the well-known places like the president palace or White House and the Congress building. There are two airports in Washington, D.C.: the Dullas International Airport and the Ronald Regan International Airport. I usually flew from Brisbane to Seoul and then to Dullas International Airport. During one of my trips there, I had to attend an International Learning Conference in Beijing. So I flew from Dullas International Airport to Chicago to take a connecting flight to Beijing. The plane from Dullas Airport to Chicago was delayed, resulting in missing my connecting flight.

I was put on the next flight to Tokyo and flew from Tokyo to Beijing. There was no extra charge because it was not my fault. The international conference was held at the Friendship Hotel in Beijing. My roommate was Dr Don Alexzander, a lecturer from the University of Queensland, an old friend in Brisbane. We used to play tennis together. We had a good time rooming Beijing by ourselves. I remember while Don and me were travelling in the train, we met a charming Chinese lady. She was intrigued by seeing me speaking English so freely with Don. Most Chinese in Beijing could not communicate in English. She was an English teacher running a centre. She started a conversation with us and invited us to visit her. She told us that she would be very happy if we could spend some time helping her to teach English there. The conversation ended when we got down at the next station. We had no time for such an offer. Most things sold at the hotel were rather expensive. I discovered that many of the restaurants serving the local populations were rather cheap. So I organised dinner trips for some of my friends at the conference. They were shocked that a bottle of beer only cost American twenty cents in one of the restaurants. In the hotel, we paid almost two American dollars for the same bottle. These restaurants only cater for the locals. So I told them that I was a local because I spoke fluent Chinese. The foods were cheap, and we had a good time enjoying cheap and delicious recipes. I enjoy eating out with friends. I also enjoy helping people to enjoy life. The next goal for me is to learn not only helping people but also influencing people.

I want to help others in influencing people in a simple way so that the world will be a better place for the future.

Touring Europe for Seven Weeks

When I was writing up my thesis, I was invited by a professor from a British university to present a paper on mathematics curriculum renewal in Malaysia. He was doing a comparative study of mathematics curriculum and achievement in sixteen different countries. The conference was attended by representatives from various European countries, Australia, Singapore, and Malaysia. The venue of the conference is in Cologne, Germany. I flew from Brisbane to Kuala Lumpur and then to London. We stayed two nights in London visiting some of the famous places first before we took a flight from London to Frankfurt. From there, we took a slow train to Cologne arriving in the evening. The hotel arranged for us was just a few kilometres from the railway station. The conference lasted three days.

This was the first time I learnt how to influence people from various different countries. To many participants, learning two languages in school was a problem for the students. But in Malaysia, Chinese school students are expected to learn three languages. It is a huge problem. The consequence is bad for average and below-average students. I joked with them that many Malaysian believed eating with chopsticks would enhance mathematics learning. This was because most Chinese students eat with chopsticks and they performed well in mathematics tests when compared with the other races. Many Malay and Indian parents now started to send their kids to Chinese schools. Everybody laughed. The presentation was just a summary of my Ph.D. dissertation. After the conference we took a train back to Frankfurt and had a bus tour to various cities in Europe. In every city we allowed two nights to look around and enjoyed the local cuisines. From Frankfurt, we stopped at Munich, Budapest, Prague, then Venice in Italy, Rome, Florence, Amsterdam, and cities in France like Nice, Paris, and back to London. We made our journey back to Singapore and then Brisbane. It is such a memorable trip that I treasure the rest of my life.

Simple Steps to Influence People to Like You

There are some interesting things I learn by attending cell group meeting, attending conferences, and interacting with newcomers. Meeting new people can be awkward. I learnt how to make a good impression and how to keep a conversation going. All of us know that relationships are vital to happiness and networking is the key to getting jobs and building a fulfilling career. There are a few critical things to bear in mind if you want to click with people and put them at ease. This is the beginning for people to like you and an opportunity to influence people.

First, when I meet someone the first time, I try to seek his or her thoughts and opinions without judging him or her. I used to ask question. I also will listen. But I avoid judging. Nobody likes to feel being judged regarding actions, opinions, or thoughts. It does not mean that I agree with someone. I learn to listen attentively to understand someone's needs, wants, dreams, and aspirations. It is always a good start to get people to like me. Even if I disagree with his thought or opinion, I used to express my surprise for such a fascinating story and tell him politely that I have never heard it expressed that way. I will ask him to help me understand the story or how he comes up with that. I form the habit not judge him but show interest. And that helps him to calmly talking about his favourite subject. Most people like to talk about themselves. People talking about themselves feel good, and they derive more pleasure than they do from food or money. I used to fall into this category because I have a lot of stories to tell involving myself. Now I have learnt not to do so. I let others tell their stories. The trouble is that most of us are not that gracious because of our ego. To achieve this habit of listening without making judgement requires constant reminder and practice. Once it becomes my habit, it manifest naturally and sincerely. I think most people will like it and not feel threaten.

Second, I learn to suspend my ego. Most of us are too eager to point out that other people are wrong. Our natural instinct is to correct someone, to point out his misconception, and to be one up with your clever little story. I used to make the mistake that I want to be right. Now I know that if I want people to like me, I do not need to be right. So please don't correct others. Note that ego suspension for me is putting my own needs, wants, and opinions aside. Consciously I keep on reminding myself to ignore my desire to be right. I also learn not to correct someone else. By self controlling myself I avoid killing rapport. Contradicting people does not build relationship. When others hear things that contradict their beliefs, the logical part of their mind shuts down. Their brain prepares to fight back as that part of the brain that handles hostile attacks is activated. The fight-or flight response lit up. It takes a lot of practice to form these habits: non judgemental, not egoistic, and listening attentively. So it's better I try to stop being clever. I learn to be a good listener! People tend to like someone who is a good listener. How to be one? When someone tells his story or express his opinion, listen and stop thinking what you are going to say next but focus on what he is saying right now. I will be curious and ask to hear more of his story that interests me. Actually listening is having nothing to say not shutting up. The difference is that if I am shutting up, I am still thinking about what I want to say. I am just not saying it. When I am thinking of my response, I am half-listening and waiting to tell my story. Instead, I focus on his thought or opinion. It takes me a long time to acquire the skill of becoming an active listener. This habit needs consistent practice and awareness. It is straightforward. Listen to what he or she is saying. Do not interrupt, disagree, or evaluate. I used to nod my head and make acknowledging comments like 'I agree or yes'. People feel good if you can repeat the gist of what he has told you. Asking questions regarding his story shows that you are paying attention. This will help to move the discussion. By asking people to tell me more, I think it makes me more likeable and get them to want to help me. But there are people who are boring and you do not want to listen to their story any more. What should I do? I always think of a question. I will tell him that his story is good, but what is his challenge at home or at work this week? This gives him a break, and he needs to think before he continues. This will change the course of the conversation. It's effective. Just give it a try next time if such situation arises.

All of us are aware that life is always tough! Most of us face challenges at work or at home. To break a silence when meeting someone, you can use this strategy of throwing this question. The question must be relevant to someone. To a working man, this question may be appropriate. What kind of challenge do you have in your work? What kind of challenge do you have in raising teenagers? People like to share their challenges like his priorities in life. Another way of influencing people is to ask for advice. People have tendency to feel good that they are respected and valued. But remember you need to be sincere; otherwise, the whole attempt will fail. It appears that advice-seeking tends to be significantly more persuasive than pressuring others. If it's a habit done with sincerity and authenticity, advice-seeking is consistently more influential than others. People will like you and not intimated. Just practise this skill, and soon people will respond and want to share more things with you.

People tend to respond when they feel at ease. If I tell someone whom I meet for the first time that I have only a minute to talk to him and I am heading for the door, he feels relax because he knows that I am leaving soon. Most strangers will put up a shield if I come forward to help him. He wants to know who I am. What do you want? Most importantly, he wants to know when I am leaving. So by telling him that I am leaving in a few seconds will put him at ease, and he is more relax to respond. Asking him whether now is a good time to do things you ask for will make him more likely to respond to your request. Remember nobody wants to feel trapped talking to a stranger. He will more likely to talk and help you when he feels safe and in control. For a stranger to trust you, you need to ensure that your words and your body language are aligned. The impression that someone appears untrustworthy is usually the misalignment of words and body language.

It takes a lot of awareness and practice to cultivate the best body language to build rapport. First, for me my words should be positive, free of ego, and judgemental, matching with my body language. A smile is a great way to engender trust. Smile matters and smile releases its power of attraction. Smile gives the brain pleasure and makes people happy. Good posture, comfortable, relaxing, and looking straight at him while I am talking, that's always wonderful. People will feel relax, more likely to respond, and I think they will like me.

The Award of Ph.D.

I enjoy reading and meeting new people. The new lifestyle of my retirement is exciting. I attended church almost every Sunday. I also attended care-group meeting every week. I spent almost two to three years of my precious time at the library. Three and a half years of research soon ended. I had finished my dissertation on mathematics curriculum renewal. The normal procedure for awarding a Ph.D. degree in University of Queensland requires three examiners: an internal one, a national one, and an international one. I received favourable assessments from all three examiners. My journey in my doctoral study thus ended. Now I can use the title Dr Wong. I went back to school to teach for a while. I did not like the working environment. So I stopped teaching and became full-time curriculum developer and an investor. I am now a self-employable person.

In my retirement, one curtain is closed. Another curtain is opened. My research into companies related to my investment portfolio took a serious turn. Now, besides writing mathematics curriculum materials, I began to look into potential growth of companies so that I could make investment. My simple philosophy in investing came under scrutiny. I was not looking to make more money but to keep myself busy and my brain working. Income from my rentals, my small retirement pension, royalties, dividends from my stocks and gains from my trading was growing. I seemed to be getting richer every day. My children are all working, and they do not need my support any more. I consider myself blessed with wealth, success, and good health. I am now grateful not only to those who has helped me but also to my creator. I am looking forward to the freedom of doing things that I enjoy, to enhance my learning capacity for new things, and finally to give back to my community the benefits I have derived. I am still exploring into the possible ways I can use my talents and resources to express my gratitude to humanity. To me, age is no longer a hindrance to new experiences and my growth. I begin to set new goals and create new dreams. I begin to experiment a new field of interest to provide encouragement and motivation for others to experience growth as well. My new contribution will be in the field of motivation, helping others to live a healthy and satisfying life. A new journey begins.

CHAPTER SEVEN

ENJOYING THE FRUITS OF LIFE AND KEEP LEARNING

Looking back at my accomplishments and achievements, my life is still full of purpose and passion. I am still using my writing skill to pen down words of inspirations for the young and old. I am still developing curriculum materials to help students learn. I feel lucky because I have already delivered for my family. I believe that I still have many worthwhile things to accomplish. I still enjoy playing tennis and meeting new friends. My garden and my orchard still cry for my touch. My young grandchildren love to be carried by me. I still have many things to do before I leave this planet. I believe that I have accomplished my four purposes of life, namely I have learnt many life lessons, I enjoy my career and callings, I discover my hidden callings, and finally, I have attended well all my arising moments in life.

At this retiring stage of life, I have all the time and all the money in the world; what would I do? I never know unless I stop for a moment and ask myself, and I may just find that I am doing it already. Most evenings I will take a gratitude walk for about twenty minutes. I will dedicate 100 per cent of that time to gratitude. I will consciously think of all the things I appreciate in my life, notice all the beauty and natural gifts that surround me, and simply reflect on how lucky I am to have the life that I have. After each walk I feel awesome, and usually, I feel a higher satisfaction towards my life. Passion and happiness are something I should pursue further. I am passionate about writing. I am passionate about investing. I am passionate about sports. These dreams of mine have been partially fulfilled. I know I still have to dream further for complete accomplishment. Most people who dare to dream big usually achieve them. Pursuing these big dreams remains my passion. I have break-through in mathematics curriculum material publications, and I want another break-through as a motivational writer. The Internet may be the necessary tool to help me seeing the light. Investment brings challenge, and trading to profit remains a test of will. Developing strategies brings active involvement of the mind. As I grow older, I need to use more thinking to keep the mind functioning well. Watching and playing competitive sports remain my passions. Any big tournament like World Cup in soccer, Master tournament in Golf, and Olympic games still excite me. Playing competitive tennis and golf bring more life to me. I need to keep in shape and be healthy. I strongly believe that I should strictly adhere to the following basics such as quality sleep, regular exercise, balance nutrition, and free my mind from unnecessary distraction to provide the building blocks for my optimum brain function.

I strongly believe that I can learn any new skill at any stage of my life. What I need is to form the habit of doing it. I also believe that it is never too old to learn. My wife tried to convince me that I could do all the kitchen chores even though I had never done it before when I was working. When I came to Brisbane, I began trying to do all those stuffs. Initially, my washing of plates and utensils were not perfect. But gradually, I learnt the art. I also started cooking, and now I am quite confident in preparing lunch and dinner for a few persons. As I mentioned in Chapter One, I had just embarked on a new meditation adventure called Quantum Jumping.

I will be sharing this new concept of jumping into a parallel universe to meet with a doppelganger or twin-self who has the expertise, wisdom, and knowledge that I am seeking. This remarkable concept has given me a new power to explore space and inter-universal travel without leaving my own room. First, I would like to share with you the basic philosophy of Quantum Jumping. According to Burt Goldman, he waited thirty-one years to formally introduce Quantum Jumping to the world. He had gathered all the scientific evidences supporting his concept of the existence of infinite number of parallel universes, and therefore, the existence of infinite number of our alternative selves who have made different choices of lives and experiencing different successes or failures. Quantum Jumping offers us a powerful strategy in creating reality visualisation in our subconscious minds to meet up with our twin-selves who are successful in their choice of vocations or hobbies that we are seeking. At the same time, Quantum Jumping has made the concept of inter-universal travel possible mentally and visually through imagination without any risk. What a wonderful idea! I have got a simple philosophy of adventure. First, I will give myself a chance to try out the concept of inter-universal travel to meet up with my alternative selves to overcome any fear and to learn new knowledge through imagination. Second, I will try to learn another form of meditation to help me reaching alpha level through Quantum Jumping. Finally, if I get succeed, I will have gained another strategy to help me becoming a better, more spiritual, and more successful person. It's all win-win situations. To add some spices to our life, we need to use whatever inspirations available from time to time. So to gain a little wisdom; increase a little knowledge; add a little pep to your steps; to gain new experiences; to make the rainy days a little brighter and to remind me how beautiful my journey of life through autumn season can be.

My personal experiences in meditation and visualisation are enriched by reading and interacting with successful people. Positive energies are contagious. Do not be drag down by negative forces from pessimistic people. Life is always a choice. Choose your friends wisely. It's not wrong to be wealthy, healthy, and generous. Try to get a taste of what it takes to get into the millionaire mindset, liberate your spirit, and also rediscover how powerful the laws of attraction are. Napolean Hill, the author of the famous book, *Think and* Grow *Rich,* gave me a powerful lead in this respect. Here is what Napolean Hill said,

> 'When you begin to think and grow rich, you will observe that riches begin with a state of mind, with definiteness of purpose, with little or no hard work. You, and every other person, ought to be interested in knowing how to acquire that state of mind which will attract riches ... Observe very closely, as soon as you master the principles of this philosophy, and begin to follow the instructions for applying those principles, your financial status will begin to

improve, and everything you touch will begin to transmute itself into an asset for your benefit. Impossible? Not at all!'

I always believe that I am not the product of my circumstances but the product of my own decisions. I take the courage to grow up and decide my own destiny. I used to ask myself this question. Do you want to be wealthy, successful, happy, or otherwise?

There is no harm trying Quantum Jumping! This unique technique of guided imagery through deep meditation can train me tapping into the power of advanced dimensions of my mind. I may accomplish what I might think impossible! I think I may acquire the state of mind for riches, or I may become the person I always dreamt off during my childhood.

I am a born-again Christian believing in the words of Jesus. His healing powers are well revealed in the Gospel. Many established pastors are using his healing power to do the healing for those who believe. I believe in the infinite power of the mind, and if you can reach any particular advanced dimension, it can trigger that healing power you desire. For a strong believer in Jesus, that faith can be triggered by an honest and committed prayer. Jesus once said, 'Ask and it shall be given.' Most of us do not believe, not only in Jesus but even in ourselves. We do not ask or visualise the possibility. Perhaps Quantum Jumping can provide another alternative possibility.

This beautiful new concept in Quantum Jumping provides me an easy way to explore the infinite power of my mind. First, I need to make my intention clear. What is the purpose of each Quantum Jumping? Once the intention is established, I will follow the procedures introduced by Burt Goldman. I can actually use my own technique or any other technique as long as I can bring down my brain vibrations to a low alpha level allowing my mind to explore possibilities to solve problems or gain knowledge from my twin-self who has all the requirements. In my few experimental jumps, I pretend that I am there merging with my doppelganger who has the skills and getting his rhythm and energy. This is like daydreaming, and finally, this habit becomes my visualisation technique exploring possibilities to become successful in any aspect of life. Sometimes, it's hard to believe because others do not believe. I will experiment with such concept because it is going to benefit me.

Searching for Fulfilment in Life through Quantum Jumping

This remarkable concept of Quantum Jumping is invented by Burt Goldman. He just got married at eighty-six years old, and now he is eighty seven. He believes, like most other physicists, that there exist an infinite number of parallel universes. Our universe includes the earth, the stars, the moon, the galaxies, and its inhabitants. Correspondingly, there are an infinite of my twin-selves or doppelgangers in these parallel universes. Each of them has different capabilities, and they are in different professions such as doctor, writer, artist, inventor, tradesman, and waiter. Quantum Jumping is a form of meditation using my creative visualisation by imagining that I can travel through space to a parallel universe to meet with a particular doppelganger who has the talent and know-how I am seeking. I can learn his rhythms, his talents, and his infinite potential so that I too can be successful in the same field. So there is no limit in my imagination and my potential growth. Everything appears to be possible through Quantum Jumping. Burt is great at spreading this type of positive energy to people like me who is seeking fulfilment in life. Age is no more an obstacle. In his seventies, he practised Quantum Jumping to become an artist, a photographer, a writer and acquired other skills. At the age of eighty-seven, he is still striving for greatness. He wants to leave a permanent mark in this world. He is a great teacher, writer, artist, photographer, and multimillionaire. He serves as a great role model for me to follow. I am a mathematics textbook writer and a state basketballer, and now I want to be a motivational writer to encourage people, young and old, to live out their potential in life. I will share my experiences in various successful Quantum Jumping and hope that you will include this form of meditation to enrich your life.

Quantum Jumping for Healing

I would like to share with you my first experience in Quantum Jumping. The course I am following is conducted by Burt Goldman himself under the publisher 'Mindvalley'. The intention of this beginner meditation course is for healing purpose. I was seated in my comfortable armchair in my study room. I was instructed to close my eyes and asked to relax allowing my infinite mind to function effectively. After a few seconds of silence, Burt led the way by counting the number three, three times in descending tone, that is, three, three, and three. Then I was told to follow by the number two, that is, two, two, and two in a similar way. Then I had to repeat the number one in the similar way. A few seconds were allowed to elapse. Then I was instructed to start counting number ten, followed by nine, eight, seven, ... until one. The purpose of this ritual is to wake up my subconscious mind to begin its exploration. I was told to imagine that I am walking in a big hall, going towards a quantum door which is closed. Slowly, I approached the door. The door opened, and I was asked to take my Quantum Jump over the door way into another parallel universe. I allowed my imagination to do the rest. The space was well lighted and the environment was totally different. My imagination started its exploration. But my intention was clear. I wanted to meet my doppelganger who was a healer in this parallel universe. I looked at him, and he appeared as such a healthy man. My doppelganger was immersed in a great white light. He lived in a healing planet. My twin self smiled at me. I smiled back and slowly approached him. He was well built and in very good shape. He reached out his hands to welcome me. He looked like me. Slowly, we merged into one, and we settled for business. All these imaginations worked well. I had acquired his rhythm and his energy, and I learnt his technique of keeping fit. He had a busy schedule going round healing others. Besides his duty, he was active in games, he ate well, and he was happy for being healthy. I learnt his eating habits, sleeping habit, his lifestyle, and his attitude of keeping himself happy and healthy. Many of his lifestyle seemed to be similar to mine. But he had something else which I was seeking, that is, his healing power as a healer. I wanted his knowledge, his energy, and his technique of healing. I was healthy, but I had a little complain regarding pain in my left arm. He told me to start swing my arms when I walk every day. I agreed, and we bid each other farewell, hoping to meet again. I imagined that I had acquired his rhythm to heal. The keyword was to swing my left arm. I used my right hand to play tennis, and the left was seldom used vigorously. I slowly walked away from him and back to the quantum door way. I crossed the door way and slowly walked back to my old position. Everything was quiet, and I slowly opened my eyes, feeling fresh to begin another day of my life.

I strongly believe that I can change my life and can heal my pain by taking action immediately. That morning I went for my hour-long walk up the hill in front of my house. I started swinging my both arms sideways fifty times and forward way fifty times. I kept repeating my swings as I walked. As I walked down the hill, I explored another strategy by walking backwards to strengthen certain muscles of my legs. This procedure has become my style of walking every morning. Some walkers saw me swing my arms sideways were amazed. A walker warned me that I might take off like a bird. I keep practicing my swing every time I walk. This has become my style of walking. Since then I had forgotten about my pain on my left arm.

I believe in practicing my meditation as often as possible. Thinking alone is not enough. Action is required. I must have practised this healing technique many times before the pain on my left arm disappeared. In the process, I had moved from a basic jumper to a novice jumper. I believe now I have become a master jumper after many repeated meditations. With more practice, I will soon be a quantum jumper.

My First Successful Quantum Jumping to Heal My Headache

One afternoon, I was having a headache. I was not comfortable to read messages from my e-mail. Everything was quite. My intent was to heal my headache. I closed my eyes and started counting three, three times; two, three times; and one, three times. Then I started counting from ten, nine, eight, ... until one. Soon, I was in deep meditation, and I was in an alpha state. I walked towards a door. When the door was opened, I jumped into another parallel dimension to meet my doppelganger, my twin-self who was happy and smiling because he did not suffer the same headache as I had. I walked towards him, and we merged into one person. My intention was to get his rhythm to free from headache. I was in this stage for a while. When everything was accomplished, my twin-self asked me to leave with a smiling face. I smiled back because I felt happy and relieved. I slowly walked back to the door and left that parallel universe and came back to my own room. All these imaginations seemed to help me. When I opened my eyes, I could see the bright sunlight coming through my windows. I was feeling fine, and everything seemed to be in order. I had forgotten that I had a headache before. This success in Quantum Jumping marks the beginning of my new discovery as a quantum jumper.

QUANTUM JUMPING TO LEARN A FIGURE OF SPEECH

One morning after my tennis game, we had coffee at the nearby cafe. One of my co-tennis players mentioned about a figure of speech known as a paraprosdokians. I had never come across such a figure of speech. He tried to explain it to me, but I did not catch the actual meaning without examples. I was too shy to ask further question. I left it that way. When I reached home, I had a good bath. After a light breakfast, I turned to my computer to read my e-mails. Before I did that, I suddenly remembered that I must try Quantum Jumping to get my doppelganger who was English specialist in another dimension for help. As usual I began to meditate, and I met my twin-self who knew exactly what my intention was. I knew that I was lacking in connection with the wonders of the world. The world was a mystery. The words we used to express our thoughts were always mysterious. Most of the sentences we write were usually straightforward. Usually, the first part of the sentence agreed with the second part. What happen if we had a sentence where the first part contradicted the second? What type of figure of speech was this? My doppelganger told me to focus on the second part of the sentence that appeared to contradict the first. Everything became crystal clear to me that a paraprosdokian is a figure of speech where the last part of the sentence or phrase appears unexpected or surprising. Sometimes, the last part may be humorous. The following are some examples:

1. Light travels faster than sound so some people appear bright until you hear them speak.
2. Plagiarism is to steal ideas from one person, but to steal from many is called research.
3. Indecisiveness is a part of me, but now I am not sure.

4. Target hitting: to be sure of hitting the target, shoot first and call whatever you hit the target.
5. War does not determine which country is the winner, only those left to suffer and rebuild.

Quantum Jumping can be a tool to explore, imagine, learn any new thing, and acquire new knowledge. The power of imagination can do wonder.

Quantum Jumping to Overcome Illogical Fear

Many parts of my life are affected by my childhood experiences. I was told by my grandmother that children must not interfere or ask questions whenever others were talking. Because of this memory, I developed the fear of asking questions whenever I did not understand certain things explained to me. Listening to all the haunted stories had instilled fear in me regarding darkness and abandoned houses. I was told not to climb tree because of the danger of falling down and breaking the limbs. I soon developed the fear for height even it was safe to be at such height. All these emotions including fear live with us as we grow up. Fear is an emotion which is a thought of like or dislike to certain degree. The opposite of fear is faith which is a positive expectation, whereas fear is a negative expectation. People seem to confuse and think that the opposite of fear is courage. A person has courage, but he still has fear. His courage emerges because of his positive expectation exceeds his degree of fear. Fear is a good guide to protect us from harm or injury. We do not jump down from a tall building or a moving vehicle for fear of breaking our legs. We run from a wild animal for fear of being attacked. But there are other illogical fears which we have to control to a certain degree to allow our potential to develop. For me, first, I need to control my fear for public speaking, the fear of asking questions, my fear for the unknown, the fear for height, and the fear of meeting strangers.

My intention was clear when I started Quantum Jumping to overcome and control these fears. I went through the process of bringing my mental state to an alpha level where my visualisation was optimal. At the entrance of the quantum door, I had a good look at my doppelganger in another parallel universe. He had a unique smile with so much confidence, and he did not suffer from any illogical fear which I had. I gave him a smile in return. Slowly, I walked towards my twin-self and merged with him. My intention was to acquire his rhythms of courage and his energy to overcome obstacles. I went along with him to observe his skill and confidence in public speaking in front of a big crowd. I noticed that he just talked to one of the members of the crowd while he spoke with ease. I needed to develop that rhythm whenever I spoke to a crowd. That visualisation seems to stay with me whenever I make a public speech. Soon after many attempts, I seem to have forgotten my fear for public speaking.

My doppelganger took me to a high platform overlooking a great forest. The scenery was amazing, and I enjoyed the view. The slow rhythm for height seemed to have dissipated and replaced with a high rhythm. I wanted more adventures of height to enjoy more of a bird's-eye view of the environments. With a few more Quantum Jumps of these nature, my fear for height seem to have vanished in thin air. I begin to enjoy good views from higher places. My life has made a great turn, and I seem to enter into another level of living, enjoying the higher grounds.

Another visualisation observation my doppelganger gave me was his confidence and attitude whenever he asked questions regarding things which he was not absolutely certain. He was polite and full of grace whenever he asked a question. People seemed to entertain his questions because he was polite and never insisted on his rights. He was assertive but polite. All this rhythm and attitude seemed to stand well when I attempted my questions. I acquired the attitude to ask politely, and people seemed to response politely. After many occasions of asking, I have just acquired another good habit of finding out things which I am not certain. This habit of finding the truth and facts seem to add another dimension to my well being and happiness. Life is never the same without these illogical fears.

Quantum Jumping to Enhance Happy Marriage

Another experience in my Quantum Jumping had a specific purpose. I wanted to contact my doppelganger in another parallel universe who was a marriage counsellor. I wanted to find the secret of keeping my love alive for my marriage of forty-three years. I went through the same process to jump into this particular parallel universe to meet my twin-self who was there to counsel me. He was also married for the same number of years as me. His 'emotional love tank' was always full, but mine was not that full. He told me to learn to speak the language of my spouse. Most of the time, the husband speaks a different love language from the wife. I was in that shoe.

My subconscious began its exploration to find the love language of my spouse. I started asking God and reading books to shed light on this issue. I remember what Jesus once said, 'Ask and it shall be given.' A few days later, I received a book entitled *The Five love Languages* written by Gary Chapman. The book was sent by my brother-in-law from overseas. He is the author of this best-selling book. He travels the world presenting seminars, and his radio programmes air on more than 300 stations. According to him, the desire for romantic love is deeply rooted in our psychological make-up. Yet many marriages end up on the rock. His remarkable concept of understanding the primary love language of our spouse and our own leads the way to his discovery. He proposes five basic love languages that will form the solid foundation for a healthy and lasting marriage. I am determined to learn this second love language. I cannot rely on my native tongue if my spouse does not understand it. If I want her to feel the love I am trying to communicate, I must express it in her primary love language. What are these five love languages which constitute her primary love language?

According to Gary, these five love languages include the following:

1. Words of Affirmation: Words of appreciation or verbal compliments are powerful communicators of love. Expressing in a straightforward manner constitutes statements of affirmation. I have never learnt this tremendous power of verbally affirming my spouse. Unnecessary negative statements, sarcastic comments,

flattery, critical comments of my spouse will be avoided at all cost. I must practise to say things for common well-being.
2. Quality Time: From now, I will give her undivided attention. We will do things together and enjoy each other's company with quality conversation.
3. Receiving Gifts: We will learn to appreciate the attitude of giving. Gifts need not be expensive. Once a while, a gift is an expression to do with love. A gift of flower or a birthday card on her birthday is a good gesture.
4. Acts of Service: All sorts of household chores done for each other are act of service. By doing these simple household works I have created a good climate for love to grow. I learn to provide help whenever she is busy. Now I enjoy cooking and cleaning the house.
5. Physical Touch: It is a way of communicating emotional love for both children and spouse. It can become their primary love language. Without it, they feel unloved. With it, their emotional tank is filled, and they feel secure in the love of their spouse. The power of touch and the body is wired for touch should not be neglected. All the 'love touches' are the emotional lifeline of the person for whom physical touch is the primary language.

The moment I dived into this river of information, I was determined to take action. I am going to practise and practise these five languages consistently, patiently, and playfully until I can speak her primary love language fluently. Hopefully, it becomes my habits. From now on, I will ensure that our 'emotional love tank' is always full.

I repeat this deep meditation as many times as possible to ensure that I put into practice what I visualise and put into action what I have learnt regarding the primary language of my spouse. I believe by now I have qualified as a quantum jumper.

QUANTUM JUMPING TO ENHANCE ABUNDANCE

I would like to share with you another of my experience in Quantum Jumping in relation to enhancing my financial freedom. I met with my doppelganger who was already a wealthy man in another parallel universe. During our meeting he whispered to me to revise and improve on my financial blueprint. If I thought like him (rich twin-self) and if I did what he did, I would get richer like him. He whispered to me to first change my mindset. If I clinked on the belief that money was bad for me, I would never be able to attract wealth. Such negative belief would never help to change my mindset. He wanted me to practise giving unconditionally without expecting anything in return. Whenever I found something inspiring, I should give generously in terms of time or money. I should give and ask nothing in return. This was the short cut to abundance. The natural law is that if you bless others generously, you will receive blessing in abundance. He also wanted me to practise prosperous spending. If I have the money, I should spend on something I really desire. If I don't, then I will be telling myself that I do not deserve it, I don't have enough money, and I have no faith in the future. If I buy it, I reaffirm myself that I am worthy of it and I believe in prosperity and I believe my future is positive. He also hinted to me that I must ask for help from sources like my network of friends or relatives and ask also from the divine or God I believe in. Jesus says that ask and it shall be given. I need to set goals for myself and imagine that I can accomplish them. By establishing this feeling, I will have a good chance of working towards my goals. If I think like an entrepreneur, I will see problems and challenges as opportunities. I will think creatively to solve problems and challenges towards abundance. Finally, if I work hard and also think of helping others, then I open myself to receiving more. By picking on worthy cause, I will more likely to resonate with others and leave an impact.

I would have greater freedom to give back to the community I love. Though I am already a wealthy man, I need to think differently from the poor or middle-class people. I need to grow mentally by being more proactive and more action-oriented.

According to T. Harv Eker, the author of the book, *Secrets of the Millionaire Mind*, if our subconscious 'financial blueprint' is not programmed for success, nothing we learn, nothing we know, and nothing we do will make much difference. The first thing we need to do is to reprogramme our 'financial blueprint' by redefining our financial freedom, learning to play to win, and increasing the size of our character to determine our response to various-sized problems. Any weakness of our current 'financial blueprint' needs to be identified and revised to help achieving bigger financial success. Be more observance. Emulate the thinking and actions of rich people. The chance is that we will increase our wealth and enhance our freedom to give back to our community. According to Russell Simmons, author of the book DO *YOU!*,

> 'In the end, the overriding factor in whether or not you realise your dreams is going to be you. Not the world. You.'

It may sound difficult. We need to learn to create a vision for our life and using the power of mantras to reprogramme our mind for success. It is not about resources we have, but it's about our resourcefulness. And it is within resourcefulness that we will find abundance. Abundance is everywhere. But we just don't see it and are not action-oriented. Instead, we just sit around complaining. We see bad economy instead of seeing a world filled of new opportunities. In spite of lacking in resources, we need to think creatively and take advantage of any situation. People with a millionaire mind create a balance in their approach to life. They are financially independent yet they enjoy life. We need to balance our need to become wealthy and economically productive with our need to enjoy life.

First instinct for us is to get rid of credit-dependent mentality, thus breaking the cycle of borrowing to consume and earning to consume. Do not be controlled by others financially. We need financial independent, and success can be achieved by living within our means and leave something for us to invest. Make sure that we are not controlled by money. Learn to enjoy your work, your lifestyle, and at the same time accumulating your wealth. Acquire this mindset, and I am confident we are on the way to financial success.

Quantum Jumping to Enhance Spirituality

The next exploration to my experience in Quantum Jumping is about spirituality. All of us have the same dream to live up to our full potential as awakened human beings. We all aspire to engage with our intuition and visualisation as our sixth sense in addition to our five basic senses: sight, hear, taste, touch, and smell. I am seeking spiritual liberation so that I am able to live up to my highest potential. I know this potential is already there in the subconscious waiting activation. In my quiet moment, I close my eyes to begin my meditation, bringing me to the alpha level required to meet my doppelganger in another parallel universe. My twin-self is a highly awakened being, and he is capable of leading me into living up to my potential, to become more of myself and more about being an awakened being. The encounter has awakened my subconscious that I am here not only to survive but also to allow my full potential to blossom. The catch word is to 'grow' mentally, and all the others like happiness, wisdom, abundance, knowledge, health, and well-being will follow.

This provides the necessary motivation for me to search for my spiritual liberation. I will allow my resourcefulness instinct to make its exploration. My journey on this spiritual adventure begins. I need to examine possible transformation, peace, abundance, and the habits of highly evolved people. I will keep my eyes open. I want to be free from narrow confines of fear, doubt, worry, and lack. I want to live from a conscious awareness of my authentic self as one true nature of wholeness. I want to discover and to express my intrinsic qualities of enlightened consciousness. This is to live to my full potential. I am seeking spiritual liberation as such.

As part of the exploration, let us turn to spiritual leader like Michael Bernard Beckwith, the founder of the Agape Spiritual Center, and also a featured teacher in *The Secret*. He said,

> 'You are not here to merely survive but to soar, to express and release the dynamic power of consciousness residing at the deepest center of your being.'

Sonia Choquette suggests that we can make use of our six senses or vibes to tap into our intuition and emotional guidance to create an extraordinary life. The mind has infinite power. I will live a life that can create a partnership with God. This will help me to discover using the sixth sensory secret that every step I take towards divine spirit by trusting my vibes, it will take a step towards me; together, I will create a life of grace, harmony, simplicity, and abundance. This spiritual liberation will enable me to achieve and enrich my life to the next level. This process will continue and enrich my life bringing out all my potential as an awakened being.

Finally, we need to consider the wisdom of Dan Millman, the author of

Everyday Enlightenment, which states the following:

> 'When people ask me abstract questions about time, or space, or reincarnation, I may respond by asking whether they exercise regularly, eat a wholesome diet, get enough sleep, show kindness to others, and remember to take a slow, deep breadth on occasion - because it seems important to bring our spiritual quest down to earth.
>
> Of course, there's nothing wrong with philosophical speculation. But let's not mistake conceptual thought for spiritual practice of everyday life. After all, what does it serve to know whether angels wear earrings if we can't hold a regular job or maintain a long-term relationship? What good does it do to pray like a saint or meditate like a yogi if we are unchanged when we open our eyes? What good to attend a place of worship on Friday or Sunday if we lack compassion on Monday?'

I will repeat this deep meditation as many times as possible until I can practise what I learnt. Regular practice will help me to become an awakening person with a sharp sixth sense. I need to practise compassion until it becomes my way of life. Always do to others such as showing kindness, what you want others to do the same thing to you.

QUANTUM JUMPING TO EXPERIENCE FLOW

We all know that in our life, we enjoy a few moments of real joy when we experience successes. These precious moments are few. As a writer,

I long to get into this rhythm allowing ideas to start bursting out from my head, and my writing can move smoothly. With this intention in mind, I closed my eyes to start another Quantum Jumping to meet my doppelganger in another parallel universe. My twin-self had experienced many such incidents which he called 'flow'. This feeling of top form is like floating with new ideas and is carried on by the flow. I was made to realise that those who experienced or attained this 'flow' develop into a better and more confident writer. Why is that so? A question I need to explore! My twin-self hinted to me to use my energy wholeheartedly and creatively! The key word is 'focus'.

I have been struggling to control my mind from flicking between different distracting thoughts, causing me to lose focus on my writing goal. Many of my friends share the same experience. They told me not to worry because I was not alone. My search for moments where I can get into the rhythm of things has become my priority to finish my book. My quest for new focus leads me to various books I read. The answer comes from an extraordinary writer.

According to Mihaly Csikzentmihalyi,

> 'We have called this state the flow experience, because this is the term many people we interviewed had used in their descriptions of how it felt to be in top form: "It was like floating, I was carried on by the flow." It is the opposite of psychic entropy, and those who attain it develop a stronger, more confident self because more of their psychic energy has been invested successfully in goals they themselves had chosen to pursue.'

The experience of 'flow' tells a story. These are occasions or days when everything falls into place and when projects move forward easily. Information seems to fall into our lap the moment we need it, and we have endless supply of ideas, energy, and inspiration. These are the moments of our life when we are rowing in the direction of the river. We are experiencing 'the flow'.

The visualisation during the alpha state of meditation seems to be able to start such rhythm of things. It will be good to have such experience when

I get into an effortless of flow. It is like getting into a smooth groove where your ideas and information move effortlessly. These are moments when inspiration takes over and your writings go on smoothly and productivity seems to be at its highest. These are joyful moments of a writer's life.

Besides, our ability to attract other things we desired, be the tangible things like wealth or money or intangible things like love or happiness, hinges on our ability to receive. Remember that there is no shortage of anything. There is no limit to the amount of joy, abundance, success, appreciation of fulfilment that we can experience. Everything that we could possibly desire exists in infinite supply. We only need to examine our capacity to contain them, and if possible, try to expand that capacity so that more will flow into our container. We cannot just sit and wait. God only helps those who help themselves. We need more effort and knowledge to ever expand our capacity to receive them.

Quantum Jumping to Overcome Negativities or Difficult Situations

Many a time in our life we face difficult situations. A few days ago, I met an old friend. He had many difficult situations. He told me that many 'bad things' happened to him. He became negative and started to blame others. When he asked for my opinions, I was not ready to provide any solution. I told him to give time to ponder over such situations and how to regain positive energy again. When I reached home, I sat on my usual chair. I closed my eyes to begin my meditation. I went through the process and managed to meet my doppelganger who was an expert in turning negative thoughts into positive energy. My twin-self hinted that we should not try to row the proverbial boat upstream. Every step we try to reach our desired goal is a struggle, and it seems like maximum effort to produce minimum results.

This encounter gives plenty of food for thought. There will be days we face problems and we become anxious, frustrated, and angry. These are the occasions or days we are rowing upstream; it seems like the harder we push to accomplish our task, the farther away we get the desired outcome. We react with resistances. We complain about it, and we blame others or refuse to deal with it altogether. This attitude only constricts our perception. When we are in this frustrated state of mind, all we can see is the 'problem' even when potential solutions exist in front of us. So as long as we remain in this energetic state, no amount of actions and accusations will produce the desired results. In our proverbial boat rowing upstream, we can row as hard we want, the outcome is going to be minimum. Take a break, drop your oars, and stop rowing. Change direction and release your resistance. This may be the key of reversing a negative spiral and getting back in the flow. Take action and address the problem by looking for suitable solution. Joy of working will return. The following steps may help us to bring back the moments of 'flow' and let the feeling of joy to return.

1. First, identify your resistance that may manifest in the form of anger, frustration, disappointment, or the project gets 'stuck'. Take note of the situation that causes you to feel less joyful and change direction by addressing the problem.
2. Second, acknowledge that you are the only one has the power to change your inner vibration. Make a choice of focusing not only on one wrong thing but on many right things. Remind yourself that altering your inner perception, you will alter the entire situation.
3. Third, close your eyes for a short meditation or listen to a good music or go for a short walk. Allow the resistance to leave your body and enable you to return to neutral energetic state. This will bring a sense of relief.
4. Finally, try to identify one feeling or quality that could cultivate in order to bring this feeling of relief into the situation. It may be patience, trust, focus, or others. Whatever it is, seal this feeling into your body. Imagine that when you open your eyes, you will see the world and everything in it through this new clear lens. Positive energy and joy will certainly return.

For me, I always have a solution when things are not going well for me. The first step is to take a complete rest and meditate through Quantum Jumping. I always have faith in my doppelganger in the next parallel universe. My imagination is that twin-self has the answer to my problem why bad things happen to me. There are specific things I can do to break free from these bad things. I will learn the rhythm and acquire the energy necessary to break free these bad things from becoming permanent features of my life. I will follow my twin-self's method of fixing them. First, I learn where all these realities come from. As soon as we are born, we are on survival mode. We learn to blend in by absorbing everything around us. We pull in the thoughts, feelings, beliefs, ideals, and rationalisation of people around us. We learn, and we survive. All these things we learn become our reality. Many experiences including relationships, finances, and others we encounter become our way of life, and we tend to duplicate them. Not all these experiences are positive and motivating. Some turn out to be destructive. That's how bad things have their source. So what do we do? The logical solution is up to us to fix them so that they do not influence our future life. Instead, we should put on a different lens and see things differently. It's time we see 'bad things' for they really are. They may be gifts the universe is telling you to work on something to change the situations. I learn not to ignore these signs or admit being 'victim' and let the bad things repeat themselves. If I do, I have myself to blame. It is my realities, and I am responsible for clearing them up. I learn to accept that these bad things are the universe's way of telling me vital information. So I have to do something to clear all these mental blocks from my life. I acknowledge that when something bad happens to me, I should be happy to know what is wrong with me. These events are pointing the gunk in my life and giving me the opportunity to get rid of them forever. So I have no choice but to act effectively. I believe the universe loves me and keeps showing the patterns and telling me to work on so that I can clear them and get on with my happy version of life.

Remember that the universe will continue to give me this gift or 'bad thing' over and over again. At the end of the day, I have no choice but to love myself enough that I will decide to keep fixing whatever comes up. So I need to keep busy, be considerate, and be kind to others.

Quantum Jumping to Search for Happiness

The search for happiness and well-being is well wired in the brain. Our duty as awakened being is to find and strengthen the network to experience them throughout the journey of our life. Happiness, although it's something all of us strive for, can often be mysteriously elusive. Looking for positive habits to help us increase our levels of happiness may sound difficult. Little do we realise that we can learn the skill that unlocks the secret of happiness. My observation tells me that the key difference between happy people and others. The formers are totally excited by life and looking forward to each day. Others spend their time longing and hoping for better days. Observation of happy people reveals that they follow certain habits. Happy people have a bounce in their steps, a smile in their face, and a sense of purpose in the hearts. Another thing about happy people is that they have relationship that work. They tend to be creative. They do work that matters to them. Happy people live a life that has meaning and purpose. We may suspect that happy people have advantage because they come from good upbringing environment. We expect others who are not happy because of horrific upbringing. There is no correlation between these two assumptions. Happy people may have some degree of financial success others do not have. The truth is that happy people can come from all different economic background. To be happy, we need to be sensitive to and pay attention to the longing of our heart. So if we learn to apply and practise these habits, we can attain happiness too. Armed with this philosophy, I am confident to meet my doppelganger who is practicing these habits of happiness, in another parallel universe.

As usual I started my meditation to meet my doppelganger. In this alpha state, I found myself merging with my twin-self who was such a happy man. I wanted to know and learn his secret of being happy.

First Lesson to Learn the Skill of Happiness

My doppelganger tries to impress on me that he never make an effort to change his past. He only makes changes to his life under his control. He makes an effort to make every day a better and more productive day. This is the first thing I learn. I need to accept things that cannot be changed. I know immediately that everything in my life is not going to be perfect. What had happened to me during childhood, during working life, and family life had passed, and I cannot change them. These happenings are perfectly all right. I need to learn to accept injustice and setbacks in my past that cannot be changed. So what shall I do? Instead, I must invest my energy on changing what I can control for the better. I will try to make every day a better day for me and my family. By doing so, every yesterday will be a day of great memory and happiness.

My doppelganger tells me that grudges are bad for happiness. He has the habit of letting them go and cremate them. The second thing that dawned on me is let go of grudges. Holding a grudge again any one encourages resentment, anger, hurt, and other negative emotions. These are standing in the way of my happiness. I need to practise forgiving and forgetting to regain my own happiness. A lot of practice is needed to achieve this. Keep trying until I achieve this. I need to do it patiently, consistently, persistently, and regularly until I achieve my goal. Letting go of a grudge frees me from negativity and allows me more space for positive emotions to fill in.

My doppelganger is such a kind person. He is also very happy. The display of kindness by him is demonstrated everywhere. The third habit for me to learn is to treat everyone with kindness. First, learn to say sorry when I make a mistake and learn to say thank you when someone does me a favour. Give a helping hand when someone is in difficulty. Always prepare to help and be helped. Kindness is not only contagious, but also proven to make you happier. Research shows that when you are kind to others, your brain produces feel-good hormones and neurotransmitters like serotonin and you are able to build strong relationship with others, fostering positive feelings all around. We need a clear picture of kindness. Mark Twain reportedly said,

> 'Kindness is a language which the deaf can hear and the blind can read.'

We all admire this quality called kindness and want it to practise consistently by all of us. Kindness is a trait not easily defined. It is a general term referring to a cluster of more specific skills, which essentially involve a specific thoughtfulness displaced towards someone. Many actions such as caring for children or animals are considered as kindness. An act of opening doors for others or an act of giving a helping hand when someone is in difficulty is also considered kindness. Many other characteristics having thoughtfulness or considerate behaviours as common trait are classified as kindness. So to be kind is to be considerate, mindful of another's well being. It is an unselfish act to get the focus off ourselves and on to others.

My doppelganger impresses me with his gratitude towards others especially those who have rendered help to him. The fourth habit for me is to express gratitude for what I have. My doppelganger is always thankful for what he has and he is able to cope with stress, have more positive emotions, and is better able to reach his goals. In fact, he keeps a gratitude journal by actively writing down things he is grateful for each day or week. I need to follow his footstep by recording things that happen in my life to which I am grateful off. Starting from my childhood days, I am grateful to my eldest sister and her husband offering accommodation for me to finish my secondary school. I am grateful to my second sister and her husband who gave me a loan to finish my university education. I am grateful to my third sister and her husband who helped me to buy my second investment property. I am grateful to my girlfriend who helped me to buy my first car. She is now my wife. There are many things in my life I grateful off. All these memories have been linked to my happy moods, greater optimism, and better physical health.

My doppelganger is always cheerful, and he does not entertain any unpleasant event happening. He lets it go. The fifth habit I learn is not to sweat over the small stuff. Many things happen in our daily life. Some are pleasant and some are less pleasant. If the issue I am mad about, I will not sweat over it. It will be irrelevant soon in a matter of time. Happy people know how to let life's daily irritations roll off their back. Learn and practise this habit to avoid being drag down and become unhappy.

My doppelganger is a typical optimist, and he always has some kind words for others. The sixth habit I need to learn is to speak well of others. My doppelganger convinces me to avoid gossiping and talking negatively about others. He explains that doing such things is like taking a bath in negative emotions and my body will soak them up. Instead, I need to make it a point to only talk positively and use nice words about other people.

Doing so will help me foster more positive thinking in my life. Happiness will follow.

Time to say goodbye to my doppelganger and we will meet again in another session to continue to learn new skills regarding other habits of happiness.

Second Lesson to Learn the Skill of Happiness

After exploring and learning six habits of happiness in lesson one, my meditation led me to other habits of happy people. I will do more learning through my doppelganger in Quantum Jumping.

The six habits to be mastered include the following:

1. Accept what cannot be changed
2. Let go of grudges
3. Treat everyone with kindness
4. Express gratitude for what you have
5. Don't sweat the small stuff
6. Speak well of others.

I have put the six habits into practice in my daily life, and I seem to be in a better mood every day and appear happier as each day passes.

Time for new meditation begins again. This time I want my doppelganger to show me other habits of happy people so that I can put them into my daily routine. Life is full of problems as the saying goes. Do we accept such phenomenon? I consulted and learnt from my twin-self regarding this issue.

Here comes the seventh habit which I need to learn. Regard my problems as challenges. I need to change my internal dialogue so that anytime I have a 'problem', I will view it as a challenge or a new opportunity to change my life for the better. I need to eliminate the word 'problem' from my mindset.

Another habit I need to learn is to dream big. My doppelganger encourages me to dream big. Just like him, I am more likely to accomplish my goals. I believe in the infinite power of my brain to achieve virtually anything I desire by dreaming big, thus opening my mind to more optimistic and positive state. There is nothing to lose by dreaming big. Hope or dream is the mother of all men.

The important habit to learn is not to make excuses. My doppelganger convinces me that it's easy to blame others for your life failures, but doing so means you're unlikely to rise past then. Happy people take responsibility for their mistakes or missteps and use the failure as an opportunity to change for the better.

The habit to learn is to live in the present. All of us have different past experiences: some were pleasant or positive and some were unpleasant or negative. So I learn not to allow my past negative events to replay in my head or worry about my future. I try to immerse in whatever I am doing now and take time to really be in the present moment. I try to practise this habit as often as possible and know what's going on in my life. I will make today the best day I want it to be. You will make every yesterday a memorable and happy day.

Another extra habit I learn is that I will not compare myself with others. Remember each of us is unique. So I do not measure my own worth by comparing myself to my relatives or friends. I learn that even regarding myself better than my peers is detrimental to my happiness as I am fostering judgemental feelings and is an unhealthy sense of superiority. I will measure my success based on my own progress alone and not that of others.

A good habit I learn is to wake up at the same time every morning. Try to get up every morning at the same time is deceptively simple. Able to do it regularly every morning will help regulate my circadian rhythm so I will have an easier time getting up and likely feel more energised. Most successful people have the habit of getting up early, and it enhances their productivity and focus. Another good habit I have is to brush my teeth after every meal. When I was in school and working, I used to bring along a toothbrush in my pocket. After every snack, even tea time, I brushed my teeth to feel comfortable. Even now I still practise this good habit. The reward is that all my teeth are as good as ever. By practicing these habits, I am more likely to become successful, healthier, and happier.

Another useful habit I learn is to surround myself with positive people. 'Birds of a feather flock together' or 'misery loves company' seems entirely true. So I try to choose my friends who are optimistic and happy themselves as I will be surrounded by positive energy. I use my discretion and avoid people with plenty of grudges. I also avoid mixing with people who are always pessimistic. I know their influence is not good for me.

I also learn to take time to listen to others. Once I am surrounded by positive and optimistic people, listening helps me to soak in the wisdom of others and allows me to quiet my own mind at the same time. By practising intense listening, it can help me gain different perspectives. By practising this habit as often as I possibly can, I soon learn that my wisdom and judgement will improve. Consequently, I feel happier.

A critical good habit to learn is nurture social relationship. All of us are gregarious animals. Positive social relationships are keys to happiness. So I make sure that I take time to visit friends, family members, and significant others.

I learn an independent habit to realise that I don't need others approval. To be successful in life, I need to listen to advices and consider different opinions. But it is important to follow my own dreams and desires without letting naysayers stand in my way. Happy people stay true to their hearts and don't get bogged down with the need for outside approval.

The most important habit for me to learn is to be honest. Honesty is the best policy. After learning that my conscience is always clear. I realise that every time I lie, my stress levels are likely to increase and my self-esteem will crumble just a little bit more. If others find out that I am a liar, it will damage my personal and professional relationship. On the other hand, telling the truth boosts my mental health and allows others to build trust in me. I started to practise this habit as early and I become a happier person.

The last and critical habit to learn is to establish personal control. I know my destiny is in my own hand. So I avoid letting other people dictate the way I live. Instead, I try to establish my own personal control in my life that allows me to fulfil my own goals and dreams. Being independent is a great sense of personal self-worth. By being aware and following these habits, I know I will achieve a happier and more fulfilled lifestyle.

Third Lesson to Learn the Skill of Happiness

The intention of this meditation is to complete the set of habits to attain full happiness. The first two lessons have covered eighteen habits of enhancing happiness. These habits need daily practice to be effective. We need patience, consistency, persistency, and diligence to achieve happiness. To refresh your memory of practicing these habits regularly to attain happiness,

1. Accept what cannot be changed
2. Let go of grudges
3. Treat everyone with kindness
4. Express gratitude for what you have
5. Don't sweat the small stuff
6. Speak well of others
7. Regard your problems as challenges
8. Dream big
9. Avoid making excuses
10. Live in the present
11. Don't compare yourself with others
12. Wake up at the same time every morning
13. Surround yourself with positive people
14. Take time to listen
15. Nurture social relationship
16. Realise that you don't need other's approval
17. Be honest
18. Establish personal control

I began my Quantum Jumping with the intention of completing my full set of habits in attaining happiness. When I was in my alpha state and facing the door which slowly opened, I could see my doppelganger jumping over that door and slowly walking towards me. We merged, and the reverse jumping happened. It became clear to me that my twin-self was here to learn from me the remaining habits which were my strong points.

First of all, I am always fit as I play tennis regularly and climb the mountain on a regular basis. These exercises seem to boost my level of health-promoting brain chemicals like serotonin, dopamine, and norepinephrine, which can help to buffer some of the effects of stress and also relieve some symptoms of depression. These regular exercises, though serve as a medical tool to lose weight, keep lean, prevent disease, and help me live longer, they also serve as a daily tool to immediately enhance my frame of mind, reduce stress, and make me feel happier.

Second, I eat well. I live on plenty of fruits and vegetables. I have fish three or four times a week and other meats intermittently. I eat moderately and consume no sugar and animal fats. I avoid soda drinks and processed junk foods totally. I drink almost two litres of water every day. Little do I realise that what I eat directly impacts my mood and energy levels in both short and long terms. My choice of foods serves well for both physical and emotional wellness.

Third, I live minimally. I am an orderly person. My observation of clutter frightens me. Clutter has a way of sucking the energy right out of you and replacing it with the feelings of chaos. This habit is often an unrecognised source of stress that prompts of anxiety, frustration, and distraction. Avoid clutter by getting rid of excess papers, files, and other stuffs that not only take up physical space but also take up your mental space. Learn the skill of placing things in orderly manner and organise your space to suit your lifestyle.

Finally, I am a regular quantum jumper. This routine helps me to keep my mind focused, calm my nerves, and support my inner peace. All these meditations and visualisations seem to lead me to physical changes in my brain and make me happier.

My doppelganger, in his reverse Quantum Jumping, seems to learn my strong points: exercise, eat well, live minimally, and meditate regularly. These four habits plus the eighteen other habits of happy people will certainly make any one who yearns for happiness to be busy pursuing these skills. The journey in this pursuit will worth every effort you put in.

Quantum Jumping to Overcome Unhappiness over Issues of the Past

Throughout our lives, we have to make many decisions regarding our career, our relationship, where we live, and how many children we are going to have. However, the most important decision is the one regarding our own happiness. Do you allow past issues or external factors to make you unhappy? You can decide to be happy regardless of external factors which are beyond your control. How do you do it? As usual, I will do a Quantum Jump to consult my doppelganger who is a psychologist and a counsellor. As soon as I merge with my twin-self, my imaginations seem to be able to provide the following suggestions to overcome my unhappiness because of the past issues. I must start changing my source of happiness from external to internal, and I will be able to conquer my emotional feelings. I must decide now not to attach conditions to my happiness. I must not insist in conditions such as getting an apology, a letter of admission, a good partner, or a good job first. When I make the commitment to be happy right now, I will truly on the path to living the life I was born to live. This powerful intention will eventually transform any disharmony because of past issues to feelings of peace and bliss. Such an intention of unconditional happiness will create a heightened awareness of anything that is standing in my way to my happiness. Such unresolved issues which are not the purpose will become obvious. Initially, it can be confusing as the feeling of discord within. However, this is a wonderful opportunity to use such feelings, as alchemy to connect to my true source of happiness. In my imagination, my doppelganger whispers to me that there are three steps I can take.

The first step is to sit with the discomfort of the feeling of such emotional pain instead of blaming others. These feelings can be very uncomfortable because of the unresolved issues. Allow such feelings to surface. Do not make any judgement or analysis. Instead, allow such feeling to connect to the heart, my strong part. Let the healing take its course. This can be challenging as my heart may be telling me things that I may initially prefer not to know. However, I know my heart is never wrong as it's the very own internal guidance system. Let the loving heart take control, and if there is anything requires forgiveness, the heart will do the rest. Allow the emotional energy to pass, and start thinking, saying, and doing things in harmony. Happiness will slowly make its appearance.

The second step is to make decisions about the things preventing my happiness. Once the unresolved issues have surfaced, allow them to pass. Start the healing process from the heart. I will have clarity of thought regarding my unhappiness and allow forgiveness to do the rest. My heart will tell me what I need to know through meditation. I will receive a kind and loving response that is custom made for me. Happiness is possible now if I decide to be happy.

The third step is to speak and act on the truth once my heart has spoken. This will allow me to flow with life instead of being stuck to my current unhappy situations. I realise now that those challenging moments are part of my happiness when I embrace them and let them flow. These moments will no longer create fear or emotional pain within me as I open my heart and transform any unresolved pain into love. I can allow my life to evolve and unfold in a way that I connect to and experience the deep well of happiness that resides within me. This powerful life force from within will help to move me forward in the direction that makes me happy. This reinforces the saying of Gandhi that 'happiness is when what you think, what you say and what you do are in harmony'.

QUANTUM JUMPING TO REINVENT YOURSELF

One morning I met an old friend whom I did not see for many years. He looked disappointed and rather sad. He had just lost his job because his company was downsizing. He had been with the company for more than three decades. He was angry because the company did not appreciate his contributions. I consoled him by asking him to reinvent himself. I told him to let thing go because he could not change his past. Now was the time to create a new life. I told him that I left my job when I was fifty-one. I loved my job because I was a great teacher. I did my best for the development and growth of my school as a principal. When I had achieved what I set out to do during the six years as administrator, I knew I had to move on and let another person continue the process. I had helped to build five spacious science laboratories, a new sixth-form block, an extended canteen, and a badminton hall with four courts. The school became the most outstanding academic institution for boys in Petaling District, and we were outstanding in all games. When all these projects and achievements were met, I knew it was time for me to move on. I knew my friend was in a different situation. But it is all the same because change means reinvention. It is not easy to leave a job or a relationship. We have to take control of who we will become or risk never reaching our full potential. I told him that I have reinvented myself several times in my life. I did not forget to choose reinvention each time I faced the situation. I shared with him that he had to forge his new path deliberately and with foresight. My advice to him was that not to wait for your future to find you and you would probably wait in vain. The best thing to confront the situation was not to think about your past but plan what you wanted to do for your future. Suddenly, I mentioned Quantum Jumping to help him reinvent himself. I shared with him the concept of Quantum Jumping so that he could contact his successful doppelganger in an alternate universe to show him the way. He agreed, and we started our meditation together in a quiet room.

Our intention was to reinvent ourselves for the future. Soon, I was in deep visualisation mood, and my successful doppelganger suggested that the following steps would be helpful to reinvent ourselves, especially my friend. First, create a vision for your future. Second, write about your intention. Third, surround yourself with visual reminders of the life you would like to create. Fourth, break up your vision into workable tasks, and finally, every day, go back to that vision of you walking towards your future. Choose courage instead of letting your fear choose your future for you.

When we opened our eyes, we were not sure what the steps meant. We left them as they were and explored their inner implications later on. We agreed to meet again the following week to discuss the steps and their implications.

A week past, and we met again. Things seemed to have changed. We had coffee together. My friend was in good mood. He had found a part-time job and he had decided to take it easy. He was keen to follow my footsteps to do some investing while doing his part-time job. We went back to discuss the five steps we need to reinvent ourselves. I gave my opinions.

First, to create a vision for my future is to imagine the situation that I need to leave behind. Start to imagine the future that I want. What type of new life or a new job that I want. I would like to picture the sun coming behind my future, the warm glow of the light on my face. Let my silent voice of appreciation regarding everything that came before pass by. Be thankful for the past and turn towards the sun. With compassion and gratitude, I imagine myself walking away from the past and into the future.

Second, write about your reinvention. I will imagine a new scene to create. Where I am going or living? What do I do in the morning, afternoon, and evening? Who are my new friends? What do I spend days doing? Write down whatever come into my head. I will look at it occasionally. I will add others that come into my head.

Third, I will surround myself with visual reminders of the life I will like to create. The images will remind me regarding the direction I am moving towards.

Fourth, I will break up my vision of the future into workable tasks. What I need to do every day to create that vision. To be an investor and writer, what do I need to know to be successful? I need to make a list of things that I need to do. Once I have listed, then I will do it and commit to keep doing it, one day at a time.

Finally, every day, I will go back to that vision and start walking towards my future. I will meditate and visualise myself walking into the rising sun and towards my dream. I will commit myself moving towards this new possibility. Reinvention is neither easy nor always smooth. I experienced plenty of resistance. We do not want to let go things that even cause us pain or things that are obviously already out of our grasp. We often struggle with limiting beliefs about ourselves that hold us back from trying new things. Each time we fall into these old habits like isolating ourselves, making excuses not to look for work, and procrastinating on a task that might advance our career, we must take the attitude not to bother why we are doing it. Just ask ourselves this: 'What can I do in this moment to keep moving forward?' irrespective of our feeling and keep on doing something to gather momentum. An old adage that says true courage isn't about not feeling fear, but it's about feeling fear and acting anyway. So it is better to choose courage instead of letting your fear choose your future for you.

Quantum Jumping to Find Ways to become a Better Leader

One Sunday morning, I met a few old friends. We had not seen each other for quite sometimes. We had a few discussions regarding leadership. One of them asked me for suggestions regarding ways to become better and more effective leader in any organisation or business. From my own experiences as a principal of an institution, I told them that an important characteristic was being likable. Being likable would help a leader not only in his or her job but also relationship and life. Many simple things like being polite, kind, cheerful disposition, and helpful could help a leader to be more successful. Another golden rule was to treat others as a leader liked to be treated. One should show others the same courtesy a leader expected from others. By holding others including staff, customers, or business partners at high regards and respect, a leader would demonstrate his or her likeability and that would motivate others to work with you. The brainstorming session managed to reveal some of the ways to become an effective leader. Characteristics such as listening, storytelling, authenticity, transparency, a team player, responsiveness, passion, surprise and delight, simplicity, and gratitude were mentioned. Not much detail for each was discussed because of time factor.

When I reached home, I was curious to go into detail the ways to help a leader to be more effective to accomplish his or her job. As usual I used Quantum Jumping as a vehicle to acquire the detailed facts regarding ways to enhance leadership. I managed to jump into another parallel dimension where my doppelganger was a great leader in a big corporation in that universe. We merged, and I got all his rhythm and energy. I observed that when his staff or customers talked, my twin-self listened carefully and completely. When I was the principal, I might have forgotten this, and I seldom listened completely. My alternate-self seemed to listen to what his staff and his customers wanted and needed. He was open to new ideas by listening more. I also noticed that my twin-self used storytelling to bring home his vision and sell his ideas. Customers and followers were usually captivated by interesting stories, and they seemed to remember better. It became a win-win situation when customers were motivated by the stories and they took action. Another observation that attracted me was his authenticity. He said who he was and had integrity beyond compare.

Vulnerability and humility were his hallmarks, and he created much positive attractive energy. His staff and customers seemed to have great inclination to help him succeed. My doppelganger was always transparent about who he was in his family life and professional life. Transparency became his hallmark. This was his great leverage for being truthful. Openness and honesty seemed to give him happier staff, customers, and colleagues. He had no secret which normally would be exposed. So he slept well without worrying what he had said before. Finally, being a happy leader he became more productive and more successful. He was a good team player. He understood that his business needed teamwork to beat the odds. He practised humility allowing others to shine, encouraging others to provide innovative ideas and following other rules for teamworks. By doing so he became a more likeable leader. He was very responsive to his staff and his customers. He demonstrated cares and interest allowing his staff and colleagues to make positive contributions to his organisation. His willingness to adapt to new technologies plus his humility made him a great leader. He showed great passion because he loved his job. He utilised surprise and delight to keep his staff and customers excited. He smiled very often, and his gesture of surprise and delight created incredible word-of mouth marketing opportunities. He was able to put complicated ideas into simple ones because he knew that his customers often responded best to simplicity either in design, form, and function. He took complex projects, challenges, and ideas and distilled them into their simplest components allowing customers, staff, and other stakeholders to better understand and buy into his vision. He knew human all crave simplicity, and he focused and delivered simplicity. Finally, he believed and maintained that thanks were the highest form of thought and that gratitude was happiness doubled by wonder. He was grateful for the people who had contributed to his opportunities and success. The qualities such as being thankful, remain humble, and appreciative were well received. I observed that he felt great and always showed courtesy and held others with high regards. No wonder he was such a likeable and successful leader.

Quantum Jumping to Attract Wealth

One evening I was in my friend's house having tea with his family. We talked about many things regarding health, relationship, and wealth. My friend mentioned poverty consciousness, and he seemed to suffer from that rhythm. That rhythm is a form of negative energy. This rhythm is going to affect your attitude towards abundance. He told me that he earned a good salary but he did not manage to accumulate any wealth. In contrast, he seemed to think that I was wealthy. I joked with him that I was wealthy because I might have an affluent consciousness. I might have turned myself into a money magnet. I casually mentioned about Quantum Jumping to change his rhythm into affluent consciousness. When his wife left the table, we were all alone. I managed to convince him that poverty consciousness was a rhythm or an attitude which could be changed. I suggested that he should try Quantum Jumping with me to change his rhythm from poverty consciousness to wealth consciousness. I directed the process, and soon we were at the quantum door and we crossed that partition into an infinite number of universes. We picked a universe where he had a doppelganger with affluent consciousness. I led him to merge with his doppelganger and allowed his visualisation to run wide. His twin-self had all the characteristics of wealth consciousness.

First thing to bring about a new rhythm of affluent consciousness, he needed to bring about self-awareness from now onwards. Each evening, he was advised to re-examine the things he had done and should have done a little differently each. He would soon find that the number of things he needed to do a little differently was slowly diminishing. Self-awareness regarding our thinking that we only deserve a small amount of everything has given us our self-limitation.

We usually indulge in self-sabotaging in whatever thing we do. As soon as we realise that we have overcome those silly thinking and doing things we usually do, we are ready to transform our life to accumulate wealth. Things like value for money when we make a purchase, we need to ask the question whether we can have an alternate and cheaper thing instead. Self awareness is absolutely necessary when a decision to buy or to improvise is made. This self-awareness will be activated every day regarding value of money. Once this is achieved, we will soon accumulate some good money and will be ready to do some investment like buy some shares or buy an investment property to get ready for retirement.

All these visualisations can be imagined, and they can be achieved with self-awareness and discipline. Soon, the rhythm of affluent consciousness will start to grow and we will slowly turn into a money magnet, an electromagnet where we control by applying our own electrical energy. All these appear to be simple. Yes, everything is simple if we learn to do it. The necessary first step is to avoid debt especially credit-card debt. The second step is to make full use of the value of each dollar we earn.

To help to save money, we need to make available a multiple streams of income besides our salary. And we need to exploit our full potentials using your mental visualisation power. Get involve in other ventures like writing, sports couching, and others to create opportunities for extra income. Finally, get interested in investing to make your dollars grow. All these characteristics are dominant features of his doppelganger in another parallel universe. I have given him a comparison between foods that I like and foods that I do not like. For foods that I like, I have a fast rhythm of three times per second, and for foods that I dislike, I have a slow rhythm of one per second. But certain foods that I dislike have good nutritional values and are healthy to my body. So I need to change my rhythm when I eat these healthy foods. So whenever I take these foods, I change to a fast rhythm so that I grow to like them. Similarly, we can change our poverty consciousness rhythm from slow to fast and acquire your affluent consciousness rhythm. Try this technique every morning for thirty seconds, and soon, you will acquire the affluent consciousness rhythm. This attitude will soon develop and you will be more courageous to make decisions to affluent consciousness. He will have supplied energy to his magnetic system, and you will soon become a money electromagnet. I managed to lead him into all these possibilities and imaginations. He promised to try, and I am waiting patiently for a few years to see the results.

Quantum Jumping into Absolution

A friend came to visit us during the summer holidays. He told me a story about his son being affected by a few past incidents. Those incidents seemed to affect his son's decision-making and career advancement. I listened to his stories with the intention to help him, and his son overcame his problems. I shared my new finding about absolution meditation to overcome past sins or mistakes. I introduced and discussed the new concept of Quantum Jumping with him. He was sceptical about the concept. I told him that I, too, was sceptical initially. But when I found that this new concept works, my scepticism vanished. He wanted some proofs that this new method, called absolution meditation, works. After some discussions with him, I soon realised that he was not trying to be difficult, he was indirectly asking for help. He wanted to believe that such new strategy would help his son; he just needed more reasons to take a step forward. I advocated that he should learn Quantum Jumping first before he could help his son. I referred him to the introductory course given by Burt Goldman. I gave him three months to become a quantum jumper before I could introduce absolution meditation to him.

Three months later, he came back to visit me. He was delighted that he had mastered the art of Quantum Jumping. He was able to convince his son to do likewise. Now he was ready to learn the art of absolution meditation. The intention was crystal clear that he wanted his son to meet his doppelganger in another parallel universe who had managed to overcome past events which he regretted, felt guilty about, or would change if he could. His thoughts might surprise you with what his mind came up with. The twin-self was able to deal with it and overcome whatever happened before. So when his son jumped through the quantum door, he would be able to tell his redeemer, his doppelganger, that he would have nothing to be shame off. I asked him to tell the whole stories and let go all of them from his subconscious. By letting all out, let the guilt vanish and change him mentally for the better. Let his intention be clear. His absolution meditation was to acknowledge the actual events that were causing him problems. I asked him to speak it out and let his subconscious be clear. After the let go, he should not be concerned about his past events, just should allow his consciousness to be directed to the place, and wherever he goes was the right place. I wanted to allow his inner conscious be his guide.

If one absolution meditation was not enough, I asked him to repeat other absolution meditations until the problems were controlled. Then he should move on with other Quantum Jumps to improve his mental strength and let the infinite power of his mind do the rest in his future life.

Nothing venture nothing gain. The journey of a thousand miles begins with the first step.

Quantum Jumping into a Long and Happy Life

Life expectancy in every culture tells us that there is always a scientific number which a person can live. But we notice that in every culture there are people who live well beyond that expected number. What do these people do to beat the expected number they are supposed to die? To search for common answers to this critical question, I fall back to Quantum Jumping asking my doppelganger in another parallel universe who has lived a happy and is enjoying his longevity. It takes me only a couple of minutes to reach him. After merging with my twin-self, I manage to make the following observations. First, my doppelganger is enjoying his life telling me that people live longer if they love their lifestyle and love what they are doing. He has full control of his career as a teacher. Although he has good partners who can help to relieve part of his burden and seem to help him making things easier, but he ultimately views his business or career as he himself. He opts to choose himself. He believes in the concept of multiple sources of income. This concept is worth emulating for financial security. The saying that it is not wise to put all eggs in just one basket is important. My successful doppelganger adheres to the practice of mastering one thing at a time. At first he masters his self-study strategy as a student and helps others to learn using his strategy. While helping his students to learn effectively, not only he benefits financially, but also he develops effective self-study approaches. Once he gets bored with one thing, he moves on to master another thing that he loves doing. This time he takes up writing as his new venture besides his career as a teacher. He masters the skill of writing, and he benefits immensely from his new publications. Money seems to be the side effect of doing what he loves to do. He does it for fun, and he never stops having fun in studying and writing. This seems to reinforce the belief that once he becomes good at mastering one thing, it becomes easier for him to master the next thing. He learns the language of mastery, and mastering a new thing is easy for him. He applies the same principle to his games. He masters tennis with so much fun, and he moves on to master golf with equal zest.

This process helps to make him look young and enterprising. He keeps fit and has a young athletic look. He does that by drinking a lot of water, and he does not eat a lot of foods especially carbohydrates. He finds fun in competing, and he has good connection with others. By doing that he improves his insulin sensitivity and manages his carbohydrate tolerance. It appears that most of his carbohydrates in his blood are converted and stored as glycogen in his muscle cells to be converted as energy when he competes in his fun games. He has fun, and he loves it.

In everything he takes up, he has a goal to accomplish and a purpose to master it most of the time. This revelation tells me that my chronological age is just a number and my physiological age is more important. My doppelganger is seventy-five years old, but his physiological age is about sixty that he is able to perform activities most normal people at sixty can do. I strongly believe my doppelganger will live well past the expected scientific age to die. He enjoys many things, and he enjoys his life. His life is usually free from stress and pressure. He lives a simple but a productive and useful life. There are always new ventures for him to think off. For example, my doppelganger is planning another new book to write and a new business to embark on. This tells me that to live happily I need to plan ahead and enjoy another new journey in life. Keeping busy and healthy becomes a daily routine. He always looks forward to new and exciting ventures each day of his life. He loves every inch of his life, and his next birthday is of no significance to him.

I bring back his rhythm and his approaches to life. Hopefully, I will also live a long and healthy life.

Quantum Jumping to Imitate the Habits of Happy People

After learning strategies to be happy, now I am interested to imitate the habits of happy people. Before I can imitate their habits, I need to make observations what are the habits of these happy people. My natural response is my imagination through Quantum Jumping. I have a powerful tool at my disposal. It only takes a few minutes and I am with my doppelganger from another parallel universe who is one of the happiest people there. I am able to merge with him and acquire his rhythm and energy. My imagination is engaged and I can visualize all his habits. The following living habits become obvious to me.

First, he is fit and healthy. He makes his body happy because he knows there is connection between his body and mind. He is just like me, happily married. He thinks positively, he exercises regularly and I believe he enjoys sex most of the time. It's simple. He knows that the happier the body, the happier he thinks.

Second, he takes ownership of his happiness. He knows he alone is responsible for his happiness. He does not harbor any blame on other people. Consequently he is able to experience more of it and quickly too. Simple his attitude is right.

Third, he does not believe everything he thinks off. He realizes that his mind is capable of throwing up negative thoughts, fears and anxieties. This is natural. But he does not have to take every thought seriously. He disciplines himself to focus on his positive thoughts and acts on them. He lets go the rest of the negative ones.

Fourth, he lets love lead him all the way to happiness. He not only allows loves abound in his life but also gives love freely. He loves what he does and loves helping others. There is certain risk while doing this but the reward far outweighs the risk. He knows the more love he shares, the happier he becomes.

Fifth, he believes in the wonders of the world. He tunes into higher power. I notice that people who believe in a power beyond tend to be happy. He is one of them. This helps him to cultivate faith that his goals and dreams will manifest. This belief is significant in his pursuit of his dreams. He lives with hope but also with actions.

By believing that he will succeed always add happiness in his journey of life.

Sixth, he is inspired and feels that his drawn to a bigger purpose than himself. He knows he is there to serve others. He discovers that the bigger he dreams, the more people he will impact, and the happier he will be.

Lastly, he has good relationship with people around him and his environment. He puts in a lot of effort in giving special focus on relationship rather than getting it. He helps others, he praises others who also help, he loves others and he supports others. The more he gives, the more he receives. Consequently he becomes happier.

On reflection, I have been a servant to many people during my working career as a teacher and an administrator. I also serve by providing curriculum materials to make learning easier. By doing so I have constantly adding values to others, and I am getting values that come back to me. It becomes natural that I also become happier. I have been honest and show gratitude to everything I get. When I come back to my own room, I quickly make a resolution that I am going to imitate all these habits so that I too can become one of the happiest people on this earth.

Quantum Jumping to Be a Successful Investor

I have been an investor from the day I started my third stage of my working life. I was late to start this critical stage of my life. I was already thirty years old when I graduated from the university with a degree in science, B.Sc. (Hons). I just got married, and I just managed to settle all my debts, the money I borrowed to get my university education. Looking back, that was the best investment I ever made. The three and a half years I spent in the university to pursue my degree had given good discipline, perseverance, and commitment. This critical thinking taught me an important lesson in life. Knowing that data is not information, information is not knowledge, and knowledge is not wisdom. Learning the skill of interpreting data is critical. This skill needs experience and learning especially in investment whether stocks or properties. I like learning. I went on to get my master's degree and eventually my Ph.D. I enjoy the learning journey all the way.

Using the new acquired skills in imaginations and visualisations through Quantum Jumping, I would like to share the wisdom with others to become successful investor. As usual, with my eyes closed, I was on the pathway leading to the gate of the next parallel universe to meet my doppelganger who was already a successful investor. I began to visualise his philosophy and knowledge related to investment in stocks. My imagination told me that my doppelganger started the habit of investment when he was very young. He started when he was in primary school. His father was a basketball enthusiast, and he told him that there were two types of valued players. This first category of players was those who were consistently good most of the time. A typical example was Michael Jordan of Chicago Bull. They might play badly in a few games. Another category of players were those who were good only in a few games and they soon disappeared from the scene. His father impressed on him that he should only keep cards of players belonging to the first type. His father gave him some pocket money, and he bought a few packets of these cards of valued players. When his classmates offered to buy some of his cards at a good price, he sold only those cards of players belonging to the second category and made a good profit. He kept on accumulating cards of players of the first category type and their value kept increasing. When he started working, he had accumulated many boxes of these cards commemorating these valued players. He sold them with good profit because of their values. He started investing in the stock market using this same philosophy. He started investing into value companies whose profits and dividends would increase consistently. They might suffer from occasional setbacks because of recession or market collapse. These value companies were fundamentally very sound, and they always emerged from any setback without much damage. He reinvested his dividends and harvested from the compounding effect of their growth. When he was fifty years old, he was already a wealthy man. He was able to retire from his job as a teacher to become a full-time investor and do the things he was interested. His methods of investing were rather similar to my own strategies of investments.

My visualisations tell me that to be a successful investor, one must avoid these three common mistakes. First, do not buy or sell with one's heart but with one's mind. My doppelganger embraces the philosophy of not buying when everyone is doing so. His basic philosophy is not to follow the herb for fear of losing opportunities of profit. He shows a lot of patience, and this helps him from overpaying for a stock even it is fundamentally sound. Some investors sell their stocks out of fear when the market retreats even the stocks are fundamentally making good money. The ability to use the mind and to acquire knowledge through one's own research instead of being controlled by emotion is critical for success in investing. This is to look well into the matter before buying or selling. The second mistake is not to ignore inflation. Sitting on one's capital without taking risk is never safe. Inflation will slowly erode the value of one's capital. Considering 4 per cent of annual inflation will devalue a capital of $10,000 to $9,600 after one year. In five years, the value will be reduced to almost $8,000. Your money is losing its intrinsic value. It is wise to make the money work for you by investing wisely and looking well into the stock or investment. Third mistake we make is to trust the wrong people. Many advisors or brokers used to talk up the matters for their self-interest. Please bear in mind most people do not have your interest in mind. Knowledge is important, but it does not make you wise. Wisdom in investment comes with using knowledge correctly to benefit one's investment.

My doppelganger likes to read, and he enjoys reading. It is a coincidence that he too believes in the fundamental principles in the Bible. He uses the biblical codes to help him benefit from his investment. Most of us have the misconception that money is the root of all ever. It is not. Money is necessary in all transaction and business deals. In fact, the Apostle Paul states clearly that the love of money is the root of all evils. This is different because the love of money influences us to become greedy and careless. We are emotionally influenced to become instant millionaires without looking well into our investments. Our attitude towards money is critical here. We embrace the philosophy of becoming wealthy so that we can be of great help to those who are less fortunate. The biblical code is clear that you practise more you will be blessed more. Jesus put much emphasis on the right attitude of investment and the righteous ways towards wealth. More than half of the forty parables given by Jesus are concerned with money. In one of his parables, he tells the following story: there was a rich businessman who was about to leave for a long journey to do his business. He called all his three servants and instructed them to help him to grow his money. To the first servant, he gave five talents, to the second he gave two talents, and to the third servant he gave one talent. Each talent was equivalent to about twenty years of a worker's wages. So a talent in today's term is equivalent to about a million dollars. The first servant invested wisely and doubled his capital and so was the second servant, who turned his two talents into four talents. The third servant was too cautious because he loved money and fear controlled him. He was afraid to lose the one talent and so he buried the talent in a safe place. When the master returned, he was filled with joy when the first two servants reported their profits in their investments. The third servant thought that he had played it safe by returning the talent. The master was angry because he did not make use of the money for investment or at least deposit in a bank for interest. The master rewarded the first two servants and gave them more responsibilities for future investment. To third servant, the one talent was taken away and given to the other two servants.

This biblical code tells us that if you are good steward of your money, you will be blessed with more. Playing safe with your money without investing it for the love of that money, you may not be blessed with more. In fact, inflation will rob you of your precious saving.

Investment is a tricky game. To be successful, we need to find good companies to invest. Companies are affected by the economic cycles. For most companies, the biggest factors driving them are often outside the control of the management. What we are seeing now, 2015, are interest rates, regulations, new technology, consumer taste, oil prices, the strength of US dollars, and even demographics. If we are observant, we will notice that there are two big trends shaping the current market: low interest rate and the strength of the US dollars. Be aware that low interest rate provides many advantages for companies to borrow and expand with minimum risk. They make use of other's assets to grow their business. In the last three years, many market observers expect interest rates to rise. But they are consistently being wrong. At the same time, the US dollars have strengthened against major currencies by about 23 per cent in the last twelve months. What a big move! What is the implication? This means that interest rates are even less likely to rise soon. Imports are cheap now in the United States and that holds down inflation. So it is unlikely interest will rise in the immediate future. The strength of US dollars is affecting companies exporting goods overseas, and they are making less profit in their transactions. That affects their growth and hiring. This is another discouragement for interest rates to rise.

Knowing these two big trends operating in the 2015, we should start looking into some sectors which will benefit from these two big trends. Your guess is as good as mine. The utilities sector is our choice. Utility companies are often seen as stodgy investments. They are highly regulated and are also their profit. They often operate as local monopolies. They need investments in big expensive projects to expand their networks and upgrade their system. Low interest rates seem to benefit them resulting in higher profit. Being local companies the strength of US dollars will give them a boost. Look out for utility companies with good yield as well as potential for capital gains. This information is necessary for investors to look seriously at companies in the service sector like Internet companies, electricity companies, and other utility companies.

Quantum Jumping to eliminate Emotion from the Investment Decisions' Equation

How do we know when to buy, sell or hold on to a particular stock? In my investment journey, I have been facing this critical problem most of the time! I read with surprise that researchers at Stanford and Carnegie Mellon found that people with brain injuries preventing them from processing emotions made much better investment decisions than ordinary people like us. This suggests that the pathways our brains use to evaluate investment information are linked to emotion inputs and not logical brain pathways as expected. It turns out that most of us are using our emotional side of our brains to make investment decisions instead of the logical ones. Perhaps this partly explains why the brain injury victims who could no longer process emotional stimuli, did better than normal investors. I have the intention to minimize my investment decisions from my emotional input. This Quantum Jumping is for that purpose. As usual it takes only a few minutes for me to meet my doppelganger in another parallel universe. My twin-self is the Warren Buffett in that parallel universe.

My doppelganger has many of the characteristics of Warren Buffett. He is bizarrely unemotional. In investment all of us know that we should do the opposite of the crowd. As quoted in cliches that we should be greedy when everyone else is scared and buy when there's blood in the streets. There are endless such quotations! But guess what? We find it really hard to do it. The herd instinct is the deepest-rooted behavior in most of us. It's been planted into our DNA since the time when our ancestors were cavemen. Until now even brilliant investors find it tough to break away from the crowd. For all of us, it is almost impossible. The exception is Warren Buffett. He is not the same. He is noted to be the most unemotional investor on this universe. He does not care whether his investment decisions make him look foolish or out of touch or what other people think of him at all. His decision not to touch technological stocks during the dotcom burst is a good example. He freely admits that he is 'wired differently' from most of us. He just follows his own investing rules unemotionally.

My doppelganger admits that he is not Warren Buffett but he has a system that will eliminate emotion from his investment decisions.

When he invests, he sticks to his system that runs on emotion free measures such as dividend yield, cash flow, profit and relative value of a particular stock. These are all the factors that ultimately drive a stock price. His system is simple based on numbers. He assigns scores for the followings: dividend (0 - 5 points); profit (0 - 5 points); cash flow (0 to 5 points) and growth potential (0 - 6 points). The maximum scores possible for any stock in his radar is 21 points. No stock will ever reach the maximum score! But once a stock reaches 12 points, it is under surveillance. My twin-self will then look into the price chart of the stock for the past two to five years to buy the particular stock when it is under valued. A lot of patience is needed to buy or sell a particular stock. On the other hand if he holds that particular stock which scores more than 12 points, he will hold on to the stock. Once the score dips below 11 points, he will sell that particular stock. By following this system consistently, he is able to win 60% of his stock picking most of the time. If 60% is good for him, it must be good for me in my investment decision making.

Comparing investment to tennis game, a player who wins 50% of his points is rated about number 350 in the ranking. This guy does not make enough money to pay for his travel expenses. Now if another player who wins 55% of his points is a serious contender and is recognized and making a good living. Players like Roger Federer and Djokovic win over 60% of their points, they have won many Grand Slams. The former has won more Grand Slam single titles than any man in history. A small edge is enough to help us make a lot of money. Casinos make tons of money by just having a 2% advantage. Gamblers lose money because of many factors and one of them is the emotional one.

People like us always think of making money in investment. My doppelganger does not think that way. He follows his system so that he does not lose money. His system tells him what stocks not to buy by removing 60% of the stocks in the market. From the remaining 40% of the market, he will more likely to pick winners. After my encounter with his system, I think I have acquired a simple tool to help me make better decisions in investment by minimizing my emotional factor.

These numbers tell me that I will only buy a stock at least 20% cheaper than its true value. And I will take my profit when the price moves 20% above that value. My doppelganger is never sentimental on any of his winners. He does not fall in love with any of his stocks. He knows that it will not return his affection. The last parting can be very costly. He emphasizes that by investing this way he does not need to take big risk to make big money. I plan to follow this system closely and hope to make some money.

Quantum Jumping to Help My Doppelganger How to Use Creative Visualisation to Realise His Dreams

I have been benefiting and improving all aspects of my Life through Quantum Jumping. This jump is different. With the usual procedure, I arrived in another parallel universe meeting my doppelganger who was struggling to live his dream. He wanted to learn from me how to use creative visualisation to shape his future and turn his dream into reality. I loved to tell my story because I knew that the basic ingredients in my story would provide the recipe for his dream to become reality. I had a very difficult time during my childhood. I was conditioned by my father that education was not important but hard work was essential for success. That was my father's experience in his life. His definition of success was different from what I knew now. I was his tool and his manpower to serve the family. For the first fifteen years of my life, I followed my father's belief and worked hard from morning until I went to bed. I did not know that my subconscious mind was programmed and conditioned to think that way. The change took place when I was given the opportunity by my eldest sister to continue my education in the city, Penang. I was sixteen years old and life was totally different. I did not have to work. I had twenty-four hours a day to live my dream. I was overaged, and I could not attain government-aided secondary school. I enrolled in a Mission Private School catered for overaged students to have a second chance in education. I attended school in the afternoon because the school had to borrow classrooms from the government-aided school. I had no room to call my own. I slept on a camp bed under the staircase. I had to get up very early each morning (about 6 a.m.) before my sister and family woke up. I usually escaped to the basketball court every morning with a ball to practise dribbling and shooting. This became my routine every morning just to escape the crowd at my sister's home. I returned for breakfast after 7 a.m., and I was free to do my study. My sister provided me a table for my study. I usually started my day with a short meditation that I learnt from my teacher when I was in my Chinese Primary School. This habit was developed to bring in my subconscious mind to help me to plan for my future. I knew that there was nothing new, strange, or unusual about visualisation. It was my natural power of imagination. I used it every day to imagine what will be when I grew up.

I was not aware of this phenomenon during my childhood because I was too busy working from morning to evening. This awakening gave me new power to make use of my basic creative energy. My command of English was weak, and I knew I had to catch up soon or I would drop off. The only source of knowledge came from my few textbooks and few other books found in my sister's house. My short meditation each morning provided me the plan for the day. My intention was very clear. I wanted to master all the subjects I had to take from my school curriculum. My subconscious mind did all the creative visualisations and decisions for me. My success depended on the decisions that I should prepare all the lessons before my teachers' instructions. I had all the time in the world, and I saw the effectiveness of such a self-study strategy in my creative visualisation. The habit was formed each day, and I followed through patiently, diligently, and consistently. The intention was reinforced each morning during my short meditation.

After one semester, my report card celebrated all my efforts. This gave me further motivation to pursue this self-study strategy more intensely. The same creative visualisation was applied to my basketball skills development every morning. I became a great ball handler with my dribbling skills and sharp shooting ability. These skills came in very handy when I took part in my basketball tournaments. I excelled in both my study and my game. My repeated creative visualisation each morning enabled me to see my own future. It is just like what you do in a restaurant. You order your meal say salmon and chips and you wait for your meal to come. So my creative visualisation is similar. I make an order to become a well-known educationist in the future, and I am waiting for the event to come to pass. I saw myself becoming a teacher, and I moved up the ladder of success to become principal. I saw myself writing down my thinking and my creations to be published. I also saw myself playing basketball in front of thousands of spectators and in different cities and countries. I dared to dream big. I was waiting for all these things to happen. I saw myself become an investor and eventually an entrepreneur. I saw myself reaching the highest possible qualification. The orders were made, and the dreams became reality. I had more than twenty textbooks and learning aids to my credit during my twenty-three years of teaching career. I served as curriculum lecturer for in service trainers for mathematics teachers. I had a bachelor of science (honours) degree, a master in education, and a Ph.D.

Financially, I was well prepared for a good retirement. I was able to live comfortably in my chosen city, and I could afford to travel around the world. In my chosen sport, basketball, I represented Penang State, Kedah State, Malaysian Veteran Team, University of Malaya, and Combined University Team in Hong Kong. At the age of seventy-five, I am still playing good tennis and I am very healthy. All these achievements were made possible through my creative visualisation and the courage to dream big. All the information and strategies I adopted were transmitted in terms of rhythm and energy to my doppelganger. He was pleased to share the rhythm and bring back all the strategies to be tried out. Hopefully, he would also succeed in visualising his dreams.

Now I agree that the subconscious mind will ultimately cast the vote on how much success, abundance, health, happiness, and freedom I experience in my life. It is more powerful than my conscious mind. I was able to rewire my subconscious blueprint through imagination, and I dared to dream big.

My doppelganger wants to know other ways of meditation. My answer is simple. Quantum Jumping is just a tool for bringing imagination into our creative visualisation with a specific intention. But according to Osho, a great meditator, every new activity we do is meditation. Walking, jogging, swimming, singing, or anything is meditation. Integration of our body, mind, and soul, the three forms of energy, through meditation, brings harmony when they function together. From the harmony, the combined energy resonates and our creative visualisation is awakened. Our imagination runs wild, and new ideas begin to spring forth. This awakening dips deep down into the core of our subconscious mind and takes control of our past conditioning, reducing its influence in our present life. The moment you are born, conditioning is in progress. The significant influence comes from our parents, relatives, and others we come in contact with. We are told what is right or wrong, what is good or bad, and what we should follow and what not. Not all of these conditioning are bad, but some of them have profound effect, creating our limiting beliefs to live and experience the life we dream of. We become conditioned to fit into certain moulds. We are guided to pursue certain subjects or a specific degree in college according to their thinking. We are expected to behave in a certain way by our elders according to societal norms. No wonder, we live our lives stuck in a pattern of 'rinse-and-repeat' behaviours, and our dreams will always out of reach. We need to find a solution to break through this pattern of self-sabotage. A possible process lies in creative visualisation through meditation. Meditation, in whatever form, is an effective way of reversing these effects. Creative visualisation becomes a powerful tool to counter the past influence and help to reprogramme our subconscious mind to experience the life we dream of. I encourage my doppelganger to take the first step by trying Quantum Jumping as a meditation exercise with specific intention. A journey of a thousand miles begins with the first step. You may be preparing a fertile ground for the creative visualisation flower to bloom. I wish him the best of luck and hope to visit him another time.

Quantum Jumping to Seek Joy in Life

After achieving all I ask for in life, such as financial security, position, and well-being including happiness in my life, what more do I want? Happiness is the constitutional right of every human being. I soon realise that happiness is from the outside and usually unhappiness will follow occasionally. So there must be a difference between happiness and joy in my life! I have a powerful network called Quantum Jumping to provide me the answer I am seeking. My availability technique using my creative visualisation takes me to another parallel universe where my doppelganger is already living his life with joy. In just a few seconds, I catch up with my doppelganger. My imagination begins to do wonder. Wonders begin when you are connected to the mysteries of the world. The world is full of mysterious things. Appreciation starts to grow as you see beauty everywhere. I always marvel at the number of different species of birds, animals, and their colours. Who created them? They are free and happy! Human beings are slightly different. Some are happy and others are not. People experience happiness and also sadness depending on the situation. My doppelganger is smiling and radiating with joy. I ask him why he is forever having joy in his life? His answer is simple. He is happy because his environment provides it. But joy is different from happiness. There is happiness and there is also unhappiness. Joy does not come from outside or other's influence. Joy comes from internal spiritual state of equilibrium, contentment, acceptance, love, and others from within. He lives in joy, and he also lives in love. To him, love is the fragrance of the flower of joy. He usually lives in joy, and he goes to sleep in peace. Happiness is usually temporary, but joy is forever.

Quantum Jumping to Help a Beginner to Start Meditation

I believe after reading this book, you may be keen to experiment meditation as a beginning of Quantum Jumping. The intention of this Jump is to meet my doppelganger who is a meditation instructor in another parallel universe, and the purpose is to seek his help for a beginner to start meditation. As soon as I jump through the quantum door, I meet my doppelganger. We merge to gain his rhythm and energy, and it becomes clear to me that there are four basic steps I can do to help a beginner to meditate.

First, a beginner should concentrate on his posture. According to my doppelganger, the traditional cross-legged meditation position has several advantages. He advises a beginner to make use of any cushion sheet to feel comfortable. In this position, the hip is higher than the knees, providing comfortable circulation. This position allows a free flow of energy through the seven energy centres. It allows a person free open breathing, and it does not constrict any blood flow. Alternatively, I prefer sitting on my comfortable chair with my feet on the ground and my spine unsupported by the back of the chair. One can lie down or stand straight while doing a short meditation. There is no restriction.

Second, a beginner must have his intention clear before he starts meditating. He should be aware that this is a process of self-discovery. The purpose is to teach him the inner working of himself, provided that he is willing to let go of timelines, agendas, and hurry.

The process of self-discovery can be difficult initially. It requires discipline to sit silently and observe his thoughts or silent them entirely. It can be frustrating initially. To be aware that by disempowering the ways of one's thinking can be uncomfortable and unpleasant. But once these thought patterns are identified, one may find it easy to discard them. So one's intention is simply to be an observer of whatever happens. One does not have to control breathing or force oneself into immobile stillness. For a beginner, do not expect anything, just be open to what will unfold. Only make observation. That's all. Let things happen naturally. Do not judge what is happening! Do not worry whether one is doing right! Once aware of what is happening within oneself, the meditation is on the right path.

Third, be focused. For a beginner, just pick a point of focus. It can be just a mental image or a physical one. Having a point focus will help in keeping the mind from wondering. It's a simple way of developing an amazing mental self-mastery. One can make use of this technique to deal with thoughts that arise. A busy mind usually has a torrent of thoughts vying for one's attention. So it may be difficult to slow the rush. Try to practise a 'catch and release' technique when one is aware of a thought and let it pass without becoming entangled in it. Many thoughts will be allowed to pass without reacting to them in any way. Just let them drift away. To silence one's thoughts entirely takes a lot of practice. A simple command like 'be still' or be focused back to one's breath is important. Meditation through Quantum Jumping has an advantage because one focuses on the quantum door. Walking towards that door and concentrating in jumping into another parallel universe to meet a doppelganger can allow other distractions drift away. By practicing this feat, one will notice that the moments of pure silence get longer and more frequent. Meditation is about to begin. The intention of the jump becomes the central focus. Merging with his twin-self allows imagination and visualisation to begin.

Finally, to be successful, one needs plenty of practice. An effective way to get the most out of meditation is to set aside time daily for it. Each meditation only requires fifteen to twenty minutes. A good way is to get up thirty minutes early and start meditation before one does anything else. This is a peaceful and productive way to start a day. Alternatively, one can take a meditation practice along with him as he goes about his day. Encountering a stressful situation, he can use the countdown method to reach a meditative state very quickly. This will soothe his emotions from escalating and help to minimise the 'fight or flight' response. This will give him a chance to gather his thoughts so that he can respond rather than react. Time is an essence. Soon he will get to know his inner mental and emotional working very well. He will gain mastery over his thoughts, enabling him to make choices that are aligned with what he wants in life. Every journey of a thousand miles begins with a single step. It's one choice to take that step to begin a productive, happy, and fulfilled journey in life.

Conclusion

After touching on many aspects of life, it's time to sit back and appreciate a practice to treasure myself by asking what I love to do before creating any new goal for a new year. I will sit back to value some quite reflections and pen down my appreciations of my life. I will continue to list down new ideas every day. I still want to be an idea machine. I still want to be happy by figuring out what made me happy and unhappy. I am still interested in the problems of others. Will this habit help me to be happy? I am aware that being happy I am able to turn outward and focus on the needs of others. I still want to master the habits of my everyday life and try to form good habits in order to find more happiness. These habits will help make things easier. Thinking of others can spark happiness. Appreciating life and the small things will certainly help. I still need to grow as growth and happiness are strongly correlated.

These are some questions I would like to ask myself. First, what ways throughout the years did I intentionally push myself of my comfort zone? Second, what people did I meet that stand out as significant? Third, what books did I read that helped me to become better version of myself? Fourth, what were the places I visited that I always remember? Fifth, what were the good moments I enjoy? Sixth, what were some of the contributions towards others I valued? Seventh, what ways was I blessed all these years? Last but not least, what were the important lessons I have learnt? All these will provide the basis for my next book.

Summary

This is a success story about the journey of life of a village boy from a poor big family. The three stages of life are classified as the learning stage, working stage, and yearning or retiring stage. These three stages of his life can be compared to the four seasons. The book has seven chapters. The first chapter consists of the author's general philosophy of life; his habits of meditation; his drill strategy to enhance skills of his game, basketball; his secrets of his study strategy; his discoveries of his talents as a writer, investor, and entrepreneur; his financial planning; his family achievements; and his super physical health. The second chapter provides the necessary ingredients, information, and knowledge that help him in building his financial security. It gives a full description of his strategies building many linear incomes as well as residual income. All these efforts make him a wealthy man. The third chapter is full of information and knowledge to help him living a healthy and fulfilled life. There are plenty examples of lifestyle for anyone who cares to live healthily. The fourth chapter gives a full description of his three stages of life including his family history, his struggle from birth to fifteen years old. It describes the experiences of a terrible childhood and child labour. This is comparable to the winter season of his life. His spring season of life begins when his sister has given him the opportunity to study in a secondary school in the city of Penang. He has made full use of the period, moving from secondary school to teacher training college and the university. His interest in his game propels him to be a basketball star player. The fifth chapter gives an account of his working life. After graduating from the university, he begins his summer season of his life. His chosen career as a professional teacher becomes his calling, and he makes full use of available talents in writing to secure his financial security. His motivation, experiences, and contribution give him an edge, and he moves up the ladder of success. He is not only a successful mathematics teacher and an excellent administrator as his school principal but also a successful writer, investor, and entrepreneur, making him a wealthy man. At the age of fifty-one, he accomplishes his mission seeing all his projects completed, he has taken his optional retirement. He leaves for Australia to pursue his doctoral study. The sixth chapter gives an account of the autumn season of his life. He continues to write, invest, and learn. He keeps fit and continues playing his game, tennis. He keeps fit and enjoys his retirement. The seventh chapter tells a new story. He embarks on a new adventure called Quantum Jumping. He provides many successful Quantum Jumps to heal his headache, to learn new concept, to achieve new abundance and wealth, to gain happiness, to increase his excitement in happy marriage, and finally to acquire joy of his life. The journey is well travelled.

www.ingramcontent.com/pod-product-compliance
Lightning Source LLC
LaVergne TN
LVHW021652060526
838200LV00050B/2310